SCHNITZLER'S VIENNA

Image of a Society

Bruce Thompson

London and New York

First published 1990
by Routledge
11 New Fetter Lane, London EC4P 4EE

Simultaneously published in the USA and Canada
by Routledge
a division of Routledge, Chapman and Hall, Inc.
29 West 35th Street, New York, NY 10001

© 1990 Bruce Thompson

Typeset in 10/12 Garamond by Columns of Reading

Printed in Great Britain by TJ Press (Padstow) Ltd, Padstow, Cornwall

All rights reserved. No part of this book may be reprinted or reproduced or utilized in any form or by any electronic, mechanical, or other means, now known or hereafter invented, including photocopying and recording, or in any information storage or retrieval system, without permission in writing from the publishers.

British Library Cataloguing in Publication Data
Thompson, Bruce
  Schnitzler's Vienna: image of a society.
  1. Drama in German. Austrian writers. Schnitzler,
  Arthur, 1862–1931
  I. Title
  832'.8
  ISBN 0-415-02378-5

Library of Congress Cataloging-in-Publication Data
Thompson, Bruce.
   Schnitzler's Vienna: image of a society / Bruce Thompson.
     p. cm.
   Includes bibliographical references.
   ISBN 0-415-02378-5
   1. Schnitzler, Arthur, 1862–1931 – Contemporary Austria. 2. Vienna (Austria) in literature. 3. Vienna (Austria) – Intellectual Life.
   I. Title.
   PT2638.N5Z894 1990
   832'.912 – dc20   89-70123
                                                                   CIP

CONTENTS

Preface   v
Abbreviations   vii
Map of Schnitzler's Vienna   viii

1 THE SETTING   1

2 THE LITERARY IMAGE   15

3 THE FREUDIAN CONNECTION   32

4 THE SEXUAL CONTEXT   55

5 THE BOURGEOISIE   91

6 THE SOCIAL FAÇADE   114

7 SOCIAL GROUPS   131

8 POLITICS AND THE JEWISH QUESTION   160

9 REALIST AND CRITIC   177

Notes   194
Selected bibliography   206
Index   210

PREFACE

This study is an attempt to establish Schnitzler's position as a chronicler and critic of the society of his day, that of the imperial city of Vienna at the turn of the century.

There have been several previous attempts to demonstrate that Schnitzler's work is a reflection of the social world in which he lived. For example, Françoise Derré's *L'oeuvre de Arthur Schnitzler. Imagerie viennoise et les problèmes humains* (1966), is a thorough and scholarly investigation of Schnitzler's social range, and Janz and Laermann's *Arthur Schnitzler. Zur Diagnose des Wiener Bürgertums im Fin de Siècle* (1977) offers a joint study of the social and psychological topography of Vienna as mediated through Schnitzler's art. Both in effect attach Schnitzler to the realist tradition of the nineteenth century, but at the point where social realism *per se* gives way to minute psychological detail.

Schnitzler's connections with Freud have been well documented and the profundity of his psychological insight well acknowledged. But critics have been peculiarly reluctant to tackle the social import of his works. This study accepts the Freudian connection and concern with psychology. But it also attempts to structure Schnitzler's treatment of the various individual members of his own society and the social groups to which they belong. It also places Schnitzler within the context of other writers, contemporary and later, who treat Vienna and Viennese society in their works. Over the years the world of Habsburg Vienna has been described at length, frequently with nostalgia and sentimentality. The cultural and artistic advances of the turn of the century have also been well charted by numerous international scholars. But in his literary works Schnitzler offers the most detailed and immediate account of the actual life of the city. His is a fictional version, but simply because he drew much of his material from his own experiences, and based so many of his characters on friends and acquaintances, it represents a unique contribution to the literature on Vienna at this time. The social groups he treats range from the aristocracy and the army to the lower classes, but essentially his works reflect his preoccupation with the world he knew best, that of the bourgeoisie.

Not all Schnitzler's works take place in the Vienna of his own time. *Der junge Medardus* is set in the Vienna of the Napoleonic Wars. *Der grüne Kakadu* takes place in Paris at the outset of the French Revolution. Other works are given more exotic settings, for example in the period of the Italian Renaissance (*Der Schleier der Beatrice*), or in the refined eighteenth-century world of the Rococo (*Casanovas Heimfahrt*). Detailed treatment of these has been deliberately omitted from this study, for they offer at most a comment on Viennese society by implication, through parallelism and analogy.

My interest in Schnitzler's Vienna has been fostered by a seminar on Vienna 1900 which I have held during recent years for students at Stirling. To many of the latter I am especially indebted for their enthusiasm and stimulating comments. I am also grateful to the University for enabling me to visit Vienna on several occasions to gather material. Some of the points made in Chapter 6 I owe to the observations of a Stirling postgraduate, Miss Marion Lines. Small sections on *Der einsame Weg* in Chapters 4 and 5 have appeared previously in *Scottish Papers in Germanic Studies*. I am grateful to the editors for permission to reprint. I owe a special debt of gratitude to my London colleague Dr Patricia Howe, who gave generously of her time, energy and expertise to criticize my initial draft, and who permitted me to read in advance of publication her article 'Mortality and Mercy in Vienna. Moral Relativism in Shakespeare's *Measure for Measure* and Schnitzler's *Das weite Land*'.

The jacket picture is taken from a postcard entitled 'Gruß aus Wien' and shows the Opera House in the background. It is reproduced with the kind permission of Dr Reinhard Urbach.

Stirling University, August 1989

ABBREVIATIONS

DW   Arthur Schnitzler, *Gesammelte Werke. Die Dramatischen Werke*, 2 vols, Fischer, Frankfurt, 1962.
ES   Arthur Schnitzler, *Gesammelte Werke. Die Erzählenden Schriften*, 2 vols, Fischer, Frankfurt, 1961.

Extracts from these editions are frequently quoted in the text and the sources are shown by the initials DW or ES, followed by the volume number and a page reference.

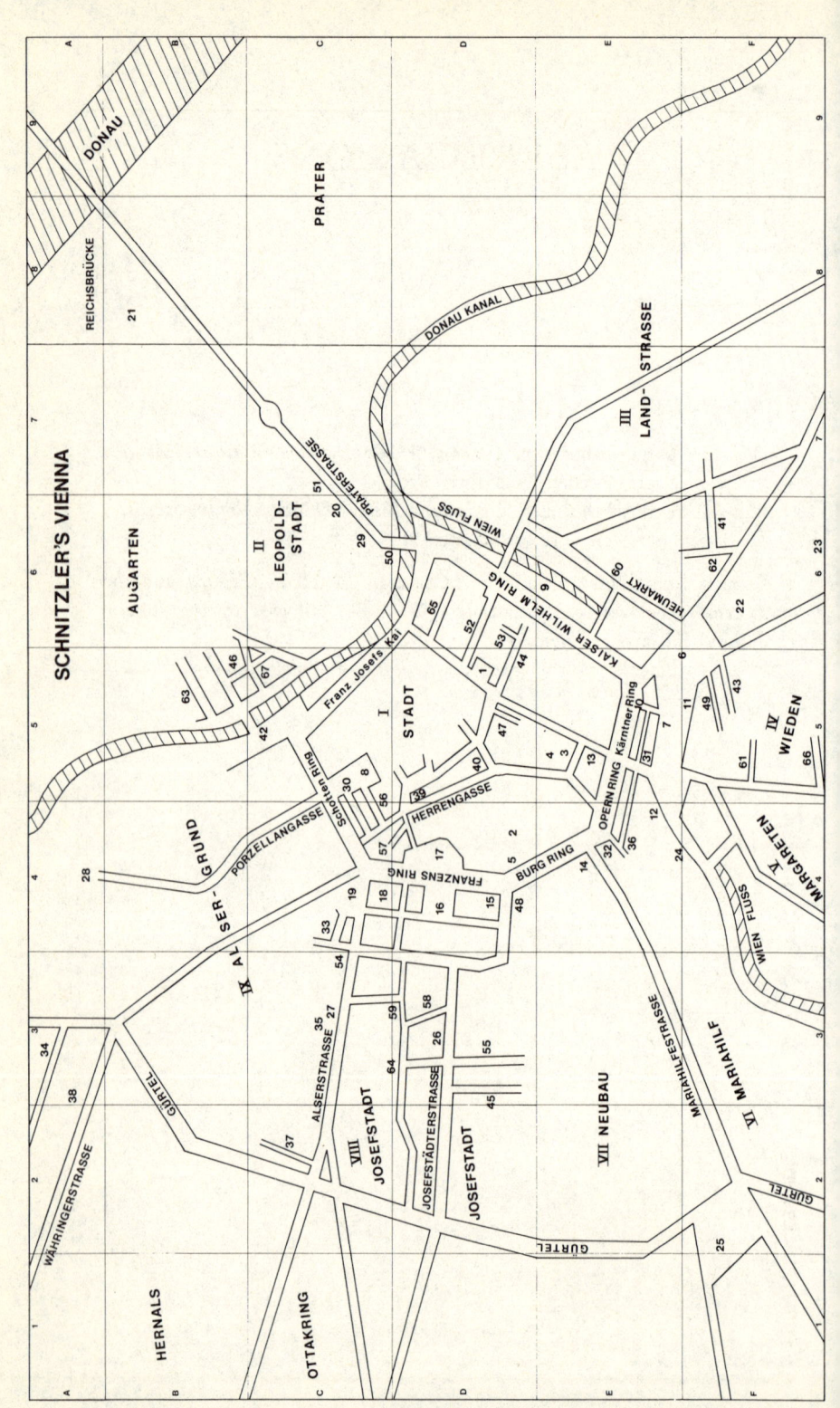

PUBLIC PLACES AND BUILDINGS

Stadt

1. Stefansdom D5
2. Hofburg D4
3. Hotel Sacher E5
4. Kapuzinergruft E5
5. Volksgarten D4

Ring Area

6. Schwarzenbergplatz E5
7. Karlsplatz E5
8. Börse (Stock Exchange) C5
9. Stadtpark E6
10. Hotel Imperial E5
11. Karlskirche F5
12. Secession E4
13. Opera House E5
14. Kunsthistorisches Museum E4
15. Reichsrat D4
16. Rathaus D4
17. Burgtheater D4
18. University C4
19. Votivkirche C4

Vorstadt

20. Carltheater C6
21. Nordbahnhof B8
22. Schwarzenberg Garten F6
23. Belvedere F6
24. Theater an der Wien E4
25. Westbahnhof F2
26. Josefstadttheater D3
27. Allgemeines Krankenhaus C3
28. Franz Josefsbahnhof A4

SCHNITZLER'S LIFE

29. Praterstraße (birthplace) C6
30. Schottenbastei 3 C5
31. Giselastraße 11 (now Bösendorferstraße) E5
32. Burgring 1 E4
33. Frankgasse 1 C4
34. Sternwartestraße 71 A3
35. Poliklinik C3
36. Eschenbachgasse (Franziska Reich) E4
37. Zimmermanngasse (Jeanette Heger) C2
38. Gentzgasse (Olga Schnitzler) A3
39. Café Central D5
40. Café Griensteidl D5

SCHNITZLER'S WORKS

Liebelei

41. Strohgasse (Fritz) F6

Reigen

42. Augartenbrücke (Prostitute/Soldier) C5
43. Schwindgasse (Young Gentleman/Married Woman) F5
44. Singerstraße (Süße Mädel/Husband) D5
45. Strozzigasse (Süße Mädel's sister) D3
46. Schiffgasse (Prostitute) B5
47. Spiegelgasse (Prostitute) D5

Leutnant Gustl

48. Café (by Volksgarten) D4
49. Gußhausstraße (Steffi) F5
50. Aspernbrücke C6

Die Toten schweigen

51. Nepomukkirche C7

Die Nächste

52. Wollzeile D6

Frau Berta Garlan

53. Riemerstraße (Cousin) D6

Spiel im Morgengrauen

54. Alserkaserne (Willi Kasda) C3
55. Piaristengasse (Bogner) D3
56. Helfersdorferstraße (Konsul) C4

Traumnovelle

57. Schreyvogelgasse (Hofrat) C4
58. Buchfeldgasse (Prostitute) D3
59. Wickenburgstraße (Gibiser) C3

Der Weg ins Freie

60. Stadtpark (Georg von Wergenthin) E6
61. Paulanergasse (Anna Rosner) F5
62. Schwarzenbergpark (Ehrenbergs) F6
63. Rembrandtstraße (Therese Golowski) B5
64. Florianigasse (Heinrich Bermann) C3
65. Fleischmarkt (Nürnberger) D6

Komtesse Mizzi

66. Mayerhofgasse (Lolo) F5

Fink und Fliederbusch

67. Schiffamtsgasse (Fliederbusch) C5

1
THE SETTING

At the time when Arthur Schnitzler was born in 1862 the city of Vienna was still the capital of the Austro-Hungarian Empire, which was to break up into its various component parts at the end of the First World War. Schnitzler's Vienna, the Vienna in which he lived, and in which he set so many of his works, was therefore the imperial city of the last fifty years of Habsburg rule, whose culture and society have been celebrated in countless songs, operettas, novels, plays, films and personal reminiscences. Many of these are tinged with nostalgia, as authors look back upon an age felt to have departed for ever. Typical is Stefan Zweig's idealized eulogy of Vienna in *Die Welt von Gestern* (The World of Yesterday, 1944), as a city set in the fine surroundings of woods and hills, rivalling the natural gaiety of Paris, absorbing the cultural influences of the various racial groups of the empire, and attracting a never-ending stream of foreign visitors and tourists.[1] But the most vivid and possibly the most accurate presentation of Viennese life is to be found in the narrative and dramatic works of Schnitzler, and it is largely to these that we owe today our impression of the social world of the closing years of Habsburg Vienna. Schnitzler's version of the life of his native city is one viewed at first hand through contemporary eyes, and represents the fullest exposition of Viennese society by any of the generation of writers living and writing in Vienna at the time. As the only true exponent of social realism of the period he offers a unique portrayal of this fascinating world.

Vienna has been praised for the splendour and beauty of its architecture, particularly the inner city with its sumptuous palaces, including the royal residence, the Hofburg, baroque churches and the famous St Stephen's Cathedral, the Stefansdom. But the new city, the Vienna of the second half of the nineteenth century, is also famed for its line of impressive buildings along the broad new Ringstraße, built in a variety of architectural styles. Historians have recognized Vienna's distinction as a highly civilized and uniquely cosmopolitan city, the political, commercial and cultural capital of a large multi-racial empire, the headquarters of the court and the aristocracy, of the bureaucracy and the Imperial Army.[2] Such a centre attracted members of all races, professions and cultural backgrounds, including Schnitzler's father, Johann Schnitzler, a man of quite humble Jewish origins, who came to Vienna from Hungary to study medicine, and worked his way up successfully to become assimilated into the higher ranks of bourgeois society. This was assisted greatly by his marriage in 1861 to the daughter of a well-established doctor, but his outstanding success as a laryngologist also enabled him to help found the Poliklinik, of which he later became director and head.

Vienna's cosmopolitanism lent the city a surface charm, which yet reflected a genuine warmth and spontaneity on the part of a population noted particularly for its capacity for pleasure and enjoyment. It contributed therefore not only to the social and cultural atmosphere of the city, but also to the character of the population, which has fashioned the legend of romantic, sentimental Vienna.[3] The superficial gaiety of Viennese social life masked, however, an antiquated and decaying social and political system. Following the military defeat at the hands of Prussia in 1866, Austria had lost its identity as a leading European power, and by 1900 it was acknowledged to be internationally weak and internally unstable. Vienna has been described as a melting pot for racial and political ideas, engendered by the fact that a centralized multi-national state had survived into a new age of rapid economic development, wholly out of tune with its anachronistic social and political system. Pan-Germanism, Pan-Slavism, Marxism, Christian Socialism, Zionism all coincided at the heart of the Habsburg Empire in the years of its decline, and by the end of the century the stability of the empire was threatened by numerous mutually hostile factions.[4]

The rulers of Austria in the latter half of the nineteenth century were faced with two main problems, namely the demands of the individual subject peoples, notably the Poles, Czechs, Slavs and Italians, for greater independence, and those of internal political groupings, such as the Christian Socialists and Social Democrats, for greater influence in government. Internal control over 'Hungary' had already been conceded by the terms of the *Ausgleich* (Compromise) of 1867, and from then on the Emperor Franz Josef and his ministers were engaged in a defensive operation to maintain the balance between the various disputing parties, often amounting to no more than a desperate process of muddling through ('fortwursteln'). A safety valve did exist in the form of a parliament, the Reichsrat, and there were occasional attempts to introduce a system of parliamentary government, but no party or group ever gained overall control, and by the turn of the century parliament was effectively paralysed. Franz Josef thus returned to bureaucratic rule. The business of administration was conducted over parliament's head by an army of professional civil servants and ministers chosen by the emperor, who was effectively governing by imperial decree. Parliament was simply a talking shop, an assembly of conflicting national and political groups. It had no influence on policy.[5]

The unifying personality of the whole epoch was Franz Josef himself. The length of his reign alone (eventually nearly seventy years) was sufficient to give the illusion of stability, but he ruled formally, and without imagination. He was reticent, tidy, meticulous, persevering. He hated change, paid only lip-service to the principles of parliamentarianism, and his philosophy of government was authoritarian.[6] As a man he has been described as mediocre and shallow.[7] Yet he was well-intentioned and highly conscientious, was devoted to his duty as administrator of his enormous empire, and lived out a frugal and spartan existence, frowning upon modern comforts and technological developments. Publicly he preserved all the traditional pageantry of the monarchy, and this, together with his devotion to public duty, made him an object of general veneration. His stoicism enabled him to survive numerous personal tragedies: his son Rudolf committed suicide in 1889, and his empress wife Elisabeth was assassinated in 1898. In his later years he withdrew into increasing isolation, and in 1902 he already described himself as mentally feeble.[8] Yet he still worked all day at his desk on public affairs and his sole aim was to keep the empire together until his death. Ironically it was he who signed the death warrant of the monarchy when his signature on the ultimatum to Serbia launched Europe into world war.

As well as in the empire at large, Franz Josef encountered problems within his own family. The Empress Elisabeth, a legendary, romantic character, and a more spontaneous and vivacious personality, detested the stiff conventions of the imperial court, and sought solace in riding, hunting and travel. Rudolf, his son and heir, also attempted to assert his independence, likewise rejecting the stereotyped conservatism of his father, and seeking to modernize and liberalize Austria. He was felt to represent new hope for the empire, but he was also a somewhat tense and unbalanced personality, and he has gone down in popular history for the tragedy at the hunting lodge at Mayerling, when he shot his mistress, the young Baroness Vetsera, and then himself. In the final years there was the new heir, Franz Ferdinand, another independent and more vigorous spirit, who had plans for reorganizing the empire on his succession, but whose policies promised to be fiercely reactionary and authoritarian. He was hated by Franz Josef, and in effect operated a rival court in the Belvedere Palace.[9] Despite his unpopularity in the Hofburg, the court nevertheless reacted with appropriate, if somewhat insincere outrage to his assassination at Sarajevo, which effectively initiated the First World War.

Viennese society of the day was noted particularly for its sharp social distinctions. In the main the various strata kept to their own circles and districts, the higher aristocracy to its palaces, or *palais*, in the inner city, the diplomatic circles in the third district, the industrialists and merchants to the Ring area, the lower middle classes to the inner districts (the 'Vorstadt'), the proletariat to the outer suburbs. This did not mean that individuals did not bridge the various social gaps. The actress Katharina Schratt, for thirty years the confidante of the emperor, was the daughter of a shopkeeper in Baden. Anna Sacher, the proprietress of the celebrated hotel behind the new opera house, frequented by the highest in society from royalty to the most prosperous of the bourgeoisie, hailed from a butcher's shop in the inner suburbs. The father of Karl Lueger, who rose to be mayor of the city, was a porter at the Theresianum, the school founded by Maria Theresa to provide the empire with well-educated civil servants. Clearly, upward social mobility was possible, but at the very top of the social hierarchy the families of the older, highly privileged nobility led an artificial, exclusive existence, dividing their time between their residences in Vienna and their country estates. Generally they took little interest in outside affairs, though some occupied the higher posts in the civil service and the army, and most took their seats on occasion in the Herrenhaus, the upper chamber of the Reichsrat. These were the families of the Habsburg archdukes and the famous historical families, the Kinskys, the Auerspergs and the Windischgrätzes, an anachronism in an age of industrial and commercial development, to be clearly distinguished from the *Briefadel*, the newly created barons, mostly bankers and industrialists, who were not admitted to the upper circles.[10]

If the aristocracy represented an exclusive, privileged caste, so too did the officers of the Imperial Army. The army was Franz Josef's own province, he controlled it, and it represented one of his few interests, its ritualistic, regulated life-style appealing to his love of order and tradition. It was an unwieldy, expensive and inefficient machine, yet it was popular with the majority of civilians. The officers lived by their own code of honour, and were virtually beyond the reach of the civil law. If an officer's honour was infringed he had the right to satisfaction through a duel; if, in turn, he refused a challenge he could lose his commission. Officially the duel was illegal and punishable by imprisonment, but until 1900 courts refrained from enforcing the law against officers, and in cases where an officer actually killed a civilian, Franz Josef usually granted a pardon. In England the duel had died out by 1850, but in Austria it persisted until the turn of the century, after which duelling became less prestigious. In 1911 Franz Josef issued a decree forbidding duels for any but the most serious reasons.[11] Up to then students at university had also represented an elite, enjoying the privilege of being permitted to fight duels without punishment, and many joined militant fraternities (Burschenschaften) in order to do so, though the more academically minded avoided them.[12]

Despite the presence of these exclusive social groups, Vienna in 1900 was essentially a city of the bourgeoisie. The wealth of the bourgeois families had been made in the 1870s, the so-called *Gründerzeit*, when bourgeois enterprises were founded on a grand scale and large fortunes were accumulated. By 1900 the most successful professional men also enjoyed comparable incomes and living standards, and visitors to Vienna were impressed by the luxury and ostentatious display of the nouveaux riches.[13] During the final years of the nineteenth century Stefan Zweig grew up in a society where prosperous families such as the Schnitzlers lived a secure, regular existence, which they assumed would go on for ever.[14] The philosophy of the middle classes was essentially materialistic, they were impressed by new technological developments, such as electric lights, modern plumbing and telephones, and soon became addicted to the new marvel, the motor car. But culturally and intellectually Vienna's bourgeoisie also formed one of the most sophisticated middle classes in Europe, and the most aspiring families used their wealth to rival the aristocracy as patrons of the arts. Under Franz Josef the nobility had gradually reduced its patronage, so that the wealthy middle classes welcomed the opportunity to step into the breach and uphold the cultural traditions of the city.[15] The members of the Schnitzler family took an active interest in cultural life. As a boy Arthur Schnitzler was a frequent and privileged attender of the Burgtheater, and he met the most successful and fashionable actors as patients of his father.

The most striking and permanent bourgeois phenomenon of the late nineteenth century was the famous Ringstraße, the avenue or boulevard constructed round the inner city on the site of the old city walls.[16] It was on or near the Ring that the wealthy industrialists and manufacturers, the financiers, the highly paid officials and professional families built their new homes. Most of the building took the form of large apartment houses, four to six storeys high, modelled on the aristocratic *palais* of the inner city. The aristocratic splendour of the Ringstraße buildings was enhanced by their façades, particularly by those of the first floor apartments, whose high windows, rich ornamentation and pillars lent them their exclusive quality. Indeed, the decorations of the façades, as of the stairways and hallways, constituted a far more important factor in determining rental levels than the size or quality of the internal features of the apartments themselves.[17] The Ring not only attracted the upper middle classes (the *Großbürgertum*), but also aristocratic families and the titled nobility, especially on the Schwarzenbergplatz. The most prosperous members of the middle classes, the manufacturers and industrialists, tended to settle along the highly exclusive Schottenring. The financial leaders, merchants and bankers, as well as the most highly paid academics and government officials, gravitated towards the Burgring, the Opernring and the Kärntnerring. In 1871 Doctor Johann Schnitzler moved from his flat in Giselastraße to occupy a more sumptuous apartment on the Ring itself, in Burgring I. But the Ring contained more than dwellings. On it were built in a variety of imitation architectural styles the ostentatious new public buildings, the Rathaus in Gothic, the Burgtheater in Baroque, the University in Renaissance style, the Reichsrat in Classical Greek. The Ringstraße was constructed at a time when the empire was already threatening to disintegrate, and the monarchy was under sentence. Few were aware of this, but the ostentatious façades and the vulgarity of much of the interior decoration, the sheer scale of the Ring and of its public buildings, represented a conscious assertion of power.[18] Edward Crankshaw has called it 'the formal admission of decadence'.[19] The buildings of the Ringstraße were also designed to harmonize with the ostentatiousness and theatricality of Viennese life, with its emphasis on pomp and ceremony. They blended perfectly with the public masquerade of the elegant clothes of the upper classes and the magnificent uniforms of army officers.[20]

Only the very affluent upper middle classes could afford to live on the Ring. The lesser merchants and professional families occupied the fourth to eighth districts, Wieden, Margarethen, Mariahilf and the Josefstadt, the academics and physicians settled in the ninth district, Alsergrund, whilst prosperous artists and writers and higher government officials built elegant villas in the outer suburbs, such as Döbling and Hietzing, and in the foothills of the Vienna woods.[21] Many of Vienna's middle-class families were Jewish, indeed there were Jews in all classes except the higher aristocracy. Many had come to Vienna from the provinces following the emancipation laws of 1867. A significant number went into the professions, became financiers and industrialists. It has been calculated that by 1910 they made up the largest segment of the legal and medical professions, and by 1914 the industry and trade of Vienna were to an overwhelming extent under Jewish control.[22] Jewish intellectuals and artists also became prominent in literary and cultural circles, and in the theatre. Before 1867 Jews had been largely restricted to the second district, the Leopoldstadt, but by the 1880s only the poorest Jewish immigrants from the east settled there: the more wealthy gradually moved into the ninth district, and then into the inner city and on to the Ring itself. Stefan Zweig describes his father's efforts as a Jew to assimilate into a higher cultural and social stratum. The acquirement of wealth was simply a means to an end, to free himself from all taints of being a Jew.[23] Indeed, only a minority adhered to the Jewish faith. Most became baptized and assimilated into the rest of the population. The trappings of the Jewish religion played no role in Johann Schnitzler's household, and his son Arthur set foot in the synagogue only for weddings and funerals. A few of the wealthiest Jews even secured titles of nobility and married into the lower aristocracy.

Beyond the Ring, in the inner districts was to be found an agglomeration of lower middle-class groups, the so-called *Kleinbürgertum*, small shopkeepers and manufacturers, employees and white-collar workers, living respectable lives, but in much more straitened circumstances. The growing industrialization had led to a rapid growth in the city's population (it increased from seven hundred thousand in 1880 to over two million in 1910), and to the creation of a large urban working class, which was crammed into the miserable multi-storeyed tenement buildings in the new outer suburbs of Ottakring, Hernals and Favoriten beyond the Gürtel, a further, outer ring-road constructed in 1890. There a large proportion of the population lived in destitution and overcrowded conditions, condemned to a lifetime of sweated labour. Both the lower middle classes and working classes were fertile ground for the new political movements, which were to dominate the political life of the city during the final twenty years of the monarchy.

The members of the bourgeoisie who built the Ringstraße were the bourgeois liberals who had enjoyed a period of political power in the 1860s. The liberals had developed a number of social services, among them the first city hospital, a public water supply and the provision of public parks. The liberals had also aspired to turn the Habsburg Empire into a genuine consitutional monarchy, with the establishment of an administration working through parliament. But by the 1890s liberalism no longer appealed to the minority groups that had settled in Vienna, or to the victims of rapid urban growth and industrialization. This did not mean that liberalism as a political principle died – right up to the fall of the monarchy the majority of the middle and upper classes felt themselves to be 'liberal', and lived their comfortable, secure lives.[24] This was Stefan Zweig's 'golden age' of security, in which everything went its orderly way and had its own established value, and the majority believed in the inevitability of material and social progress.[25] Gradually, however, the liberals lost their political influence, for although the administration was still largely an upper-middle-class affair, genuine political life was being conducted not in parliament, but in the streets and the public halls.[26] In 1882 members of the radical wing of the liberal party drafted the Linz Programme, a package of social reforms with a German nationalist flavour, which paved the way for the main movements of the left and right, which, by the turn of the century, were to replace liberalism as a political force. In 1889 Victor Adler formed the new Social Democratic Party, drawing support initially from the working-class district of Ottakring. As early as 1890 a demonstration marched through the streets of Vienna, to the fear and consternation of the respectable middle classes,[27] and in 1894 workers and members of Adler's party held a mass demonstration for universal suffrage, a campaign that was eventually to be successful in 1907. Adler's appeal fed on the dissatisfaction bred by the critical housing problem, high rents, long working hours and low wages, and the party offered its members opportunities such as youth associations and further education. All this bore fruit in 1918 when the Social Democrats gained control of Vienna and presided over the establishment of the First Austrian Republic.

Between the two extremes of the liberal wealthy bourgeoisie and the working classes, were the lower middle classes, the small tradesmen, shopkeepers and manufacturers who made up the *Kleinbürgertum*. They fell prey to a new party formed in the 1890s by Karl Lueger called the Christian Socialists. This was essentially anti-Semitic in nature, and appealed to their hostility towards the large-scale manufacturing enterprises, which threatened their livelihood and were largely in Jewish hands. Lueger also exploited their hostility to 'Jewish socialism', for many of the leaders of the Social Democratic Party, including Adler himself, were also Jews. Lueger's party was thus anti-liberal, anti-capitalist and anti-Jewish, it was in alliance with the Catholic Church, and appealed to the small-minded prejudices of the so-called 'little men' of Vienna.[28] If the working-class outer suburbs supported Adler, the inner districts, the *Vorstadt*, belonged to Lueger.[29] His popularity was such that he was elected mayor of Vienna in 1895, and embarked on a programme of municipal socialism that made Vienna one of the most progressive cities in Europe.[30]

Lueger's anti-Semitism was economically based, rather than racist in origin, and was less fanatical than that espoused by Georg von Schönerer's Pan-German Nationalist Party. Schönerer's nationalism was directed as much against the Czechs and the other subject races, as against the Jews, and was fuelled by proposed language concessions to the Czechs and by the government's attempts to appease the demands of Slav nationalism. Schönerer was aiming for the eventual break-up of the empire and the unification of 'German Austria' with the German Reich. He did not achieve such a mass following as Lueger, but his rabble-rousing methods encouraged street demonstrations and fighting, and the violence even erupted in the Reichsrat. His supporters consisted mainly of university students and other professionals who felt threatened by Jewish competition, together with the more fanatically anti-Semitic small businessmen. His brand of anti-Semitism provided an ugly anticipation of the policies of Austrofascism and of the Nazi regime, and it is significant that Adolf Hitler, who was in Vienna at the time, was deeply impressed by Schönerer's violent methods.[31]

Anti-Semitism in Vienna took various forms, the most tangible manifestations being the exclusion of Jews from the diplomatic service, from the higher ranks of the army and from the more responsible positions in the civil service.[32] They were also denied the top professorships in the University, and there were attempts by the Christian Socialists to reduce the influx of Jews into the education system generally. Despite their respectable social position, members of the Schnitzler family did not escape the wave of anti-Semitism which swept through Vienna in the 1890s. Doctor Johann Schnitzler had particular problems in his Poliklinik, and his son Arthur had already experienced a degree of anti-Semitic prejudice as a student at the University and as a military cadet in the Imperial Army. But not all Viennese were anti-Semitic, and the majority of the population was apathetic and even tolerant over the issue.[33] Anti-Semitism was first agitated by the great crash on the Stock Exchange in 1873, for which Jewish financiers were blamed. The rapid increase in the Jewish population, the growing competition in trade and industry, the influx into the Leopoldstadt of Galician Jews from the east, exacerbated the situation. The anti-clerical stance of Jews in parliament and in the press, likewise their leading positions in the socialist movement, accentuated their unpopularity with the Christian Socialists. In response to anti-Semitism more Jews attempted to assimilate, but in the face of the fanatically racist Pan-German movement many espoused the Zionist solution inspired by Theodor Herzl. It was in Vienna that Zionism, which aimed at the establishment of a Jewish homeland in Palestine, was born, ironically at the same time that Hitler's personal anti-Semitism was taking root.

This account of nationalist passions and the dawning of new political movements gives a somewhat false impression of the general tenor of life in Vienna at the time. The coming dissolution of the empire, the fall of the monarchy as a result of racial and political activism, were sensed only by a minority of the more sensitive and far-sighted intellectuals. The middle classes were for the most part politically apathetic, there was a mood of resignation in the civil service and of frivolity amongst the aristocracy. Much of the city was hell-bent on pleasure-seeking and amusement. The capacity for enjoyment on the part of all segments of the population, the easy-going, leisurely pace of Viennese social life, have become an established cliché. Even the politicians never really took themselves seriously. They savaged each other in the Reichsrat, and then sat down to drink beer or coffee together. The repertoire of the theatre was more important than economic or political events, actors better known than politicians. External affairs on the world stage were largely ignored as peripheral to what really mattered.[34] The members of the lower middle classes also lived mainly for their holidays and visits to the operetta and the wine cellars, where they would listen to Strauß waltzes and sentimental, nostalgic songs. This was the final version of the myth of gay Vienna, singing and dancing whilst the empire crumbled. Even the families of the working classes spent their few holidays in the inner city listening to band music and watching the soldiers.[35] To some extent the housing conditions helped to fashion the social habits of the Viennese, and fostered the popularity of the cafés, taverns, wine cellars, public houses, parks and the Prater entertainment centre, to which the working classes and the members of the lower middle classes could escape.[36] But one should not underestimate the role played by the public festivals and the rich cultural life of the city, in which the various social groups found their sense of unity, and their shared consciousness of 'being Viennese'.[37] It is also important to remember that this was a period of outstanding artistic achievement, and that there were many who found the easy-going attitude of the Viennese and the surface charm of their life-style insufferable.[38]

For at the turn of the century there was a sudden flowering of artistic and intellectual life in Vienna, the like of which has been rarely seen at any time elsewhere. In particular there was a spirit of innovation and rejection of accepted modes of thought and creation. In 1897 a number of painters broke away from the established Künstlerhaus to form the Vienna Secession under the presidency of Gustav Klimt. Klimt was reacting in particular against the ornately decorative art of Hans Makart, who had decorated the opulent *palais* of the Ringstraße and painted the elaborate frescos of the new Burgtheater, shaping the taste of Vienna's upper middle classes for a whole generation.[39] Klimt developed a uniquely personal style, called *Jugendstil*, in the anti-realistic, subjective mode, under the influence of *art nouveau*. But his own art was still decorative in conception, and in 1908 came a more radical rejection of decorative art by the architect Adolf Loos, who with his colleague Otto Wagner demanded that new forms of art should adapt themselves to human needs, and be both aesthetically satisfying and functional.[40] Wagner's blocks of flats built in 1910 in the suburb of Neustift had, for example, bare and unadorned façades. In painting too the new movement of Kokoschka and Schiele paved the way for Expressionism. In music the innovations of Bruckner and Mahler prepared the ground for the explorations in free tonality by Schönberg, Webern and Berg, and the eventual adoption by Schönberg of the twelve-tone system. But this latter, major advance in music did not really take place until the 1920s, and it is Mahler's music which has been singled out as the most characteristic musical expression of the mood of the *fin-de-siècle*, with its nervousness, intoxication with colour, mixture of *Weltschmerz* and ecstasy.[41] At the turn of the century Vienna was also the centre of the medical world, and Freud was publishing his treatises on the division of the psyche into conscious and unconscious realms, and on the role of sexuality and uncontrollable, instinctive drives in human life. In philosophy Ernst Mach also began to question accepted concepts of the personality. But in 'official' medical circles Freud's pioneering work went unrecognized, and the implications of his views about the role of sexuality in human life offended the sensibilities of middle-class Vienna. Similarly the public remained largely hostile to the new avant-garde tendencies, the innovations of Bruckner and Schönberg, the architectural creations of Wagner and Loos, the paintings of Klimt, Schiele and Kokoschka.[42] Moreover the more fastidious members of the intelligentsia still preferred the 'safe', light music of Johann Strauß.[43] But this in no way invalidates Edward Crankshaw's striking claim that intellectually and culturally 'Vienna was never more vital than when it was dying'.[44]

In literature there were similar innovative developments. In the 1890s a group of young authors, including Schnitzler himself, Hermann Bahr, Hugo von Hofmannsthal, Richard Beer-Hofmann, Karl Kraus, Peter Altenberg and Leopold von Andrian used to meet in the coffee-houses of Vienna to discuss topics of cultural interest, and to read poetry. As a literary group they have been conveniently labelled as the Jung Wien circle, but at the time they were also known as the 'Griensteidlgesellschaft', after the coffee-house where they chiefly met. The Viennese coffee-houses flourished in the manner of literary or cultural clubs, where men and women gathered to read or converse, or indulge in dilettante writing. In particular the intellectual younger generation escaped from the constrictions of their stultifying bourgeois environment, and found a vitality and spontaneity lacking in their educational and home background. Yet although the world's press was available to them there, their activities were essentially cultural, and they took little note of political developments either in Vienna, or further afield.[45]

In many ways Schnitzler himself was very much a part of this society. As the son of a wealthy member of the professional bourgeoisie, as a student at the University and, briefly, as an officer cadet in the Imperial Army, he participated in the frivolous, pleasure-seeking life-style of the privileged classes which accompanied the political decline of the empire. At the same time he also contributed to the intellectual and cultural flowering of the period. Like his father, Schnitzler studied medicine, but though he did not work with great interest or diligence, he qualified in 1885 to become a house doctor at the Allgemeine Krankenhaus, and in 1887 he became an assistant at Theodor Meynert's psychiatric clinic. For a time, then, he played a part, albeit a peripheral one, in the great advances in psychological medicine, an experience that was to leave an indelible mark on his literary works. Then, in 1888 he set up his own private medical practice in the home of his parents in Burgring I. But he practised only spasmodically, preferring the company of poets and writers in the coffee-houses of the inner city, first the Café Central in the Herrengasse, and then the nearby Café Griensteidl. The first meeting of the Jung Wien circle took place in 1890, and meetings continued regularly in private apartments and houses during the first years of the decade. In 1892 the death of his father enabled him virtually to give up his practice altogether and to devote his energies almost entirely to literature. It was now that he began to play a truly significant role in the cultural life of his city. As a man Schnitzler was fully integrated into the social fabric of the city, and was ideally qualified to become the most prolific chronicler and one of the most effective critics of the society that he knew so well.

2
THE LITERARY IMAGE

The image of Viennese society sketched briefly during the previous chapter has been recreated in a considerable body of the literature of the twentieth century. A whole generation of writers who lived through the final years of the empire tended to look back to a golden age, which became idealized in the memory. For Claudio Magris this process has effectively led to the creation of a myth, because of the distortion of the past that has necessarily taken place in their works.[1] The culture and values of Habsburg Vienna have been satirized and ironized over the years, but they have also been exalted. Indeed it is no exaggeration to claim that the life and society of Vienna at the turn of the century has exerted a greater fascination over writers since its passing, than during its heyday. This apparent paradox is due partly to the fact that the young generation of writers of the 1890s who regularly met in the coffeehouses of the inner city had little interest in social and political affairs, and in their works rejected a representation of social reality in favour of the more inward aspects of life.[2] It was not their intention to reproduce the image of the city or its social life. In view of this general trend, and of his own close association with this group of writers, Schnitzler's detailed recreation of the social image of Vienna is all the more startling.

The deliberate cultivation of modes of literary expression which countered the notion that art should constitute a detailed reproduction of reality, represented a challenge to the principles of the Naturalist movement in vogue at the time in Germany. Naturalist writers such as Holz and Hauptmann emphasized the importance of a detailed objective presentation of social problems, and of environmental and hereditary factors. The writers of *fin-de-siècle* Vienna espoused a more poetic and subjective mode, turning away from outer reality into the inner, spiritual world of the private imagination. Their lack of political and social engagement led to an aesthetic withdrawal into a cult of the self, and they came to form a cultured and self-conscious elitist group. In part the Viennese writers were simply furthering an anti-Naturalist trend already initiated in Germany by the poet Stefan George, who cultivated a superior form of intellectual art, characterized by its creation of moods and reproduction of sensual impressions. But the impetus was really provided by Hermann Bahr's admiration for the so-called 'decadent' writers of France, notably Paul Bourget and Maurice Barrès.

In the late 1880s Bahr spent some years in the bohemian atmosphere of Paris, and when he returned to Vienna in 1890 he imported his enthusiasm for the new mode of Impressionism, or 'nervous romanticism', as he called it. Bahr's views are set out in his essay 'Die Ueberwindung des Naturalismus' (The Conquest of Naturalism, 1891), in which he emphasizes the importance of the role played by the 'nerves' in French decadent literature. He predicted that Naturalism would be superseded by 'a mysticism of nerves', for it is through the account of nervous sensations that the true state of mind may be conveyed.[3] As Bahr later recognized, his preoccupations found their scientific exposition in the philosophical views of Ernst Mach, who had published his *Analyse der Empfindungen* (Analysis of Sensations) in 1886. Mach argued that neither external objects nor personal consciousness have an independent, permanent existence, but are ever-changing subjective ideas constructed out of the complex of our physical or mental sensations. The identity and validity of the individual personality are thus questionable, it being an arbitrary construction. In Mach's views Bahr and the writers of Jung Wien found scientific evidence for the shifting inner life of the soul. All moods and feelings are determined essentially by sensory perceptions, colours, sounds, smells, shapes, temperatures.[4] Hence the 'cult of the soul' of the 1890s, hence also the cult of the artist figure, whose nerves are so finely tuned that he can pick up private sensations and transform them into art. With the same cult may be associated the aestheticism of the period, the conscious refinement of the senses, and thus of the personality itself, through the collection and contemplation of beautiful objects or works of art.

The purest literary manifestation of Bahr's brand of nervous impressionism was the early lyric poetry of the young Hugo von

Hofmannsthal, sensual, intensely mannered, self-consciously aesthetic and introspective, expressing the fine vibrations of his soul. But mention may also be made of two short novels by two other writers of the Jung Wien circle, Leopold von Andrian and Richard Beer-Hofmann. Andrian's *Der Garten der Erkenntnis* (The Garden of Recognition, 1895) is the story of the son of a prince who dies when still a youth. The novel is highly stylized and affected, and is chiefly concerned with conveying the boy's neurotic state of mind and problematic relationship with the outer world. Social reality is almost completely absent. There are references to Vienna, where the novel is set, but it is a heightened, idealized reality, steeped in baroque tradition and religious symbolism. Beer-Hofmann's *Der Tod Georgs* (The Death of George, 1897) is also written with conscious artistry in rhythmic prose. Again it is set in Vienna, but the novel has a poetic aura about it, and is written very much in the spirit of *fin-de-siècle* aestheticism. It has a complex structure of visions, dreams and day-dreams, and the gardens and parks of Vienna, with their lakes and ponds, are the correlatives of the hero's inner self, in which he lives out the narcissistic life of the aesthete. The novel is almost bereft of outer action, but rich in internal psychological observation and self-reflection. The Viennese setting is entirely immaterial.

The flight from reality on the part of some of the authors of the Jung Wien circle into a private spiritual world of the soul, represents in part a rejection of the society around them, and (possibly) a semi-conscious awareness of its decline. Another flight from reality, but rather in the opposite direction, is provided by the popular Viennese operetta. If society masked its decline behind frivolity and superficial sensuality, embodied in the social whirl of court dances and the glittering uniforms of army officers, then this aspect of the façade found its popular artistic expression in the sentimentality, banality and superficiality of the sweet sugary world created by Johann Strauß and Franz Lehar, reflecting an anachronistic pseudo-aristocratic society and system of values. That the world of the operetta is merely an illusion, providing an escape into a temporary happiness, is suggested by the music and atmosphere of one of the more sophisticated operas of the period, Richard Strauß's *Der Rosenkavalier* (1911), the product of the composer's collaboration with Hugo von Hofmannsthal. In the *Rosenkavalier* waltz has been found the expression of the death of old Austria, the ironic and melancholy music, which is both magical and mournful, expressing the sadness of the passing of a social era.⁵

Despite the influence of the Jung Wien circle on the one hand, and the popularity of the operetta on the other, not all the literature of the period was of the escapist variety, for an older generation of socially conscious writers, notably Ferdinand von Saar and Maria von Ebner-Eschenbach, was still active. But both were concerned essentially with the empire at large, rather than with the specifically Viennese milieu, and both were preoccupied with evoking the atmosphere of a bygone age rather than with the tensions of the modern, developing city. For example, the majority of Saar's *Novellen aus Oesterreich* are set in the earlier period of Franz Josef's reign, and lament the passing of old values. Many of Ebner-Eschenbach's stories are set in the castles of her native Moravia, and present a generally peaceful and idyllic picture of the rural life of the empire. Nevertheless both writers were aware of the changes taking place within Austrian society, and sensed the approach of a new age, with new social and political values. Many of Saar's *Novellen* are not simply sentimental evocations of the past, but present precise analyses of contemporary decline, his awareness of the coming downfall of Habsburg Austria providing one of the main themes of his work.⁶

An example of Saar's treatment of contemporary political developments may be found in the story *Die Familie Worel* (1905). This is set, somewhat unusually for Saar, in a city, though not in Vienna itself. Yet it illustrates well Saar's conservative standpoint, and introduces the theme of the rise of socialism, industrialization, and the conflict between impoverished workers and the authorities. Worel has been employed as factotum of an aristocratic estate, but he becomes involved with local nationalist politics, begins to assert his independence, and leaves to take a more lucrative post with a cabinet-maker in the city. The decision is a disaster. Worel gets into financial difficulties, and the family has to exist in deprived circumstances in a wretched tenement building. Through his mouthpiece, the count who narrates the story, Saar draws an unsympathetic, moralistic conclusion. As he contemplates the wretchedness of the family, in its cramped, unhealthy conditions, he recalls its former more comfortable life in the fresh air of the country estate. As far as he is concerned, they are paying the penalty for forsaking the security offered in service to the traditional aristocratic household. Social changes in Vienna itself are charted in *Geschichte eines Wiener Kindes* (A Child of Vienna, 1892), a gently moralistic story set in a modern atmosphere of opportunism, shady deals and loose morals. In the course of the novel Saar makes it clear how distasteful he finds these developments. He sympathizes with the older inhabitants of Döbling who are saddened by the changes which will soon absorb their peaceful suburb into the rapidly expanding industrial city; he disapproves of the unscrupulous materialism and risky, possibly illegal speculations of the world of business and finance; he satirizes the new Women's Movement, and also the upstart bourgeois nouveaux riches, aping aristocratic manners and introducing dilettante culture into their household.

In contrast to Saar's inability to countenance new social and cultural currents, Ebner-Eschenbach presents a more tolerant and balanced viewpoint in *Der Herr Hofrat* (The Counsellor, 1902). For in this Viennese story she satirizes the rigid conservatism of a temperament that lives in the past and refuses to accept new ideas and modes of life. The Hofrat's attitude is reflected in the Biedermeier style of the décors and furnishings of his spacious apartment in the inner city, likewise in the regularity of his habits and life-style; but above all in his overt hostility to recent artistic and cultural developments. He laments the passing of elegance and beauty, and their replacement by dissonance and ugliness; he attacks modern psychological research, literature and art forms, with their emphasis on sexuality; similarly he deplores the sexual licence prevalent in the life of the city. There is a new stridency in Vienna. He feels threatened on all sides by giant advertising placards. He is nauseated by the bare and tasteless tower blocks which dominate the comfortable and modest little houses of the suburbs, and threaten to transform Vienna into a brash American-style city, signalling the collapse of Austrian and European culture. Clearly there is more than a grain of truth in what he has to say, but his bitter pessimism seems exaggerated as he foresees only anarchy and the wholesale destruction of his beloved culture and traditional ordered life.

Marie von Ebner-Eschenbach's satire of the conservativism of the bourgeoisie finds many an echo in the attitudes and publications of the younger generation of writers. In particular Hermann Bahr recognized that Viennese society was too rooted in the past to accept the challenge of the modern age. He was first taken to Vienna by his father in 1877, and was made to admire the

Ringstraße. But although he appreciated its significance for the older generation, it became a symbol for him of historical liberalism that could not keep up with modern developments. At the same time he felt that it was a false symbol, lacking respect for the real traditions of the city.[7] Bahr's hostility towards the vanity and artificiality of bourgeois society, likewise his distaste for the frivolity of the Viennese life-style, is expressed in his essay 'Wien' (1907), a malicious dissection of the Viennese character.[8] It also surfaces in a number of his literary works, many of which have a contemporary Viennese setting. For although Bahr had advocated initially that the new anti-Naturalist literature should be concerned with inner moods generated by sensual impressions, he did acknowledge that it should at the same time be based on contemporary reality, and should confront the major problems of the times.[9] Many of Bahr's later works in particular reflect this view, and one of his favourite topical themes was the Women's Emancipation movement and the abolition of the sexual double-standard, which he treated with sympathy in *Das Tschaperl* (The Fool, 1898), and in his most successful play *Das Konzert* (1909). Several of his works depict the theatre world of Vienna (*Das Theater*, 1897), and the political scene is treated in *Der Apostel* (1901), in which he exposes the corruption and incompetence of politicians. In his time Bahr's plays were popular and entertaining, but Bahr himself acknowledged that they lacked truly substantial plots and were too loosely conceived to endure.[10] Nevertheless, of the literary products of the Jung Wien writers they do come closest to the degree of social realism that Schnitzler himself achieved.

The most famous social and political commentator of the period was the satirist Karl Kraus, his main vehicle being the pages of his own private journal *Die Fackel* (The Torch). The first issue of *Die Fackel* appeared in 1899, announcing Kraus's hostility to all that was empty or corrupt in Austrian life and society. From the beginning he attacked incompetence and inefficiency in the bureaucracy, the public services, the political parties, the financial world, the police, the army, the universities, the theatres and the bourgeois liberal press.[11] He went on to confront the façade of bourgeois morality, the sexual hypocrisy and profession of lofty principles, which concealed a basic materialism and suffocated the spontaneous emotional development of the individual. In his rejection of the bourgeoisie Kraus was close to Bahr, but at the same time he was hostile to the aestheticism and impressionism of contemporary Viennese culture, and felt alienated from the Jung Wien circle around Hofmannsthal and Bahr. Kraus was more of a practical social reformer, calling for reforms in a range of social institutions, including the judicial system, the schools and universities. He advocated shorter working hours and better conditions for workers and employees, changes in the law to put an end to corruption in banking and commerce. These demands allied him closely for a time with the Social Democrats, a position in tune also with his hostility to the liberals and to the anti-Semitism of the Christian Socialists. But he later became disillusioned with the world of politics, and recognized that the political and racial divisions within Austrian society, and the essential weakness and incompetence of the establishment and government, could lead only to the collapse of the empire. Kraus was indeed 'the most articulate prophet of impending Apocalypse',[12] his sense of the coming disaster finding retrospective expression in his vast documentary of the First World War, *Die letzten Tage der Menschheit* (The Last Days of Mankind, 1922).

The one member of the coffee-house circle to be spared Kraus's contempt was Richard Engländer. He was the son of a wealthy Jewish merchant, but in fact was the only truly bohemian avant-garde character of the Viennese circle. His life-style accorded with the popular image of the decadent *fin-de-siècle* artist figure. He filled his time in coffee-houses with drugs, alcohol, newspapers and discussions in the company of fellow artists, and frequented prostitutes and girls of the demi-monde. He wrote under the name of Peter Altenberg, his characteristic genre being the short prose sketch depicting a brief scene from everyday life, with only a minimum of story-line, and an open suggestiveness regarding the lives and attitudes of the characters. Altenberg's impressionistic vignettes are reminiscent of the French prose poems of Baudelaire and Mallarmé, but his sketches also stand very much in the tradition of the Vienna feuilleton. They present fragmentary depictions of the local milieu, sometimes sentimental, often ironic, communicating a kind of splintered reality or mood, detached from the political or social context. To some the feuilleton was an escapist genre, representing a flight from reality into the sphere of personal sensations, impressionistic perceptions of Viennese life and culture that the writer observes, but in which he does not participate. Indeed Kraus attacked the feuilleton for its sentimentality and aestheticism. But he was attracted to Altenberg because of the authenticity and honesty of his sketches, which are noteworthy for their documentary truthfulness, their accurate depiction of reality and their social import.[13]

Altenberg's best pieces are like instantaneous photographs of the Viennese suburbs, concentrated précis, or 'extracts' of life, as he called them.[14] *Blumenkorso*, from his first collection *Wie ich es sehe* (As I See It, 1896), describes the scene as a coach, bedecked with flowers, moves off from the flower shop for the traditional May Day parade. Altenberg's prime concern is with the social gulf between the lady who hires the coach and the women left behind in the vicinity of the flower shop. For the tired, pale shop-girl the festival is a means of increasing her meagre income; for the young mother walking in the street with her child, the coach is like an unattainable piece of fairyland; the prostitute leaning out of her window would love to hire it herself, but the notion remains only a dream. But the most telling point is the last. The flowers are not real, but artificial. The whole coach is a façade, and far from possessing the natural scent of roses, its flowers have an unpleasant, musty smell, symptomatic of the atmosphere of the city itself.

The theme of the gulf between rich and poor finds a more aggressive expression in Altenberg's short piece entitled *At Home*, whose setting is a house in Grillparzerstraße, a fashionable street near the Ring, between the University and the Rathaus. Here the social divide is explored in terms of mistress and servants. The month is October, and the lady of the house has returned from her summer holiday in the country. But so also have the servants, as full of hatred now, as they resume their work in the 'prison' of the city, as they were when they left for the woods and mountains. Meanwhile workmen have taken over the house to carry out interior decorations, a threatening hostile force metaphorically described as an army entering a battle under the command of the head housekeeper, the field marshal. Through the military imagery Altenberg suggests that the workers (like the servants) are on the march, and the idle rich will soon have had their day. Altenberg's social criticism is not always so obvious. In many of his pieces, particularly those set in the lakeside resorts of the Salzkammergut, the sense of the end of an era, of a society 'very much on the brink',[15] is conveyed more by the evocation of wistful melancholy autumn days. And when he writes of Vienna, his sketches produce only a fragmented glimpse of individual aspects of the life of the city. In this respect his brand of social realism may be contrasted with Schnitzler's, whose works present a much fuller and more detailed account of Viennese life.

Because of their very nature, and perhaps because of their author's time-bound viewpoint, Altenberg's sketches scarcely represent a coherent overall view of Viennese society as a whole. Indeed, it was only after its passing that Austrian authors attempted to recreate and come to terms explicitly with the atmosphere and values of the last phase of the empire. A notable example is afforded by Hugo von Hofmannsthal. In his early works Hofmannsthal showed little concern for social and political problems, and he was a leading figure amongst the Griensteidl poets who expressed their disenchantment with social reality in aestheticism and self-preoccupation. Many of the central characters of his early verse dramas are themselves young aesthetes, sensitive creatures obsessed with their own inner life. At the same time Hofmannsthal was clearly aware of the limitations of aestheticism and of the inadequacies of a life spent amongst beautiful objects. This is apparent in his presentation of Claudio, the hero of *Der Tor und der Tod* (The Fool and Death, 1893), a young aristocrat preoccupied with his own feelings and works of art. This play is really a drama of the soul, and Claudio's emotions are portrayed in long, lyrical monologues, typical of the mood of the 1890s. But although his preoccupations have heightened his sensitivities, they have drained him of vitality and have removed him from the reality of social life. He is eventually forced to review his attitude and acknowledge the importance of human relationships and moral responsibilities. Claudio has been seen as a typical young aristocrat of the time, a man without function in society, without substance as a real human being.[16] But Hofmannsthal's world at this stage is still far removed from reality, the poetic image of Vienna is abstract and timeless, and its decline is presented only in symbolic, allegorical form. Nevertheless the play has been seen as a turning point in his development and a signal of a greater concern with social problems.[17]

During the early years of the twentieth century Hofmannsthal attempted to revive the Austrian popular cultural tradition and affirmed the traditional way of life of the natural community as a remedy for the rootlessness of urban industrial society. But it was only with the advent of the First World War that he began to identify himself with a civilization that was positively Austrian and Habsburg. Hofmannsthal regarded the war as a defence of the old supra-national values of the empire against barbarous and petty nationalism, and when the monarchy collapsed and the empire disintegrated, he experienced a profound sense of loss and desolation. In the post-war years his nostalgia for the traditions of imperial society became embodied in his social comedies *Der Schwierige* (The Difficult Man, 1921) and *Der Unbestechliche* (The Incorruptible, 1923). Only in these later works does the world of Habsburg Austria really come to life.

Der Schwierige is set in the elegant world of the Viennese aristocracy in the period immediately following the First World War. But the political, social and economic realities of the early days of the newly declared First Republic are ignored, and the social institutions of the old order are still preserved as though nothing has changed. Hofmannsthal's depiction of Viennese high society has therefore been seen as a poetic, idealized recreation of a world that refuses to acknowledge the reality of its demise. Most immediately the play provides a record of the polite, mannered conversation of the salons of the aristocracy. But the main focus of this delicate comedy is the central character, Count Hans Karl Bühl, an intensely private man who attempts to conceal his feelings and intentions from the insufferable inquisitiveness of those about him. But the result is that others make assumptions concerning his attitude from his words or behaviour, which are neither justified nor true, and Hans Karl resents these misinterpretations of his conduct as an intrusion into the privacy of his own being. He takes refuge behind a façade of evasion and non-commitment, avoiding social intercourse because of the complex tangle of misunderstandings that inevitably results. The result is that he is accused of being indecisive and unreliable. Paradoxically he also exercises a powerful fascination over others because of these very qualities. His nonchalance and reserve are admired as an expression of dignity and grace; his evasiveness and indifference are signs of an inner composure and serenity; in his reluctance to express opinions, in particular a refusal to criticize others, he exudes a charming urbanity and bonhomie.

The figure of Hans Karl has been idealized as a celebration of the specifically Austrian virtues of grace and good manners, which are viewed positively in the play in the face of new elements undermining the decorum of Viennese aristocratic society.[18] The spirit of the modern age is represented by the energy and determination of the brash and tasteless Prussian, Baron Neuhoff, by the blatant self-interest of the ungracious and vulgar new servant, and at a more comic and pathetic level, by the ineffective and simplistic attempts of Hans Karl's nephew to demonstrate a new decisiveness and strength of will. That Hofmannsthal wishes to view the contrast in terms of one between Austrian and Prussian qualities has been suggested by an essay which he published in 1917, entitled 'Preuße und Oesterreicher'. In this the qualities of strength, self-confidence, efficiency and ambition are attributed to the Prussian, those of humanity, charm, self-irony to the Austrian.[19] Thus Hans Karl's person has been seen as a combination of the most attractive features of the 'Austrian character'.[20] In the play itself the most flattering description of Austrian society is expressed by the man who aspires to join it. Neuhoff praises a civilization, a culture, that is in full flower, unpretentious and urbane, its exclusiveness tempered by its charm and gracefulness. That his words are insincere is seen later, when in Hans Karl's absence he mocks the Austrians as living shades, inhabiting a world detached from the reality of social and political developments, essentially empty and concerned only with superficial trivialities. This judgement is as exaggerated in its harshness as his former words of praise were flattering, but it serves to set the idealized picture of Austrian society within a specific historical context, and to remind us that it has now passed from the world stage. At the same time it suggests that Hofmannsthal was as sensitive to its failings as he was captivated by its charms. His affectionate portrait of a dying aristocratic society is unashamedly nostalgic, and represents a highly personalized view, but at the same time it is imbued with gentle irony. It is also arguable that Hans Karl's discretion and reserve are essentially 'negative' characteristics: the surface charm may indeed be no more than an empty shell. Likewise it is important to bear in mind that with his indecisiveness, evasiveness and lack of drive, he remains one of the great *comic* characters of Habsburg Austria.

Hans Karl's rival as a representative figure of imperial society is a man presented so negatively as to be literally 'without qualities', namely Ulrich, the central figure of the novel by Robert Musil, *Der Mann ohne Eigenschaften*. Musil was born into a well-established Carinthian family with a military background. He trained as an engineer, but eventually devoted himself to literary and journalistic work. His major work is the fragmentary, but still enormous novel *Der Mann ohne Eigenschaften*, the first two books of which were published in 1930 and 1933. Like Hofmannsthal Musil is also taking a sympathetic, but ironic backward look at the Habsburg world. As with *Der Schwierige*, its setting is Vienna, and there are references to specific Viennese buildings and institutions, the Herrenhaus, the Hofburg, the Belvedere, the Burgtheater and so on, likewise to contemporary social trends such as duelling and anti-Semitism. The picture is drawn so successfully that the novel is said to have captured the atmosphere of *fin-de-siècle* Vienna better than any other historical or literary work.[21] It satirizes all the stock Austrian features, the superficiality and frivolity of social life, the pedantry of the bureaucracy. Its world is inhabited by effete aristocrats, petty officials, capricious women, arrogant officers of the Imperial Army. Yet the novel was not intended to provide an accurate or complete picture. Musil's aim was to present Vienna as a spiritual entity, to capture the 'soul' of the empire and lend it a metaphysical significance.

Musil gives an impressionistic, and at times deliberately vague, picture of the city. Although the setting is specifically identified as the Vienna of 1913, the account is imprecise and timeless, a feature reflected initially in the mixture of architectural styles seen in the house of Ulrich in an unidentifiable outer suburb. It is also a period of transition, but its general direction and ultimate destination are uncertain, for its rulers lack determination and conviction. When Musil comes to comment specifically on Austria as an amalgam of features, he singles out the quality of moderation, which he captures in a series of negatives. Motor cars drive along the roads of Austria, but not too many. Occasionally a ship will be despatched to South America or to East Asia, but not too often. There is a display of luxury, but not nearly as refined as in France. Sports are pursued, but not so fanatically as in England. Vast sums of money are spent on the army, but only sufficient amounts to maintain Austria's position as the second weakest of the Great Powers. The satirical note continues with more bite: according to its constitution Austria is liberal, but it is ruled by the clerics. All citizens are equal before the law, but not all in fact are citizens. There is a parliament, that makes such violent use of its freedoms that it is usually closed. The eighth chapter of the first book provides in this fashion a series of general stock observations of the weaknesses, and the attractions, of the Austrian state machine, which Musil sums up with the name he gives it – Kakanien (from the initials k.k., or 'kaiserlich-königlich' which preceded all named imperial institutions). The name is not a fictional disguise, but an attempt to find a symbol to evoke the spirit of the empire.

Because Musil's prime concern is to capture the aura or feel of an epoch, he is less preoccupied with a story-line or with psychological detail. Indeed the later stages of the novel move into the realms of mysticism and intellectualism. At the end of Part One of the first book, however, Musil creates narrative interest when he initiates what he calls the 'Parallelaktion' with the formation in 1914 of a committee to consider an appropriate means of celebrating the emperor's seventieth jubilee in 1918, which is to be called 'The Austrian Year'. As Musil is writing with hindsight in 1931 the whole process is tinged with irony. The celebration is pure fantasy, and the fatuous attempt on the eve of the Great War to have Franz Josef portrayed as the emperor of peace also has little credibility. The 'parallel action' has been seen as a satire on the Austrian incapacity for choice and action, as the plans put forward become ever more extravagant and irrelevant,[22] and the efforts of the committee exhibit the desperation of a society to perpetuate its traditional mission long after that role is felt to be redundant.[23] Likewise the central character is presented as the typical Habsburg subject, evading his social and political duties, and displaying indecision, apathy and detachment. In his 'man without qualities' Musil captures the inertia of pre-war Vienna, as its citizens and rulers turn a blind eye to the intellectual and cultural resurgence of the new century.

Another writer who took a backward look at the empire in the 1930s was Joseph Roth, notably in his two major fictional accounts of the passing of the Habsburg world, *Radetzkymarsch* (1932) and *Die Kapuzinergruft* (1938). Both titles are resonant with historical associations: the first is named after the march by Johann Strauß the elder in honour of the one-time Commander-in-Chief of the Imperial Army; the second refers to the vault where the Habsburgs lie entombed. Like that of Musil, Roth's viewpoint is essentially critical, though he shows some sympathy for the representatives of the old order. He is also less inclined towards abstraction, and his novels conform to a more conventional pattern, with clear narrative development within a specifically identifiable reality. Even more intensely than Musil, Roth is concerned with the empire as a whole, rather than with Vienna as a social and political entity. Indeed the city itself provides the setting for only a few brief sections of *Radetzkymarsch*. The Trotta family, whose decline and demise accompany, and in effect symbolize, the end of the monarchy and the empire, has its origins in Slovenia in what is now northern Yugoslavia. The father Franz Trotta is Bezirkshauptmann (administrative head) of a district in Moravia; his son Carl Joseph, a lieutenant in the Imperial Army, is eventually stationed in Galicia, in the last Habsburg outpost on the remote eastern border. Roth himself grew up in a Jewish community in Galicia, and he first came to Vienna to study at the University immediately prior to the First World War. He also worked there briefly as a journalist in the post-war period, living in the Jewish quarter in the Leopoldstadt, thus socially far removed from the high society frequented by Schnitzler and Hofmannsthal. Roth published in the left-wing Viennese paper *Der neue Tag*, and his early novels were essentially socialist in spirit. Only in response to the onset of National Socialism in the 1930s did he experience an irrational nostalgia for the monarchy, though he was still highly critical of the forces that led to the collapse of the empire.

The contrast between Vienna and the outer reaches of the empire is brought out most strikingly in *Die Kapuzinergruft*, but it is already implicit in the structure of *Radetzkymarsch*. Despite the remoteness of the setting of much of the novel, Vienna is presented very much as the hub of the empire, the centre of political activity and influence. The Bezirkshauptmann is the emperor's representative in his administrative district, he accepts his orders direct from Vienna, which he regards as his true home. When his son Carl Joseph finds himself in disgrace with his regiment, it is from Vienna, indeed from the Hofburg itself, that his case is cleared. But Vienna also has its darker sides. It is there, in the twilight world of the inner city, that Kapellmeister Nechwal pursues his worldly pleasures, that the degenerate painter Moser peddles his pornographic pictures, that Carl Joseph enjoys his degrading affair with Frau von Taußig. Vienna is also castigated by the far-sighted prophet of doom, Count Chojnicki, as the origin of all ills: the emperor is senile, the government a collection of fools, the Reichsrat a gathering of well-meaning, but pathetic idiots, the atmosphere of the Ringstraße is contaminated by democrats and socialists, the Burgtheater by 'Jewish swine'. When Carl Joseph visits Vienna and watches the Corpus Christi procession he is dazzled by the pomp and ceremony, as the vast panoply of imperial grandeur passes before his eyes and those of the enthusiastic and seemingly contented citizens. The whole spectacle appears to belie Chojnicki's pessimism. But this is precisely Roth's point: the procession, simply because it is a spectacle, blinds Trotta to the reality of decline. The ceremonial décor is but a façade, the participants ghosts from the past. In *Die Kapuzinergruft* the attack on Vienna is even more savage and explicit. The theme of Vienna's sophisticated decadence and depraved artificiality, in contrast to the rude health of the provinces, pervades the first half of the novel. Indeed Roth implies that the decadence of the pre-war generation, its frivolity, scepticism, irresponsibility and arrogance, were the real causes, and not just the symptoms of the decline of the monarchy. Roth's narrator identifies himself as a champion of the subject peoples of the remote rural areas, and Vienna is described as a sick parasite, feeding off the innate strength and natural resources of the Crown Lands. Hence Roth appears to adopt a federalist, rather than centralist position. The essence of Austria is not to be found at its centre, but on the periphery. This is reflected in *Die Kapuzinergruft* in Franz Ferdinand Trotta's tribute to his father's dreams of a kingdom of the Slavs within a tripartite empire of the Habsburgs, the implication being that had the grievances of the subject peoples been heeded more positively, the empire may well have been saved for the Habsburgs.[24]

In *Radetzkymarsch* this standpoint is also suggested by Carl Joseph's desire to return to his roots in Slovenia, but the whole thrust of this earlier and more substantial novel is different. Here it is Roth's purpose to show that the attitudes and institutions at the heart of the empire in Vienna are reflected in all parts of the empire itself, and that the forces which might otherwise have fostered unity and uniformity are themselves the instruments of decay and disintegration. The district which the Bezirkshauptmann administers is a version in miniature of the empire, as governed by Franz Josef. The meticulous, inflexible bureaucracy of the provincial district, and the routine manner of life of its governor, reflect the artificial protocol regulating the life of the court, and stifling the human being in the person of the emperor. Decisions are taken without regard to circumstances or consequences, there are reports of disturbances and uprisings of racial groups, which the Bezirkshauptmann regards as a direct insult to himself, but whose far-reaching implications he prefers to ignore. The decadence of Viennese society extends to the Imperial Army, in which gambling and drunkenness are rife, and whose officers cling to an outmoded and futile code of honour, at present blissfully ignorant of the fate which awaits them in the Great War. The army also carries within it the seeds of the empire's collapse. The spirit of revolution lies latent in the ranks, there are reports of spying and of desertion, and the loyalty of officers cannot be counted on. Moreover there are divisions along political and racial lines at the highest level, as shown by the varied reactions to the news from Sarajevo, which arrives, ironically, on the night of the celebration of the anniversary of the regiment.

Radetzkymarsch ends with a series of deaths. The report of the assassination of the archduke is followed by the outbreak of war, and by the futile death of Carl Joseph in its early days; the madness of Chojnicki heralds the demise of Franz Josef, and then, immediately afterwards, of the Bezirkshauptmann. Neither the emperor nor his most loyal administrator could live to see the demise of Austria itself. The atmosphere of death has been building up throughout the novel, with grotesque images of worms and ravens feeding off rotting corpses, and references to the invisible hand of death passing over the chalices from which the unsuspecting officers drink their wine. The Great War in effect means the fall of the monarchy and the death of the empire, which for Habsburg loyalists such as the Trottas means 'the end of the world'. It is understandable that Roth should view the collapse in these apocalyptic terms. The sense of a declining, disappearing world likewise pervades the works of others writing with the benefit of hindsight, notably Musil and Hofmannsthal, and of later authors viewing the period at an even greater distance, such as Franz Werfel and Heimito von Doderer.

It is also not surprising that writers who felt the need to come to terms with the loss of a world which effectively ended in 1918, should present Vienna primarily in terms of the capital of the disintegrating empire, harbouring the seeds of its decay, rather than as the busy, expanding commercial and industrial city that it actually was in the pre-war period. This image is rarely seen. Nevertheless not all authors, whether contemporary or later, felt the need to view either the period or the city itself solely in its imperial context. In Stefan Zweig's account of life in Vienna in *Die Welt von Gestern* there is little sense of a great empire existing beyond the immediate horizon of the city.[25] Several of his works have a Viennese setting, but the city, like any other, functions simply as a fund of psychological material. The short story

Phantastische Nacht (1922) is set in Vienna in 1913, and though it contains a stock critical analysis of the decadent life-style of bourgeois society, the central character is concerned solely with his own personal development. The accounts of the crowd at the Prater stadium and of the dancing throng in the cheap drinking hall serve to convey the wild, orgiastic turmoil of the pleasure grounds of the 'people'. The Prater and the Viennese simply provide a convenient forum for Zweig's observations. The majority of Zweig's works were written in the 1920s and 1930s, and few of his novels are set in the Vienna of the pre-war period. Only in the early chapters of his autobiography do we find a significant presentation of the Vienna of his youth.

In his predilection for psychological themes, and in his use of Vienna as a background for his observations of his fellow human beings, the writer who comes closest to Zweig is Schnitzler. But as Zweig's senior of some twenty years, Schnitzler does use for his forum, in the majority of his works, his own contemporary Vienna of the final years of the monarchy. In his analyses of human relationships within the social world in which he moved, Schnitzler provides us with a unique record of the life pursued by particular social groups of the *fin-de-siècle* period. His attention to the realities of contemporary life sets him apart from the majority of the Jung Wien writers of the 1890s. At the same time the picture he presents of Vienna is much more detailed than that offered by the older generation of social realists, von Saar and Ebner-Eschenbach, and his works are permeated with the names of Vienna's streets, parks, squares, districts and buildings, full of associations for those who know the city well. Because of his more immediate, and almost exclusively Viennese perspective, he cannot produce the kind of far-reaching and wide-ranging analyses of social and political trends found in the novels of Musil and Roth. Nor does he approach Hofmannsthal's celebration of Austrian virtues in the refined world of Viennese high society. Schnitzler's characters are no idealized or symbolic figures, but men and women of flesh and blood, with genuine emotions and clearly defined attitudes. Yet because they are also recognizable as social types or representative figures of specific social classes or groups, the overall impression created in his stories, novels and plays is of a substantial, and at times critical, examination of his own society.

3

THE FREUDIAN CONNECTION

In many of his early works, particularly the shorter prose works, Schnitzler's main concern is with the individual psyche, rather than with the wider social scene. His central characters tend to be isolated figures, preoccupied with private emotions, and the world depicted is a limited one, perceived from their own narrow, often tortured viewpoint. These works clearly reflect his interest in his fellow beings, as well as his early professional preoccupations. Pointed fairly forcibly in the direction of medicine by his father, he graduated in 1885 with qualifications in anatomy, gynaecology and surgery. He spent a year as a resident houseman in the Allgemeine Krankenhaus, worked in various departments with well-known specialists, started his own private practice, and became editor of the *Internationale Klinische Rundschau*. Yet from an early stage he did not feel truly dedicated to medicine, and longed to escape from a career which he felt had been imposed upon him.[1] However, his appointment in 1886 as an assistant in the psychiatric clinic of the famous neurologist Theodor Meynert, opened up a new avenue of interest for him. He studied the works of leading psychiatric authorities such as Charcot, Bernheim, Freud and Breuer, and undertook specialized work in hypnosis and the problem of hysteria. Schnitzler's practical work in the field of hypnosis attracted the interest of students who attended his 'sessions' in large numbers. But it led to no professional advancement in this field, and as his literary work began to predominate over his medical activities, his interest in psychology found its true reflection in his detailed analyses of his characters. It is this aspect of his work that won the admiration of eminent psychologists, notably Theodor Reik, who published the first critique of Schnitzler's works from a psychological angle as early as 1913,[2] and Reik's mentor Sigmund Freud.

A typical early example of Schnitzler's psychological studies is *Der Andere* (The Other Man, 1889), which consists of the diary jottings of a man whose wife has recently died, recording his daily visits to her grave. Initially the work is a study of his state of mind. There is a sense of an unhealthy preoccupation with his emotions as he shuns all contact with the outside world, jealously guarding his 'eternal pain'. One day, however, he becomes aware of the proximity of another mourner at the cemetery, who actually kneels at the grave of his (the writer's) wife. As the implications sink home, his brain races, and the narrative takes on an excited tone:

> Und da stand ich . . . dem Wahnsinn nahe . . . Wer ist dieser Mann, der es wagt, auf dem Grabe meiner Gattin zu knien? . . . Was war er ihr? . . . Wie erfahre ich's? . . . Wo finde ich ihn wieder? . . . Plötzlich verzerrt sich mir die ganze Vergangenheit . . . Bin ich denn toll? . . . Hat sie mich denn nicht geliebt?
> (ES I, 44)

> (So there I stood . . . close to madness . . . Who is this man who dares to kneel at my wife's grave? . . . What was he to her? . . . How can I find out? . . . Where can I find him again? . . . Suddenly my whole past is distorted . . . Am I mad? . . . Did she not love me, then?)

The diarist is forced to review the years of his marriage, but is left in a torturing void of uncertainty, not knowing whether to cherish his wife's memory as hitherto, or to hate her for her treachery. A feverish search of her possessions provides no clues, and the truth remains elusive. Schnitzler's concern here is less with the reality as such, than with the individual's perception of it, and his use of the first person narrative concentrates the material and narrows the viewpoint.

A similar effect is produced by the story *Die Fremde* (The Stranger, 1902), in which Schnitzler presents another short study of a marital relationship, again from the limited and perplexed perspective of the deceived husband. But here the real object of interest is the personality of the wife, and the story provides more details concerning her background and behaviour. Albert von Webeling has conceived an irrational passion for Katharina, a girl with a quiet, dignified, but mysterious manner, who has recently suffered a brief period of mental illness. Albert is drawn to aspire to her hand, she agrees without enthusiasm, and remains a strangely enigmatic, detached and impassive creature throughout the period of their engagement, existing apparently in a world of her own. Then, without warning, after two weeks of their honeymoon, she leaves him. The narrative takes the form of Albert's review of their relationship, before he shoots himself in despair, and throughout the account Schnitzler provides no analysis of her mental condition and no clarification of her behaviour. Instead the reader is given a series of clues, from which we may make our own deductions. Some of these are to be found in Katharina's past. Her brother committed suicide for financial reasons; her fiancé Baron Maaßburg jilted her in consequence; she then became infatuated with a musician, and experienced a dream in which he was found dead: the dream comes true, for the musician commits suicide the next day. She then lapses into a state of depression, but apparently recovers, though her distant manner is still suggestive of mental problems, and there are indications that during her engagement to Albert she is leading a double life. There are references to secret meetings with other men, and when Albert follows her into a church after she has left him, she stares in oblivious rapture at a statue of the warrior-king Theodorich. Following Albert's suicide the reader is told that after the incident in the church she was picked up by an Italian gentleman, by whom she has since become pregnant, and who has abandoned her. Schnitzler is here presenting a case study, and the reader is being invited to indulge in psychological analysis. A trained psychiatrist may interpret Katharina's case as follows: Katharina suffers psychic traumata due to her brother's suicide and her subsequent broken engagement, a guilt neurosis based on a death dream come true, and a subsequent episode of schizophrenia. This leads to a flattening of emotions, loss of moral inhibitions, distractability and a tendency towards promiscuous behaviour.[3] The interpretation carries with it the authority produced by scientific training, but a reader lacking this expertise will remain as baffled by the story as the unfortunate husband.

Die Fremde is an extreme example of Schnitzler's psychological studies, simply because a knowledge of psychiatry seems necessary for a full understanding of the character under scrutiny. In many such stories, however, the object of analysis is the character through whose consciousness the narrative is presented, so that we gain a more immediate insight into the mental state. In *Der Witwer* (The Widower, 1894) the widower Richard discovers amongst his wife's effects secret letters to her from his best friend Hugo, which make all too clear the intimate nature of their relationship. When the unwitting Hugo visits Richard to express his condolences, the two men hold a polite, and rather strained conversation, until Hugo suddenly reveals that he has meanwhile become engaged to a girl whom he has known and loved for some time. The news triggers off in Richard a violent reaction. He suddenly stands up and fixes Hugo with large staring eyes. Pale with rage he tells Hugo in a strange, distant voice of his knowledge of the affair, drags him bodily to the piano and throws the letters in his face. This to Hugo is a new, hitherto unknown Richard, and he can only assume that his behaviour is caused by conventional jealousy. But because the encounter between the two men is preceded by a long section of interior monologue, revealing details of Richard's state of mind, the reader is aware that the psychological situation is more complex than this. Initially Richard shows signs of being overwhelmed with grief at his wife's death. But he promises himself that salvation is imminent in the form of the impending arrival of his friend Hugo. As his thoughts dwell on their relationship the reader becomes suspicious of a profound closeness to Hugo, with whom he used to pursue long, serious conversations, well into the night after his wife had retired to bed. When Richard discovers the letters, he expects to experience the 'honourable feelings' of pain and rage, but instead he views the situation with dispassionate clarity and understanding, recognizing that the root cause of the affair was his own loss of sexual interest in his wife. Far from being overcome by jealousy or hatred, he hopes to continue his close relationship with Hugo, which will be more rewarding than his marriage ever was. The death of his wife and the discovery of her infidelity have thus made Richard aware of the nature of his own feelings for Hugo. Consequently the news of Hugo's engagement comes as a far worse betrayal, and Richard's feelings of intense disappointment surface violently in the final dramatic scene.

The insight afforded the reader into Richard's thoughts and feelings enables him to deduce the reasons for his unexpected attack on Hugo. Though the attack is violent, and symptomatic of emotional instability, in no sense can Richard be regarded as a 'mental case'. Some of Schnitzler's psychological studies do, however, take the reader into the minds of characters suffering from neurotic, or even psychotic disorders. Once again his favourite situation is that of a character who has recently experienced the loss through death of a wife or mistress. Two of the most striking cases are those presented in *Blumen* (1894) and *Die Nächste* (1899).

The narrator in *Blumen* (Flowers) is a young man who has learned of the recent death of a former mistress, whom he had previously jilted. The affair had been terminated on his discovery of her infidelity, and he had remained unmoved in the face of her attempts to renew the relationship, which included a monthly delivery of flowers to him. The news of her death (presumably of a 'broken heart') is a shock to him, yet he feels no pain or remorse, and he appears to have put the whole episode behind him in the company of his new mistress, Gretel. Nevertheless he is visited by a sense of guilt at his emotional indifference, and the turning point occurs when the regular bunch of flowers arrives, commissioned before the death, but delivered subsequently to it. The man is deeply affected by this greeting from beyond the grave, he becomes morbidly fascinated by the flowers, and keeps them in his room throughout the winter, until they wither and smell of death and decay. He is aware of the irrationality of his behaviour, realizes that he is afflicted with an obsessive and neurotic attachment, but he is continually drawn back to them, weeping before them as before the grave of the beloved. The flowers, then, act as a catalyst for his repressed feelings of guilt, and the story represents a searching study of his resultant depressive condition. The spell is not broken until the spring, when Gretel brings him fresh flowers, and throws out the old. At a stroke he is cured of his condition, and emerges to face life again, refreshed and invigorated.[4]

Die Nächste (The Next One) is another detailed study of a psychological disorder suffered as a result of a bereavement. The central character Gustav has spent the winter mourning the death of his wife, which has left him with an intense feeling of loneliness. Occasional contact with people offers release, and he even begins to sense an interest in other women, but he suffers guilt feelings as a result, and consequently withdraws even more into himself – in effect he finds himself in what amounts to a psychological vicious circle. The solution appears to be offered in the form of a woman whom he picks up in the street, who is obviously sexually available, and who reminds him in some ways of his wife. The encounter causes him to dream of his dead wife, then to fantasize physical relations with her. But this again is followed by a sense of sin, of defiling the purity of his wife's memory. Nevertheless he seeks out the woman again, and eventually has relations with her in her flat. But the sensation that he is actually making love to his wife gives way to anger, for he suddenly feels that she is deliberately impersonating his wife to tempt him to betray her. Unable to control his rage he murders her, feels then at peace with himself, and hands himself over to justice. Gustav's feelings of guilt are now so intense that he can release himself from them only by destroying the object that has initiated them. For the professional psychiatrist Gustav's action is symptomatic of a schizophrenic condition, for at the moment of the murder he loses consciousness, and briefly thereafter does not realize what he has done. This psychotic condition is preceded by a pre-psychotic state, during which he exhibits paranoid tendencies and the symptoms of anxiety neurosis, prompted by his sense of guilt.[5] At an early stage of the story, even before his encounter with the woman, an episode is described in which he shows an irrational fear of the dark (which induces weeping); when he looks at his reflection in his mirror he sees the image of a stranger; he then flees into bed and covers himself with the blankets, not daring to put out his candle.

Through his use of interior monologue and direct exposition of the character's consciousness, Schnitzler enables the reader to experience directly a psychotic condition, the symptoms of which are described, but without technical explanation by a narrative voice. Such stories, of which there are many, particularly in his early years as a writer, read like case histories, as presented to a physician on first contact with the patient, from which a medical diagnosis may later be made. As works of literature Schnitzler's psychological studies, written in a cold, analytical style, involving a clinical exposition of symptoms without narrative interpretation or explanation, clearly have their limitations, as Schnitzler himself was well aware.[6] Nevertheless the meticulous accuracy with which his case histories are drawn testifies to his thorough knowledge of depth psychology, and professional psychologists have confirmed the validity of his understanding of the individual human psyche.

The links between Schnitzler's character-studies and Freud's preoccupations were recognized by Freud himself in a letter to Schnitzler in 1906. In it Freud acknowledged the general agreement between Schnitzler's analyses of psychological problems and his own, and expressed his astonishment and envy that Schnitzler the writer should have reached conclusions that Freud himself had arrived at only after painstaking research.[7] These sentiments were repeated in 1922 when Freud paid tribute to Schnitzler as an independent master of depth psychology, voicing his impression that Schnitzler had an intuitive knowledge of psychological processes, a knowledge that Freud himself had gained through laborious work with his patients.[8] To describe Schnitzler's insights as intuitive is something of an exaggeration. His training at Meynert's clinic (where Freud had also worked), and his practical work on hypnosis and the technique of suggestion as a treatment of mental illnesses, testify to his early professional preoccupation with the subject. He also kept up to date with current developments, reading various of Freud's publications as they came out.

It is easy to see why Freud should admire Schnitzler's work. In Schnitzler's elucidation of the symptoms of neuroses or psychological disorders, leaving the reader to function as an analyst of the condition, Freud recognized his own cases. Their mutual interest in erotic crises and aberrations, their shared awareness that neurosis has a psychic rather than a physical cause, that the trauma of bereavement can, for example, trigger depression and anxiety neurosis, testify to the similarities in their thinking.[9] Moreover it has been acknowledged that in some ways Schnitzler actually anticipated some of Freud's discoveries. Evidence is provided in particular by some of the early prose works written before he had an opportunity to read Freud's first psychoanalytic publications. A prominent example is the story *Der Sohn* (The Son, 1892), which describes an example of a psychopathological condition induced by infantile trauma.[10] A mother has been attacked by her son with an axe. As she dies she insists that the guilt is not his, but her own, for just after his birth she had attempted to smother him. The doctor attending her is moved to consider the possibility of the influence upon the child's psychological development of this first look from the mother of despair and hatred, and of this first night spent in unconscious fear of death. It has also been demonstrated that Schnitzler anticipated Freud's major work *The Interpretation of*

Dreams (1900), and numerous Freudian dreams have been identified in his works.[11]

At the time when Freud and Schnitzler were medical students in Vienna the emphasis both in physical and mental disorders was on diagnosis, rather than on therapy. Mental illnesses were thought to have a physical aetiology, and Theodor Meynert, who revolutionized the study of the brain's anatomy, did not believe that such conditions could be cured.[12] Freud's early experiments in psychotherapy, entailing the use of hypnotism and cocaine, were therefore ridiculed by the medical authorities. Despite professional opposition, however, Freud's pioneering work in the treatment of neuroses, and the development with Breuer of his theory of psychoanalysis, aroused considerable interest in Vienna. After he had given up hypnosis he developed the method of free association, which he originally called the 'Redekur'. This technique consisted in the painstaking process of listening to a patient speaking about everything that came into his or her mind in a particular context, until the psychic origin of the mental disorder could be identified. The very identification of the source could play a prominent part in the eventual recovery of the patient.

During his years as a student Schnitzler was exposed to the fallacies and erroneous teachings of the time, and although he followed with interest Freud's various publications, he did not accept automatically all of Freud's theories or claims. For example, there is little evidence in his literary works (apart from in *Blumen*) of an interest in the curative process of psychoanalysis. Nevertheless he had had some personal experience of the treatment of neuroses, and his use of interior monologue, or even diary notes, which allow a character to express thoughts in an unstructured, haphazard way, has been seen as the literary correlative of Freud's technique of free suggestion and association. The mind of the neurotic is revealed directly to the reader, who is like an analyst, circling round the malady and then 'homing in' on a crucial piece of evidence that exposes the nature of the disorder.[13] Thus the interior monologue is made to reveal, through a kind of free association, the inner self of the character, whose words and actions function as symptoms of inner tensions. The reader analyses the fictional character as did Freud the patients on the couch.[14]

Schnitzler's interest in psychiatry persisted into his later life, when he wrote some of his more successful studies. To some extent their appeal depends on a fuller and more comprehensible analysis of the mental condition. But what also makes them more readable as literary works is that the condition is explored within a clearly defined social context of human relationships, which has its own validity within the story. It is in these works that the interests of Schnitzler the psychologist begin to blend with those of the social realist.

Flucht in die Finsternis (Flight into Darkness, 1931) is Schnitzler's final work published in his lifetime, though its conception goes back as far as 1909. The story concerns Robert, a civil servant with a background of seemingly insignificant mental problems. The sudden onset of madness in an acquaintance arouses in him the fear that he might succumb in the same fashion, and he extracts from his brother Otto (who is a doctor) the promise that he (Otto) will allow Robert to escape his condition through a painless mercy-killing. The arrangement is confirmed in a letter which is left in Otto's possession. During the course of the story various symptoms of mental instability do indeed occur in Robert, and he fears that Otto will use the letter to determine his fate. His fears develop into an irrational suspicion that it is Otto who is mad, and is out to trap him. He arranges an elaborate flight, but when the alarmed Otto follows him, Robert actually believes that Otto threatens his life, and shoots him dead. He flees from the scene and is himself found dead three days later.

Schnitzler's presentation of Robert's case has been praised as a remarkably accurate and complete picture of paranoid schizophrenia, the following symptoms being among those singled out to support the case: overconcern with his own health, withdrawal symptoms, emotional instability, many paranoid delusions developing into a compulsive obsession, even the physical symptom of a hysterical ptosis of the left eyelid, and eventually the final homicidal episode in which he kills his brother under the delusion that he is acting in self-defence.[15] Schnitzler's main achievement, however, is to present the case so convincingly that the lay reader can follow the processes taking place, and also understand exactly what it is like to be so afflicted. Through his use of interior monologue he presents a vivid study of Robert's condition 'from the inside'. At the same time the reader is permitted occasional moments of insight into the behaviour and reactions of other characters, which facilitate recognition of the falsehood, or 'madness', of Robert's vision.

The first overt piece of evidence to suggest the possibility of mental illness is a memory-gap, which occurs as he talks with his brother's wife Marianne. His mind wanders to the conclusion of a previous love-affair with a girl called Alberta, but he is unable to recall the precise moment of parting from her. Suddenly he is struck by the possibility that he may have murdered her without realizing it. The rapid pursuit of these thoughts produces visible physical symptoms, for he realizes that Marianne is looking at him in alarm, and he has to pull himself together. Over the next days he is periodically tortured by the thought that he may have attacked Alberta; he begins to imagine that he is being followed and observed, under suspicion of murder; further, that he may have murdered another acquaintance, Paula Rolf, who disappeared without warning from a hotel where they were both staying. Neither of these delusions is substantiated, but they are replaced by the more powerful delusion that his brother Otto is mad, and is plotting against him. The sense of being observed by police spies seeking his arrest is replaced by suspicions that Otto is having him watched, with a view to having him confined to an asylum. As he makes his elaborate plans for escape, Schnitzler takes us into the first-hand experience of the persecution complex, as his mind races to confound the imagined pursuit:

> Halte ich es denn für möglich, daß Otto einfach durch die Tatsache meines Verschwindens wieder zur Vernunft kommen könnte? Ist es nicht viel wahrscheinlicher, daß er meine Abreise als ein neues Zeichen in seinem Sinn deutet, daß er meinen Aufenthalt zu entdecken sucht, mich verfolgt oder verfolgen läßt und am Ende – findet?! Nein, das wird er nicht. Ich werde schlauer sein als er. Finden sollen sie micht nicht! Wie wär's, wenn ich einen Selbstmord vorspiegelte? Kein übler Einfall. Doppelselbstmord. Ich und Paula. Wir lassen einen Brief zurück.
>
> (ES II, 975)

(Do I really think it possible, then, that the simple fact of my disappearance might bring Otto to his senses again? Is it not much more probable that he will interpret my departure as a new sign, that he will try to discover where I am staying, will pursue me, or have me pursued, and in the end – find me?! No, he won't. I will be cleverer than him. They won't find me! What if I staged a suicide? Not a bad idea. A double suicide. Paula and me. We will leave a letter.)

This convincing study of the onset of madness has been particularly praised for the clarity of the analysis of the shift in Robert from the conscious fear that he may be going insane, to the unconscious experience of true insanity.[16] It occurs after the arrival of a letter from Alberta, which effectively destroys his delusion that he may have murdered her. Robert is relieved, feels restored to mental health, yet cannot rid himself of his suspicions that Otto is still pursuing him. His explanation is that he, Robert, is after all sane: it is Otto who is mad. From this moment Robert enters the world of a genuine delusion, unconcerned at his own state, concerned only with the health and intentions of his brother. The change is given a physical symptom as he looks at his reflection in the mirror, and experiences a similar sensation of loss of identity to that which Gustav also feels in *Die Nächste*. Robert is horrified at the pallor of his cheeks, his widely staring eyes and dishevelled hair, the strange shape of his lips. The gap between Robert's view, and the reality he fails to see, reaches its culmination when Otto comes to him in the hotel to which he has fled, and moves to embrace him. Otto expresses 'fear, pity and love': Robert sees only 'malice, threat and death' (ES II, 984). The inner view produces its own reversal of the truth.

The separation of Robert from reality is also reflected in his egocentricity, which is apparent in his social relationships. This is particularly the case with the two women with whom he is briefly associated during the course of the story. One is the poor, lonely and unhappy music teacher, whom he meets in the street, walks with, entertains to dinner and eventually sleeps with, and to whom he brings a glimmer of happiness, only to abandon her. His relationship with Paula Rolf is equally one-sided. There is no indication that he loves her, and he asks for her hand peremptorily, sensing that she understands him and could bring him salvation ('Rettung'). He will take her for what she may give to him, not because he feels he has anything to offer her. In effect he is a social animal only 'externally'.[17] There is no genuine communication between himself and others, and he frequently feels hostility to those closest to him. In his portrait of Robert, Schnitzler is presenting the tragic *social* effects of madness, for his self-centred, cold-hearted nature has disastrous consequences for others, as well as for himself.

Flucht in die Finsternis is a case study presented not just for its own sake, but within a context of social relationships. The patient's illness has a destructive social effect and ruins the lives of those with whom he comes into contact. The story is actually set in Vienna, but the precise location is irrelevant to its main concern, and apart from references to the Westbahnhof and to the park in Dornbach, the movements of the characters within the city itself are left deliberately vague. Similarly the locality of the flat in *Blumen* is not identified, and in *Die Nächste* the woman's home is located only in an unnamed side-street off the Wollzeile. Schnitzler's most celebrated psychological study, *Fräulein Else* (1924), is also set in a social context, that of a hotel in the Dolomites. But here the central character is presented sympathetically as the unhappy victim of society, and the world of Vienna hovers threateningly in the background as a determinant factor.

Else is the daughter of a Viennese lawyer, and is on holiday with wealthy relatives. She receives a letter from her mother informing her that her father is in serious difficulties, under suspicion of embezzlement, and is in urgent need of thirty thousand florins. Her mother asks her to procure the money from a family friend, Herr von Dorsday, who is staying at the same hotel. Else does succeed in extracting a promise of assistance, but on the condition that she appear naked before him. Her fears for her father force her to fulfil the condition, but in full view of all the other hotel guests. At which point she is overwhelmed by a hysterical seizure, is carried to her room, where she commits suicide with a dose of veronal.

In *Fräulein Else* Schnitzler again affords the reader direct access to the mental processes of his central character, this time through the medium of sustained first person inner monologue, right up to the moment of her lapse into unconsciousness and death. Else's reasons for complying with Dorsday's condition, and her subsequent suicide, are comprehensible at a conscious level in terms of extreme love for her father, and then of the shame she suffers at her loss of social respectability. But Schnitzler's exploration of Else's spontaneous thoughts, her dreams and semi-conscious ramblings presents a more complex picture than the above simple 'rational' explanation would imply. In the early stages of the story, Else indulges in sexual fantasies of an exhibitionist nature, but with tendencies towards narcissism. This means that the libido is turned in upon the self rather than directed on to another person, and actual sexual relationships are inexplicably repulsive to her. Neverthless she expresses an overpowering desire to be 'looked at', most strikingly when impressed by her own beauty as she contemplates her nakedness in her mirror, by the excitement she feels as she anticipates displaying herself in public, and by the thrill she experiences when she actually does so. All this is sufficient to suggest that Dorsday's condition is what she subconsciously desires.[18]

These tendencies are accompanied by a subconscious death-wish, expressed notably in a death-dream, in which she lies in state in the family home, whilst Dorsday gazes upon her body. But as Schnitzler strips the layers from Else's consciousness, both in the dream and then during her hysterical seizure, there is evidence of a yet more profound desire. Else's death-dream is beset by Freudian symbolism, naval officers with swords raised as a guard of honour to her funeral, snakes that bite her foot, and a matador figure who must open the gate to the cemetery. As yet the identity of the latter figure is repressed, but when all inhibitions are released by the dose of veronal, this figure is supplanted by that of her father, who will take her hand, and with whom she will 'fly' through the world. For the Freudian interpreter, the association of the father figure with the sensation of flying provides clear evidence of a repressed Oedipal complex, and an indication that through her suicide she eventually fulfils the condition implied in her dream, namely that she may unite with her father only in death.[19]

Although interpretations of Else's actions through the method of depth psychology have undoubtedly been encouraged by the very nature of Schnitzler's exploration of the psyche of his heroine, there are nevertheless further aspects of her behaviour and situation of which account must be taken for a fuller understanding of the story as a whole. If one examines the personality and situation of this nineteen-year-old girl, one is struck primarily by her innocence and helplessness. Else is the daughter of an (outwardly) well-to-do Viennese family, and has hitherto led the respectable life of a bourgeois girl. Any experiences of a sexual nature have been strictly limited – and off-putting. We understand that a young man made advances to her three years previously at the Wörthersee, which she found improper, but obviously exciting; two years ago a certain Albert, with whom she believed herself to be in love, bit her lips. Since then there have been only two attachments. One is the faithful Fred, to whom she feels no sexual response, and who is too poor to have come seriously into the reckoning as a future husband; the second is a Dr Frierop who swept her off her feet at a dance, and then disappeared, possibly because of her father's indiscretions. Schnitzler thus provides a background of frustration and disappointment that accounts both for her sexual fantasies and for her distaste for the realities of sexual relations, even with a future husband. For Else well knows that the marriage which might await her amounts to a form of domestic prostitution, such as that already contemplated for her with a certain fifty-year-old Direktor Wilomitzer. But Else refuses to 'sell' herself in this fashion, for in principle she wishes to wait for a husband she loves. Unfortunately, due to her parents' threatened circumstances, this prospect has now receded, for no one will marry the daughter of a fraud.

There is thus considerable social and financial pressure on Else to fulfil Dorsday's condition, even apart from the love which she has for her father at the conscious level. But the choice to do so in full public view is taken deliberately, not only to deny Dorsday the pleasure of his private enjoyment of her beauty, but also to expose the immorality of a money-conscious society that has forced her into this position:

> Alle, alle sollen sie mich sehen! – . . . Dann bin ich nicht mehr das Fräulein Else, das man an irgendeinen Direktor Wilomitzer verkuppeln möchte; alle hab' ich sie so zum Narren; – den Schuften Dorsday vor allem.
> (ES II, 364)
>
> (Let them all see me, all of them! – . . . Then I shall no longer be that Miss Else who is to be paired off with some Direktor Wilomitzer or other; this way I'll make a fool of all of them; – especially that scoundrel Dorsday.)

Through her public exposure of herself, Else advertises the plight of women in her society as objects of pleasure, to gratify the desires of wealthy males. Likewise her death has a social dimension, for she feels that in effect she is being murdered by society ('You're all murderers, you've all murdered me').

A consideration of the social causes for Else's behaviour in no way reduces the significance of the work as a psychological study. Nor does it invalidate the conclusion reached by the process of psychological analysis, namely that the patient suffers from a suppressed incestuous love for her father. But this too has a possible social cause. Denied healthy sexual development, Else's pre-conscious love for her father has remained embedded in her subconscious, for it has not been abreacted in the normal way.[20] *Fräulein Else* is essentially a psychological study, but set within an identified social context, and it is precisely because Else's condition is partly the result of her social situation that Schnitzler presents such a sympathetic portrait of her. Though the setting is far away from Vienna, the social values of the city are exposed and explicitly condemned by the heroine herself, and though the story did not appear until 1924, it has been generally accepted that the values presented are those of pre-war bourgeois society.[21]

Another psychological study which carries with it its social implications is *Frau Beate und ihr Sohn* (Frau Beate and her Son, 1912), a story set in the lakes and mountains of the Salzkammergut, so well known to Schnitzler through his frequent holidays there. *Frau Beate* occupies a prominent place in Schnitzler's prose works, primarily because of the dramatic nature of its conclusion. Beate is a widow bringing up her seventeen-year-old son Hugo, and anxious to protect him from the seductive wiles of an exactress, Fortunata. But ironically Beate succumbs herself to the advances of Hugo's schoolfriend Fritz, with whom she indulges in a brief, passionate affair. When Hugo reveals his knowledge of this, and his torment at his mother's depravity, she and Hugo escape their shame by drowning in a lake together in a lovers' embrace. The manner of this mother-son *Liebestod* has obvious incestuous overtones, and has prompted interpretations of the work along Freudian lines, from Theodor Reik onwards. Indeed for Reik the Oedipus complex, represented by Beate's repressed Oedipal longing for Hugo, is the central theme of the story.[22]

It is true that Beate is deeply attached to her son, but initially there is no evidence to suggest that her feeling amounts to anything more than the natural anxiety of a widow left to bring up her child alone. Her sense of loss when she realizes that Hugo is now attracted to other women is also perfectly natural in the circumstances. Nevertheless there are brief subtle anticipations of the final outburst of incestuous feelings. During her affair with Fritz the figures of the two boys, Fritz and Hugo, are occasionally merged. As she looks invitingly and seductively into Fritz's eyes her arm is round Hugo's shoulders and her fingers are fondling his hair. When the affair is over and she is determined to take Hugo away with her, she imagines him taking Fritz's place, and that people will see them as lovers. Hugo is frequently mentioned in physical, sexual terms. She admires his tousled fair hair and attractive mouth, and as she contemplates her loss of him to other women she regrets that never again will she stroke his cheeks and kiss his sweet lips. Several times she notes Hugo's similarities to his father, and at the moment of death the husband–son images combine, as she imagines she is kissing the husband 'who never really knew her'. Boy-lover, husband and son form a complex, intermingling pattern in her mind until they fuse in the final incestuous embrace.

But to focus on incest as the central theme is to ignore other aspects of Beate's development, particularly her discovery within herself of her latent sexuality, and her changing attitude to her marriage and her husband. Since her husband's death Beate has remained faithful to his memory, 'as chaste as a young girl', oblivious to the sorrowful yearnings of the local bank manager, and to the blatantly cheeky gallantries of the young Doctor Bertram. The disturbance of her composure occurs when Hugo falls prey to Fortunata. Beate's thoughts wander to the lawless world of the theatre, and to her actor husband, whom she had loved and wooed (against the wishes of her strait-laced parents), so that she could make love to the characters he played, the Hamlets and Cyranos, heroes and villains, lovers and kings. Gradually she begins to sense that Doctor Bertram is eyeing her in a mocking, suggestive fashion, and to register the unspoken telepathic communications from the bank manager. On a picnic expedition she is conscious of the physical interest in her of the males, and she responds involuntarily with encouragement. It is uncertain whether their interest is actual or the product of her highly charged imagination, stimulated further by wine and frivolity, but there is no escaping the sexual feelings which surface from the depths of her being:

> Und wieder sah sie den Direktor, der nun schweigend an ihrer Seite einherging, flüchtig an, aber erschreckt beinahe spürte sie um ihre Lippen ein Lächeln, das aus dem Grunde ihrer Seele gekommen war, ohne daß sie es gerufen, und das untrüglich, beinahe schamlos, deutlicher als alle Worte, sprach: Ich weiß, daß du mich begehrst, und ich freue mich daran.
>
> (ES II, 74)

(And again she glanced fleetingly at the bank manager, who was walking in silence at her side, but almost in alarm she sensed a smile on her lips that had come involuntarily from the depths of her soul, and which spoke to him, blatantly, almost shamelessly, more plainly than any words: I know that you want me, and I am glad.)

The surrender to Fritz and the collapse of her moral inhibitions is the culmination of this process.

Beate's reaction against her moral degradation commences when Fritz tells her in pillow-talk of the rumours of a previous relationship between her husband and the wife of the bank manager. As Beate recalls her husband's numerous infidelities, her anger erupts at her exploitation as housewife and mother at the hands of this faithless man. But then she is forced to acknowledge again that she in turn loved not him, but the roles that he played and the masks he wore, that her marriage and her subsequent front of bourgeois respectability were but a façade, and that she herself is no better than the despised Fortunata and the licentious world of the theatre. Beate's recognition of her own depravity is confirmed when she overhears her lover Fritz boasting of his conquest of her, and she realizes that to him love is no more than a frivolous game, in which she too has taken part. Now her greatest fear is that Hugo will come to hear of the relationship, and will reject her. Rather than endure this she would sooner die. Here then is the initial motive for her suicide, and it is only a step further, when faced with Hugo's actual distress, to take him with her in a joint suicide.

Beate's story is a frank and powerful study of a woman's discovery of her own sensual nature, which is not to be explained solely in terms of subconscious incestuous urges. Furthermore the exposure of the façade of bourgeois respectability broadens the scope of the work beyond its essential Freudian elements. For Beate's adventure with Fritz is not the only episode to disturb the genteel and civilized atmosphere of the Salzkammergut resort. There are rumours that the young wife of a local doctor spends a night out on the lake with a servant, of young girls sunbathing naked on the shore. Beate senses that there is something 'in the air' this summer.[23] Like *Fräulein Else, Frau Beate und ihr Sohn* is a case study, but set within the context of a broader social situation.

A further study of latent sexuality, but which is given a specifically Viennese setting, is *Traumnovelle* (Dream Story, 1926). Primarily the story is a study of a marital relationship, but because of the nature of Schnitzler's approach it amounts in effect to a double case study. It was particularly admired by Freud, who recognized Schnitzler's intuition regarding the function of the dream related during the course of the work. The story also exposes the underworld of unconscious drives in the human soul, as discussed in Freud's 'The Ego and the Id', which was published in 1923.[24]

Fridolin and Albertine have returned from a masked ball at which each has danced with other partners, and in jest discuss the romantic significance of the various encounters. The conversation takes a more serious turn as both are moved to confess that there have been occasions when they have previously been tempted to infidelity: Albertine felt a strong attraction towards a young Dane whilst on holiday the previous summer; Fridolin had encountered a young girl during his morning walks on the beach. The discussion wanders to his pre-marital affairs, and she responds in turn with an admission that had Fridolin attempted to seduce her before their marriage, she would not have resisted. The frankness of their confessions disturbs them, and each then embarks on a night of adventure, Fridolin in the dark world of Vienna's night-life, Albertine in that of her dreams.

Fridolin's night begins innocently enough. He is called out to a patient, who dies before he arrives. But then the dead man's tearful daughter, Marianne, reveals her love for Fridolin. Fridolin does not respond, but the experience reminds him of Albertine's confessions, and he is filled with bitterness and anger, an indication that his subsequent pursuit of adventure is motivated not by erotic desire, but by a determination to express for his own part a sexual freedom that he thinks he has discovered in his wife. What follows is an excursion into a fantastic realm, seemingly far removed from the security of his own orderly existence, though it begins in the very 'real' world of the streets around Vienna's Rathaus. The further he is lured into this nightmare world, the more unreal ('ghostly') become the people whom he has left behind, and he feels released from the inhibitions of bourgeois propriety. He is tempted by a prostitute to her room, but though he shrinks back from sexual contact, he moves on to an ill-lit café where he recognizes a former medical student Nachtigall, now leading a disreputable life as a pianist in shady establishments of the demi-monde. At Nachtigall's instigation he is taken to a secret mansion where masked naked women dance with the male guests. But first he requires a costume and mask of his own, and the adventure takes on further nightmarish qualities as he hires a costume (at one o'clock in the morning) from a sinister-looking costumier. Fridolin finds his daughter attractive, but she appears to be indulging in some theatrical game with two judges. The atmosphere of the secret mansion is even more macabre. In a darkened hall, walls hung with black silk, men dressed as monks and ladies as nuns converse against a background of solemn church music. Suddenly the whole scene is turned into a wild orgiastic dance, the monks disrobe to become colourfully dressed gentlemen, and the nuns naked dancers, their identities protected by veils and masks. Fridolin is drunk with the possibilities of sexual pleasure, but he becomes aware that no sexual fulfilment is available beyond the experience of the dance. The erotic and yet formalized dancing of this secret society is ultimately non-fulfilling. At the same time its ruthlessness and underlying barbarity are revealed when Fridolin is identified as an 'outsider' and his position threatened. He is saved by the intervention of one of the 'nuns', who offers to 'redeem' him, but again the brutal code that reflects the sado-masochistic sexuality of this group is clear – by saving Fridolin the young girl is sentencing herself to rape and, we eventually learn, to death. Fridolin is taken away, to be dumped in the snow outside Vienna, and eventually finds his way back home, where the unsuspecting Albertine lies asleep.

Immediately Albertine awakens from a dream, the details of which she feels impelled to relate to him. The manifest content of the dream is inspired by aspects of her preceding conscious experiences. The fantastic fairy-tale setting was triggered by an actual fairy-tale, read to her by her daughter before she retired to bed; the melody of a dance from the masked ball is heard; in the dream Fridolin makes love to her on the eve of their wedding, a fulfilment of her confessed wish; a figure looking rather like the Dane appears repeatedly, and eventually drags her into an orgy with innumerable naked couples; Fridolin is captured by soldiers and priests, is whipped, but offered release on condition that he become the lover of the princess of the land, who is the girl on the Danish beach; Fridolin refuses, is crucified, and Albertine laughs at him – to awaken laughing in her bed. The latent content of the dream is clearly discernible. Social pressures have denied Albertine sexual fulfilment before her marriage, and a variety of partners since. At the same time the dreaming Albertine feels a burning shame at her immorality, an indication of her thankfulness that she had never carried her urge for a pre-marital affair through. Her anger at Fridolin's confession of desire for the Danish girl is expressed in the dream by her sadistic pleasure at his suffering and death. Yet the dream-Fridolin's refusal to accept the princess's condition suggests an ultimate faith within Albertine's subconscious in his fidelity. Hence Albertine feels no sense of guilt at her dream. She reveals it voluntarily, and smiles at him happily and innocently. The dream has functioned as a safety valve, providing an outlet for her desires and anger. As far as she is concerned the marriage is saved.

But what of Fridolin? Interestingly Schnitzler allows him to revisit the scenes of his night's adventures, partly because he is not yet prepared to accept the significance of his wife's dream as a force for reconciliation, but also because he has not yet understood his own role in his own experiences. When Fridolin returns to the scenes of his adventures he finds himself – in the sober light of day – in a disappointingly real world. The café is shut and Nachtigall has disappeared; when he returns the costume to the costumier, he finds that the attractive daughter is nothing but a prostitute kept by her father to entertain paying clients; the prostitute whose room he visited has been detained in the clinic for sexually transmitted diseases; when he locates the secret house in Ottakring, he is handed a letter warning him not to pursue his inquiries further; finally he suspects that a certain Baroness D, who is reported to have poisoned herself, is the 'nun' who redeemed him. He hastens to examine her body in the mortuary, but finds the corpse repulsive and is indifferent to her identity. Moreover he realizes that throughout his search for her he has had the image of Albertine before his mind's eye. The lesson of Fridolin's adventures is now clear. In themselves they provided no sexual fulfilment, erotic desire leading only to frustration and danger, sexual activity being associated with death and disease. Gradually Fridolin throws off his desire for erotic adventure and sexual freedom, to find ultimate fulfilment with his wife.

The two sequences have functioned in similar ways for the two parties and contain similar themes (nakedness, sadism, orgiastic rituals). Albertine has escaped into her dreams to satisfy her unfulfilled yearnings, which now remain healthily repressed in her subconscious. Fridolin's adventures, whilst not taking place literally in a dream world, have taken him metaphorically into the 'dark world of the soul', in which the boundaries of reality and nightmare have become blurred. Albertine's dream is based on the reality of her subconscious urges; Fridolin's adventures have dreamlike qualities.

We are left with a marriage now based on mutual understanding and appreciation. The psyche of each partner has been probed, but the work ends in a social situation, that of the family unit. An island of respectability and security in the dark, unsavoury world of Viennese society, with prostitution and consequent disease at the lower end, decadent orgies involving the highest aristocracy at the other. For Fridolin is convinced that he has stumbled on an establishment secretly catering for the perverted (and ultimately sterile) pleasures of a degenerate section of the nobility. There is a reference to a prince's daughter who took poison after being unmasked as one of the 'nuns', and there is a clear suggestion that the death of the unfortunate baroness was politically arranged, and then hushed up by the police. In this frankest of works dreams offer a more innocent form of release for secret passions than an excursion into the sordid establishments of the sexual underworld.

The foregoing analyses certainly confirm to a considerable extent the parallels existing between aspects of Schnitzler's works and Freud's thinking. Like Freud, Schnitzler penetrated the outer surface of human behaviour and explored the depths of the individual human psyche and its unconscious drives. Yet despite Freud's expressed admiration for Schnitzler's work, and the adulation which he received from Theodor Reik, Schnitzler felt that Reik's own psychological interpretation of his works was too one-sided and dogmatic.[25] In view of Schnitzler's attention to psychological detail, it is understandable that his characters should lend themselves so invitingly to the process of psychoanalysis. On the other hand it is a problematic issue as to whether such an analysis of fictional characters represents a valid approach to literary criticism. A work of literature is something more than a clinical dossier, or case history, and explores aspects of a character's experience beyond the immediate confines of his or her subconscious urges. Only then do the characters of a literary work become humanly real. As we have seen in those of his more mature works which focus on an individual psyche, Schnitzler tends, in contrast to Freud's case histories, to present the individual consciousness within the broader context of human relationships and social background. Thus his psychological profiles appear richer and fuller, as they implicitly contain historical and sociological commentary.[26] In effect Schnitzler the literary creator goes beyond the narrow, scientific methods of the professional psychoanalyst. It is also true that despite the presence in Schnitzler's works of a considerable number of mental 'cases' of the neurotic and psychotic type, he is not excessively concerned with mental illness in the broadest sense of the term. Many of his more detailed and subtle studies are of perfectly normal and healthy individuals.

It should be stressed that Schnitzler is by no means the only Viennese writer of the time interested in depth psychology. We have already seen that the writers of the Jung Wien circle were more concerned with mental processes than objective reality, so that it is possible to view Schnitzler's preoccupations as part of a general Viennese trend. Schnitzler himself, for example, interpreted Hofmannsthal's story *Das Märchen der 672 Nacht* as an admirably accurate dream sequence.[27] But Schnitzler's own exploration of the world of the soul is far more scientific and clinical than that of his contemporaries, and the specific social context within which the majority of Schnitzler's characters are presented lends his works a completely different, and individual, dimension. This context is normally the social world of the Vienna of his day, and works set away from the city itself, such as *Frau Beate* and *Fräulein Else*, generally come within the general orbit of its social mores and values. Thus in Schnitzler's most successful stories the study of the psyche is blended with an indication of the social sources of psychological maladies, and even critics examining a story such as *Fräulein Else* from the viewpoint of psychoanalysis, recognize that by implication it constitutes a scathing denunciation of the values of a particular society.[28]

For many commentators the instances of mental illness prevalent in Schnitzler's works are associated with his preoccupation with death and decay, and are a reflection of the sickly, decadent mood of the *fin de siècle*.[29] At the time the marked increase in Vienna in cases of neurotic illness led to fears among Schnitzler's contemporaries that the very fabric of Viennese society was itself responsible for this development. This was variously attributed to such forces as the increasing pressures in daily life caused by industrial development, a speeding-up of life and a sense of participation in world-wide disasters due to improvement in communications, the increased sophistication and restlessness of city life, and the treatment in literature and other art forms of disturbing and exciting subjects, which encouraged sensuality and a contempt for ethical principles.[30] The growing insecurity and the questioning of values, beliefs and life-styles aggravated in Austria by the social and political problems of a disintegrating empire, and by the conflict between new ideas and established traditions, have also been recognized as important factors.[31] For Freud himself, however, the most significant factor in the increase in neuroses, particularly in cases of female hysteria, was the prevailing code of sexual morality, which smothered and repressed natural sexual desires, and was responsible for resultant anxieties. In his essay '"Civilized" Sexual Morality and Modern Nervous Illness' (1908), Freud attacked a code of sexual behaviour which made unnatural demands on individuals, particularly women. In bourgeois society it was assumed that women should abstain from sexual activity until marriage, and that those who were not married or who were widowed should remain abstinent for the rest of their lives. Freud's observations had convinced him that such restrictions placed upon the individual were harmful to emotional health, and also that sexual intercourse confined to the marital state did not provide full compensation for the restrictions imposed before marriage. Husbands reacted by seeking pleasure elsewhere, under a veil of secrecy demanded by society, wives fell victim to neurotic and hysterical conditions.

Schnitzler's psychological studies are not all in tune with this sexual theme. The reactions to bereavement, for example, do not appear to have their origin in sexual frustration (*Blumen, Die Nächste*). In *Flucht in die Finsternis* the origin of the psychotic condition is not explored, but it does not appear to be sexual. *Fräulein Else, Frau Beate* and *Traumnovelle* are all relevant to Freud's observations, particularly the latter story, though any neurosis that Albertine might suffer is apparently avoided through her dreams. Many of Schnitzler's works are concerned with sexual relationships, and the theme of infidelity is prominent, suggesting that this means of escape from sexual restrictions was a more frequent phenomenon than Freud implies. It is with this major aspect of Schnitzler's works that the next chapter will be concerned.

4

THE SEXUAL CONTEXT

The three works which have contributed most to the establishment of Schnitzler's reputation abroad, particularly in Britain, are the early plays *Anatol* (1888–91), *Liebelei* (1894) and *Reigen* (1898–99). Because of the nature of their theme – the relationship between the sexes – Schnitzler has inevitably come to be seen as a writer primarily concerned with sexuality and with the sexual behaviour of his society.[1] From his published autobiography and diaries it has become apparent that Schnitzler was an enthusiastic participant in the sexual life of the city, and his preoccupations in these early works clearly reflect his own experiences and attitudes. Hence they carry conviction as a picture of the Viennese sexual scene.

Anatol is a cycle of one-act playlets, written originally as a series of curtain-raisers, linked by the theme of Anatol's love-life. Anatol, a wealthy young bachelor, appears in each episode, but each time with a different mistress. Because we learn nothing of Anatol's life as a whole, beyond his various affairs, the overall impression is of an obsessive preoccupation with sex. Anatol's attitude is that of a collector and conqueror of women. He is a philanderer, for whom women are fleeting objects of pleasure, to be picked up and cast aside at will. He meets girls in the street, at a dance, in an omnibus, but cannot recall the specific cases in question; he speaks of them in the plural, as types rather than as individuals. He is arrogant and condescending, regarding it as his destiny to tread all women underfoot, as he marches triumphantly over them.

It is part of Anatol's self-esteem to see himself as a breaker of female hearts, and he savours to himself the memory of his conquests. But many of his relationships are the fond creations of his own imagination, as he invests them with the aura of his sentimentality: Bianca of *Episode* he remembers through the atmosphere generated by the occasion, as he sat at his piano, her head in his lap, her tousled hair sparkling in the soft green and red light of his painted lampshade. Anatol's meticulous attention to the refinements of mood and décors provides another dimension to the aestheticism of the 1890s. Indeed he has been aptly called the 'aesthete of the bedroom'.[2] But it is a private experience. His soul is open to delicate external sensations, but these do not have the same magical effect on others, and his aestheticizing has blinded him to the truth of his partner's feelings. That he has created a false illusion of love is illustrated by the more down-to-earth and cynical view taken by his mistresses. For Bianca, Anatol is as much a part of her large collection as she is of his, except that she can recall nothing of the relationship at all. For Annie of *Abschiedssouper* (Farewell Dinner), Anatol is simply a meal ticket. When he meets her with the intention of breaking the news that this is their last dinner together, she forstalls him with the very same information. The conversation takes on a hostile note when he counters her revelation that she has a new lover, with his revelation of the existence of his new mistress, with whom he has already dined tonight. The relationship deteriorates into a cynical competition as each vies with the other to reveal the more vicious and hurtful instances of deception and infidelity. Male and female present mirror images of each other, as they become locked in this symbolic battle of the sexes.

An equally cynical version of sexual relationships is provided by Schnitzler's other cyclic drama, *Reigen* (The Round Dance). This is a cycle of ten scenes, using ten different characters who meet each other in pairs, the unifying factor being the occurrence in each scene of the act of love, indicated tantalizingly in the text by a series of dotted lines. The cyclic structure produces a chain reaction of recurrent infidelity, as the soldier moves from the prostitute to the chambermaid, the chambermaid to the young gentleman of the house; he has an affair with a married lady, who then goes home to the marital bed; her husband picks up a young girl in the street, she enjoys a liaison with a poet, who in turn takes an actress for a weekend in the country; back home the actress is visited in her bedroom by an admiring count, who subsequently gets drunk and goes off with the prostitute who began the cycle, and which can thus begin again. The characters are revolving in perpetual motion, linked together throughout the various social strata of Vienna by the common act, which reduces them to the same basic level. There are recurrent motifs: intricate preparations for the act, coded signals of intention and encouragement, intermingled with false protestations, anxious calls for reassuring expressions of love, hasty departures from the scene in the moment of subsequent disillusionment. Towards the end of the cycle Schnitzler's commentator is the count, who acknowledges that whilst the act promises so much, it is preceded by a period of anxious uncertainty, and the pleasure it affords is momentary and fragile, the aftermath a feeling of desolation.

Both *Anatol* and *Reigen* examine the theme of sexuality as a universal activity, at the basic level of male-female relationships. But these plays are also set within a specific social context, and much of their interest resides in the variations in human behaviour, as revealed in terms of the social divisions and groupings of the city. Anatol himself is from the upper ranks of the bourgeoisie, presumably living on a private income. His mistresses tend to be on a lower social level, from the lower middle classes, or from the bohemian world of the theatre or the ballet. Only exceptionally does he take a mistress from his own social circle. The contrast between Anatol's social world and that of the majority of the girls is expressed in terms of social geography, of the 'Big World', the 'Große Welt' of the wealthy inner city (the Stadt), and the 'Little World', the 'Kleine Welt' of the suburbs (the Vorstadt). Anatol goes out to the 'Kleine Welt' to seek the love he does not find in his own world; in turn the girls of the suburbs come to the inner city for love, in the Vorstadt they find only marriage. The division is carried further into the types of female to be found in the two areas, the idealized figure of the so-called 'sweet young thing', the 'süße Mädel' of the Vorstadt and the respectable married lady of the inner city. The contrast between these two figures is best illustrated in the scene *Weihnachtseinkäufe* (Christmas Shopping). Anatol and Gabriele, the married lady, encounter each other on the fashionable streets of the inner city; their conversation is strained and full of innuendo, but we deduce that in the past Anatol has paid court to her affections, and has been a source of considerable embarrassment to her. For although through facial expression and tone of voice, she has given several indications of her interest in him, for the sake of propriety she has refused him. In exasperation Anatol has turned to the 'süße

Mädel' of Hernals, who can give of her love in a manner that Gabriele cannot match. Gabriele is a victim of restrictions placed upon her by society, brought up in ignorance as a young girl, and instilled with the fears of what might result from extra-marital infidelity. Thus her bitchy, disparaging comments about the tasteless vulgarity of the Vorstadt, and her obvious jealousy of the easy-going virtue of the 'Mädel', are seen in a far more sympathetic light when she reveals that it is only a lack of courage that prevents her from surrendering to Anatol's advances. Similarly striking is the fact that whilst her sense of propriety recoils from Anatol's account of the time he spends with the 'Mädel' in her room, she also betrays her excitement that they may be *alone* together!

The predicament in which Gabriele finds herself is created essentially by the conventions governing the sexual behaviour of her own class. In principle, at the turn of the century, any form of 'free', extra-marital sex was contrary to the strict code of gentility and correctness observed by the upper middle classes. But in practice the code discriminated against women, who were required to observe a manner of behaviour that was wholly artificial, and may indeed have been responsible for the many instances of neurosis and hysteria which Freud found amongst his female patients. Pre-marital sexual activity was virtually impossible for young bourgeois girls, who led chaste, restricted lives, until being married off to a usually older man, well established in business or a profession. Single women who blatantly stepped out of line forfeited their right to a respectable marriage, and adulteresses, if discovered, could become social outcasts. The young Schnitzler in particular was sensitive to the hypocrisy of a society which 'sold' its daughters in marriage for money or titles, yet which also condemned adulteresses out of hand.[3] And Stefan Zweig gives a full account of the restrictions under which Viennese bourgeois women lived, to the extent that even the costumes of the day were unhealthy and unnatural.[4] In such an attire a woman was protected like a knight in armour, and could move herself neither freely nor gracefully. It was forbidden for women to wear trousers, even to say the word 'hose', and girls had to bathe in long white shifts. Girls were never left alone, but were escorted and protected.[5] Their reading matter was strictly censored, and purity meant being actually ignorant about sex. Thus two young people were not allowed to be alone together, 'in case something might happen', and a woman was supposed to have no desires, unless they were aroused by her husband. If she did not marry she was to remain ignorant and inexperienced, an object of mockery for the rest of her life.

By contrast men were able to escape the rigours of the code so long as they did not violate it openly, and pursued their affairs with discretion. Most extra-marital relationships were with prostitutes, who were on the streets in great abundance, and were also in plentiful supply in cabarets, bars, dancing halls and taverns. Some were legalized and registered with the police, operating from brothels that were scarcely more comfortable than army barracks, or on designated streets. Higher-class prostitutes who catered for the needs of the aristocracy and the wealthy bourgeoisie actually advertised for clients in the newspapers. But the vast majority pursued their trade illegally, surreptitiously and in constant fear of arrest.[6] The increase in prostitution at the time was due to some extent to economic factors. The demand was created by a new generation of bourgeois males with wealth and ample time for leisure pursuits. The rapid growth of the population of the city led to employment problems, especially among women, and thus produced the supply. There were other forms of 'prostitution' which were not expressly categorized as such. The more 'enlightened' fathers hired a servant girl to sleep with their sons (or themselves), but only the very rich (young or old) could afford to take a mistress and install her in a flat. Often they chose the comparatively emancipated women from the bohemian world of the theatre. Very few succeeded in establishing a relationship with a married woman, but many managed to help themselves to shop-girls and waitresses, who were often so ill-clad, tired and overworked that the young men dare not be seen with them in public. The solution was available in the form of restaurants supplying 'chambres séparées', where they could not be seen dining with such creatures. There were also small hotels in dark side-streets where rooms could be hired by the hour, secretly and in guilty haste. In addition sexual diseases were rife, and doubtful cures had ugly and painful side-effects. Problems such as abortion payments, blackmail (because such abortions were illegal), support for illegitimate children, the theft of wallets in brothels, all made the sex life of the young much less natural and pleasant than it might have been. The hypocrisy of the bourgeois façade can be seen in the fact that despite the availability of sexual pleasure, the subject was not to be mentioned within the sanctity of the bourgeois home. The artificial, unnatural propriety of the bourgeoisie contrasts strikingly with the decadent licentiousness of the aristocracy, the freedom enjoyed by the actors, artists and writers of the demi-monde, and the widespread immorality of the working classes of the outer suburbs.

Prominent examples of the more easy-going girls of the suburbs, with whom the young gentlemen of the inner city sought their liaisons, are to be found in the various 'süße Mädel' described in Schnitzler's autobiography and diaries, and depicted in his early plays and stories. Most are from the lower ranks of the lower middle classes, the *Kleinbürgertum*, but some are possibly from the proletariat (Hernals, where the 'Mädel' of *Weihnachtseinkäufe* lives, was predominantly a working-class suburb). Thus although the 'Mädel' may be celebrated as a comparatively liberated girl, who can give freely of her sexual favours in an uninhibited, natural fashion, Schnitzler also makes clear the disadvantages and inferiority of her situation. She is picked up at a dance or café by a man of superior social standing. He may offer her some material reward, but she gains only limited access to his social life, and cannot be introduced into his family circle. At home in the suburbs she suffers economic misery, working long hours in shops or taking in sewing. Her brief and casual affairs may afford her some relief, but in reality they only illustrate how vulnerable she is to blatant, unscrupulous exploitation. The only way for such a girl really to escape from the misery of the Vorstadt was to become an actress, though she often had to 'sell herself' in order to get parts on stage. The bohemian world of the theatre formed a separate social sphere of its own, where the lower and upper middle classes merged. By entering it girls of the Vorstadt gained access to the inner city, and were more likely to get invited to fashionable restaurants. For example, Annie (*Abschiedssouper*) has bettered herself socially by becoming a ballet-dancer, and Anatol entertains her in the famous Hotel Sacher. But in accepting Anatol's meals she is only acting out her deprived and subservient role, and it is significant that her real love is for one of her own class, who is a mere member of the chorus, and who will not be able to afford such opulent fare.

The two plays which depict most graphically the distinctive attitudes to sexual behaviour of the various social groups of the city are *Liebelei* and *Reigen*, the former concentrating on the lower and upper middle classes, the latter covering the whole spectrum of society. *Liebelei* has been translated as 'Dalliance' and 'The Game of Love', but in essence the word conveys the casualness and superficiality of the love affairs depicted. The play is particularly interesting because attitudes actually cut across the class divide. As in *Anatol* the male characters Fritz and Theodor, who are students and lieutenants in the reserve, are apparently both from the wealthy bourgeoisie. Fritz's father, for example, has an estate in the country, Fritz has a luxurious and elegant apartment in the fashionable third district not far from the Ring and the Belvedere Palace, and both lead indolent, superficial lives. The female characters Christine and Mizi are from the lower middle classes of the Vorstadt. Mizi has worked a twelve-hour day as a shop-girl. Christine's father has a perfectly respectable profession – he is a violinist in the orchestra of the Josefstadttheater – but is ill-paid. Christine lives a dull, modest life at home, sewing, and copying music.

The play is a study of sexual attitudes, the norm being represented by Theodor and Mizi. Theodor indulges in fleeting and superficial amorous affairs, avoiding all emotional involvement. He terminates affairs with the same ease with which he begins them, and has no conscience at his light treatment of women. He regards it as the destiny of girls from the Vorstadt to indulge in casual relationships with men above their social standing, and it is their function to provide amusement and relaxation. For her part Mizi responds in kind. She accepts the short duration of the affair and the casualness of their relationship, Theodor's lack of interest in her life, her ignorance of his. She is dazzled by the elegance of Fritz's apartment, and when she sees the photograph of him in his magnificent uniform it is apparent that she has already earmarked him as Theodor's successor. That Theodor could just as easily move on to Christine is clear from his attempts to place their relationship on a more intimate footing.

What gives this play its extra dimension is that the two main characters do not conform to this standard norm. Fritz has already broken Theodor's rules in the degree of his involvement with a married woman – and this is to cost him his life in the duel with her husband. Fritz has taken this relationship so seriously that Theodor has even feared that it is his intention to elope with her, with all the social disadvantages that this would entail. In any case Fritz has taken risks, in the form of letters and rendezvous at his apartment, so that her husband's suspicions have been aroused, and she has taken on a nervous condition, involving a paranoid fear of being continually watched. In effect she has paid the penalty for showing the courage that Gabriele (of *Weihnachtseinkäufe*) lacked. Fritz's relationship with Christine was originally engineered by Theodor to distract him from this other highly dangerous affair. He introduced them a few weeks ago. Since then they have met occasionally, and there is evidence enough to suggest that they have already become lovers. Certainly the Burgtheater actors assumed that Christine and Fritz had slept together; even the fact that the two were alone together in a room provided sufficient grounds for suspicion, and gave them cause for concern as to the way the play might be received by their genteel audience.[7] Unfortunately Christine has sought more from the affair than the conventional Mizi–Theodor relationship would provide. Instead of being satisfied with a casual affair, she wants genuine love. Mizi castigates Christine for surrendering herself physically and emotionally to her first lover, and it seems that Christine's father even harbours hopes that Fritz might actually marry her. But Christine is far too realistic to imagine that Fritz has any such serious intentions. Time and again she acknowledges that the relationship is not 'for ever'. But what she does expect is a genuinely close relationship for the duration of the affair, involving a mutual interest in each other and a degree of personal involvement beyond the superficial and trivial 'Liebelei' indulged in by Theodor and Mizi.

At first Fritz tries to play by the rules by keeping his life a secret from Christine. Yet he does display a conscience over his exploitation of her feelings, and after the arrangements have been made for the duel he begins to show an interest in her life and welfare, and even a potentiality for a genuine relationship. The process is continued in Act Two when he visits her in her room, exhibiting such a sympathetic interest in her life-style that she experiences in a brief moment of emotional intimacy something of what she has been looking for. But as Fritz knows full well, this moment is itself a 'lie', for Christine is unaware that he is about to fight a duel over another woman. The full extent of Christine's tragedy is revealed in Schnitzler's sensitive exploration of her reaction to the news of Fritz's death in Act Three. What destroys her is not the loss of Fritz, nor the end of the affair itself – though she did not expect it to end with such brutal and sudden finality – but her discovery that she apparently meant so little to him, and played such a secondary role in his life. Christine's reaction to her realization of her inferior position and exclusion from his immediate circle of family and friends, is a protest at the role imposed on her by society's standards.

Schnitzler's presentation of the love affair against a specific social background is firmly established in Act Two when he takes us into Christine's own circle. For Christine's involvement with Fritz and her hopes for the relationship are also contrary to the standards of her own class. Here the spokeswoman for the lower middle classes is Katharina Binder. It is important not to misunderstand her. In her criticism of Christine's behaviour she is apparently the voice of strict moral condemnation, as though the absolute restrictions on sexual behaviour imposed on the girls of the upper bourgeoisie had filtered down into the Vorstadt. But this is not entirely the case. Katharina's objection is that Christine flaunts her relationship with Fritz to the extent that she might jeopardize her chances of a respectable marriage within her own class. For the *Kleinbürgertum* expected its daughters to marry a solidly established man from their own circles. It was tacitly acknowledged that they might seek the company of young men from higher circles for a little pleasure and relief from the limitations of their environment, but they were expected to do so with discretion and to maintain the appearances of respectability if they were to marry the local carpenter or stocking manufacturer. Christine has hitherto enjoyed the reputation of being 'decent' and 'modest', good bourgeois virtues both, and it is important that she should preserve this. Katharina herself has apparently something of a shady past, though as a respectable woman now, she prefers not to be reminded of this.

In this penetrating analysis of *Kleinbürgertum* attitudes Schnitzler's most interesting character is Christine's father. Unwilling to see his daughter simply wait to be married off to an acceptable party with a good steady job, or to waste her youth and drift towards spinsterhood, he has raised no objections to her pursuit of happiness with Fritz. Weiring comes across as a sympathetic, enlightened, though unfortunately misguided middle-class father, an 'un-bourgeois' figure in fact,[8] whose presence in the play reinforces the impression that Schnitzler is here encouraging his audience at least to question the social conventions and strict class divisions of his time.

Although *Reigen* is essentially concerned with the theme of sexual behaviour as a universal human activity, transcending the class barriers and reducing all to the same basic level, Schnitzler reveals considerable variations in attitude and behaviour, both before and after the sexual encounter, which are related to the social group of the characters. A cursory glance at the cycle's structure suggests that Schnitzler is moving gradually up the social scale, beginning with the prostitute, soldier and chambermaid, and moving on via the upper bourgeoisie to the aristocracy in the person of the count. The reappearance of the prostitute at the conclusion completes the circle, and her scene with the count provides a symbolic link between persons from the lowest and the highest levels of society. Not all of the characters in the latter scenes of the cycle, however, 'fit in' with this basic structure. In particular the 'süße Mädel' comes from the *Kleinbürgertum*, and the poet and the actress do not really rank above the characters from the upper bourgeoisie who appear at the mid-point of the cycle.

To some extent the order of scenes and appearance of characters are determined by the sheer logic of social relationships. For example, it is perfectly natural for the young gentleman and the chambermaid to be alone with each other in the family home; for their part the poet and the actress are well acquainted with each other. The encounters are all socially 'feasible', and provide a cross-section in socio-geographical terms of the sexual mores of the city. The soldier is accosted by the prostitute by the Danube at the Augartenbrücke, not far from the café in the Schiffgasse, from where she generally operates, and where she later picks up the count (soon she will be moving to a more salubrious establishment in the Spiegelgasse in the inner city). The soldier and the chambermaid meet at a cheap dance-hall in the Prater. Her place of employment is in the home of the young man in the Porzellangasse in the ninth district, but when the latter hires the flat for his encounter with the married lady, he chooses an area some distance away, in the Schwindgasse just beyond the Ring on the other side of the city. The husband has been pursuing the 'süße Mädel' for some time on her walks through the city streets (there is a reference to the Singerstraße). He takes her to a *chambre séparée* in the Riedhof in the Josefstadt,[9] but puts the machinery in motion to establish a longer-term relationship, to be pursued in rather less public surroundings (presumably in a flat or room hired regularly and discreetly for the duration). Ironically the poet in turn is hoping to take her away for a few weeks to the country for a brief affair.

The only scene in which the sexual act is performed 'legally' is the central one between husband and wife. But instead of presenting a relationship based on spiritual intimacy and mutual trust, Schnitzler shows us a marriage in which neither partner really knows the other, and in which conversation tends to be calculated, barbed and full of hidden innuendo. Indeed it is significant that the scene involving the bourgeois married couple occupies a place at the heart of a play which is built upon a structure of infidelity, and within this structure provides the extreme example of mutual deception. The husband rations his sexual interest out between his wife and other women, offering fatuous explanations for the intervals in which his interest in his wife has waned. For her part the young wife reveals a pointed curiosity concerning his opinion on faithless wives, whom he proceeds to condemn as socially unacceptable creatures, and to pity for the lives they lead 'full of lies, malice, vulgarity and dangers', without realizing that his own wife is in this very situation. On either side of the marital encounter the two scenes depicting bourgeois characters are those involving the most carefully contrived preparations for the sexual act. The whole opening sequence of the scene between the young wife and the bachelor is an extended piece of deception. The pretence that the flat is his own (when both know it is hired) follows upon his nervous preliminaries for the occasion, as he perfumes the atmosphere and gets rid of traces of previous sexual activity. Her expressions of shame and guilt are presumably genuine, and symptomatic of her awareness of the risks she is taking, but she offers him occasional encouragement calculated to make him bolder, and as the ultimate moment of intimacy draws inevitably closer she begins to take charge of the whole operation. Indeed once in bed she displays a confidence and experience that help her to cope mockingly and successfully with his over-excitement, nervousness and consequent impotence. For Schnitzler's contemporaries one of the more shocking aspects of *Reigen* was the lack of embarrassment shown by this supposedly cloistered and repressed lady, the frivolity with which she treats sexual matters once she has 'capitulated', then again her amusement at her husband's pontifications and the playful coquetry she displays in the marital bed. Her manner disarms the young man, and vexes her husband, but it exposes the unnaturalness of a code of conduct which decrees that she must pretend to the young man that she has no intention of satisfying his wishes, and that she must simulate to her husband a childish ignorance of sexual behaviour and relationships.

The young wife's deceptively innocent attitude is to some extent matched by the reluctance and modesty shown by the 'süße Mädel'. Initially she has been very forward in agreeing to go to a *chambre séparée* so quickly after the initial encounter. Then she offers little resistance to the aggressive physical advances of the husband, and her eagerness during the act itself catches him off-guard. But she makes excuses for her behaviour by claiming that the husband reminds her of her former lover, and then puts the blame for her enthusiasm on the wine. Her sense of Vorstadt propriety is shown in the strictness with which she deals with her schoolgirl sister who brazenly flaunts her relationship with a boyfriend in the Strozzigasse; she herself covers her own checkered history by attributing her acquaintance with the world of the *chambre séparée* to a visit she has made with a friend and the friend's fiancé (a version she also later gives to the poet!). The 'süße Mädel' is a charming mixture of healthy, natural affections, to which she spontaneously gives play both with the husband and the poet, and a token sense of decorum and modesty, which requires her to play by the social rules and makes her ashamed of her nakedness after the act.

The characters who precede and follow the members of the bourgeoisie are poles apart on the social scale, but closer in attitude and manner than might be expected. When the soldier meets the prostitute in the opening sequence there is no need for pretence. The transaction proceeds with sordid haste, though also with a healthy frankness. The sexual act is here presented in its most fundamental form, having no basis in a human relationship. The following scene between the soldier and the chambermaid is almost as primitive, as the soldier rushes her out of the dance to achieve physical satisfaction as quickly as possible. Though he makes some attempt to establish a superficial relationship with weak jokes and laughter, and though she offers a degree of resistance, the atmosphere is one of rapid sexual indulgence, blatantly pursued without the inhibitions of social propriety. More delicately, but scarcely less blatantly, the chambermaid herself takes the sexual initiative with the young man of the house, and is flattered and amused by his response. The characters at the lower end of the social scale are more open and less inhibited about their intentions than the bourgeois characters. Their counterparts in this respect are the characters who appear in the later stages of the cycle, the poet, the actress and then the count. The poet has no inhibitions about taking the 'süße Mädel' to his room, and he is aggressive and dominating as he forces his attentions upon her, his only constraint being his desire first to create an aura of romanticism around the relationship. Similarly the count is primarily concerned that the time and atmosphere for the occasion should be just right, preferring to make love in the late evening, after dinner, than in the morning 'before breakfast'. The poet and the count have aesthetic, rather than social or moral reservations. The actress, however, though amused and fascinated by the count, is much more down-to-earth. She first plays a deliberate game with the poet, mocking his romanticism, but is then practical and straightforward about the sexual arrangements, and is perfectly frank about her other affairs. To her the poet is a plaything, and her belated confession of affection ('I am dying of love for you') is an obvious dramatic pose.

Although the sexual act is presented in *Reigen* as the great social leveller, the individual attitudes and behaviour of those involved reflect, as we have seen, the various social strata of the city. Across the social divides it is also possible to detect variations in attitude according to the sex of the characters. In the early stages of the cycle the male characters tend to take a more cynical, unfeeling attitude to the encounters than their female partners, who attempt to protract the relationship beyond the immediate intentions of the males. The opening scene is not a conventional encounter between prostitute and client because there is no payment. The prostitute is hoping to find a lover, and it is only when the soldier has lost all interest in her after sexual fulfilment, that she attempts to revert to the more normal relationship and demand some financial recompense. Similarly the chambermaid also wishes to establish a relationship with the soldier, and resents his loutish behaviour, when he goes back into the dance-hall to seek another partner. Surprisingly she is successful and the relationship is indeed sustained (she is seen writing to him in the next scene), but it continues on his terms only. He will escort her home only when he is ready, even if this will get her into trouble with her mistress, and he plays the role of the aggressive, inconsiderate and insensitive male. At a rather less uncouth level the young gentleman is also somewhat brusque with the same girl. Whereas she attempts to persist in the new intimacy of the relationship, he quickly puts her in her place and resumes his role as the young master. She has initiated and enjoyed the encounter, but as far as he is concerned she has simply served her purpose. Despite his nervous excitement and frantic protestations of love and adoration, he even takes the same view of his relationship with the married lady, as he looks back with cool satisfaction, after adding this rather special addition to his collection.

As Schnitzler moves up the social scale and enters the world of the bourgeoisie and then that of the theatre, the females become more emancipated in attitude, and the assertiveness of the males is expressed in the form of a refined superiority and patronizing chauvinism. The husband pontificates to his wife about virtue and purity, and attempts to teach her the way of the world as a parent talking to a child. Wary of the possibilities of disease, he cross-examines the 'süße Mädel' as to the details of her sexual past, and gives her strict instructions to avoid risky company (an order she immediately disobeys when she spends her afternoon with the poet). The poet too behaves in a superior, condescending way, creating out of her an idealized figure of natural innocence and simplicity. In these scenes the females are more than a match for these pompous and affected males. The 'süße Mädel' is a very spirited and, despite the poet's assumptions, intelligent girl, who quickly sees through the husband's claim that he lives in Graz ('You're married, aren't you?'). The actress is a truly 'liberated' woman, who plays a dominant, occasionally mocking role, talking down to her lovers as 'my child', 'you frog', 'you arrogant dog' and 'my little philosopher'.

Overall, the male characters in *Reigen* make up a rather unattractive group, whereas the females are presented more sympathetically, either as victims of male attitudes, or as emancipated figures, attempting to liberate themselves from their assumed role in a male-dominated society.[10] As was noted by several of his contemporaries, in many of his early works in particular Schnitzler appears to sympathize more with his female characters than with his males.[11] More recently it has been pointed out that around the turn of the century, as he began to take an interest in the social problems of women, there is a growing tendency for his works to present the sexual scene from the female viewpoint.[12] It is not surprising therefore that several commentators have claimed him as a feminist writer, and his growing popularity has even been attributed to the ease with which so many of his works lend themselves to feminist interpretations.[13] Schnitzler's appeal in this direction is not entirely fortuitous, for the feminist or Women's Movement was indeed active in Vienna at the turn of the century. The *Allgemeiner Oesterreichischer Frauenverein* was founded in 1893, its initial aims being to secure better educational and career opportunities for women.[14] But one of the principal targets of feminism in Vienna was the abolition of the double standard of sexual morality. Initially, as in Victorian Britain, this did not necessarily imply an opening up to women of the same freedoms enjoyed by men, but a demand that men should suffer the same sexual repression that morality imposed on women. The movement became associated with moral purity.[15] But in Germany, and in Vienna too, more radical groups began to adopt a more liberal moral attitude, and the movement became identified in Viennese intellectual circles with the issue of sexual freedom for women, as well as for men.[16] Leading figures such as Rosa Mayreder advocated for women a full sexual as well as an intellectual development.[17]

It would be misleading to imply that all intellectuals in Vienna who argued for a more liberal attitude to sexual behaviour were supporters of the Women's Movement. Notably Karl Kraus attacked the sexual double standard in his essay 'Sittlichkeit und Kriminalität' (Morality and Criminality, 1902), yet ridiculed the political and professional aspirations of the movement, and remained an implacable enemy of the concept of woman as man's equal. Nevertheless the recognition of a need for a more honest and tolerant sexual morality did lead to a widespread demand for social reforms in related areas: the legal equality of man and wife, the legalization of abortion, an improvement in the status of unmarried mothers, the recognition of 'free unions'. Much of which coincided with the aspirations of leading feminists.[18]

Schnitzler's connections with the movement are mainly indirect, but the following factors may be mentioned to suggest a mild interest on his part. He was for a time on friendly terms with Ellen Key, a leading international figure of the feminist movement and a fervent advocate of women's educational and sexual rights;[19] Lou Andreas-Salomé, who enjoyed a degree of notoriety as a 'new' or 'free' woman, selected Schnitzler as an escort to coffee-houses and Prater restaurants during her visits to Vienna;[20] he was linked romantically with Clara Loeb, whose novel *Mimi* (1897) has an emancipated figure as its heroine; he read works by feminist authors such as Lily Braun and Gabriele Reuter; he met and spoke approvingly of the suffragette Else Jerusalem;[21] he expressed sympathy for girls seeking abortions, and progressive views on the legal rights of unmarried mothers, and on the 'free unions'. In 1905 he wrote that the cohabitation of two people with a child should still be deemed a marriage, whether or not the relationship had been legally sanctioned, and that a legal contract should in any case only be required to regulate the couple's financial obligations.[22] He was much in demand at women's clubs and 'women's evenings' and was put on a committee to discuss divorce reform.[23]

It is, however, his literary works that have provided the clearest evidence of feminist sympathies. In the first place a number of his female characters have been explicitly identified as emancipated figures. One is the intelligent Marcelina, who asserts her intellectual independence in *Casanovas Heimfahrt* (1917).[24] The political variety has been perceived in the progressive young socialist Therese Golowski in the novel *Der Weg ins Freie* (1908).[25] On the whole, though, the intellectual career-girl type is a rarity in Schnitzler's works. Those who do enjoy professional independence are mostly actresses, and here Schnitzler's main concern is with sexual emancipation. The most notorious example is the actress in *Reigen*,[26] but in the earlier play *Das Märchen* (1891), a 'fallen woman' who has already had two lovers and so deprived herself of the possibility of a respectable marriage, liberates herself from the prejudices of bourgeois society to pursue her career as an actress in St Petersburg. The actress tends to live her emancipated life outside the constrictions of marriage. But a number of married women who assert their independence of the submissive role required of them have also been deemed emancipated, from the young wife of *Reigen*,[27] to the married lady of the fragment *Ritterlichkeit*, who indulges shamelessly in sexual freedom to the same degree as her husband.[28]

Perhaps the most original example to have been mentioned is Leopoldine of *Spiel im Morgengrauen* (Gambling at Dawn).[29] Married to a man considerably older than herself, she asserts her authority over him to such an extent that she permits him to sleep with her once a week in exchange for control over his financial affairs, allowing him 12 per cent interest as pocket money. She has thus rationalized the relationship as one between client and prostitute, but as she dictates the terms, she has in effect reversed the traditional roles of husband and wife. Leopoldine also asserts her authority over her former lover, Lieutenant Willi Kasda. Kasda had spent a night with her some years previously, but had left her in the morning with the ultimate insult – ten florins in payment for services rendered. Now Kasda is in considerable financial trouble – he owes eleven thousand florins, and his position as an officer is at stake. So when he meets again the now wealthy Leopoldine, he seeks to reawaken her feelings and exploit their former relationship to his own financial advantage. But after this second night together, she leaves him not the large sum he requires, but a single one thousand florin note. Despite her love for him she first wishes to teach him a lesson. He treated her as a prostitute – and so she is treating him. She will not yet write off his debts – a night's love is not worth such an exorbitant amount – but she will pay a generous market value for his services. The roles of superior, condescending client and prostitute are here reversed, and Leopoldine has again behaved in a manner usually associated with the masculine role, determining the nature and financial terms of the relationship.

The mere presence in Schnitzler's works of a number of seemingly emancipated female characters is not in itself sufficient to confirm his advocacy of female emancipation. For example, it is not necessarily the case that Schnitzler is presenting Leopoldine's behaviour in an unambiguously positive light. For in one sense the lesson which she teaches Kasda backfires – the humiliated officer commits suicide! In making her lesson to him a priority, Leopoldine obscures her genuine love for Kasda, and the result is a tragic misunderstanding.[30] In other ways too Schnitzler is often concerned as much with the negative aspects of emancipated behaviour as with the positive assertion of freedom. Many emancipated figures pay the price of a perpetual fear of discovery, which may result in social disgrace. Even the otherwise confident young wife of *Reigen* begins her extra-marital affair nervously, in secrecy and fear, shrouded in veils, in an unpleasant hired apartment, and has to resort to dangerous lies and deceptions. In the story *Die Toten schweigen* (The Dead Keep Quiet, 1897) Emma has to meet her lover in wind-swept dark streets in the Leopoldstadt, and pursues her affair in the seclusion of a jolting and rattling carriage driven by a drunken driver. Frau Rupius of *Frau Berta Garlan* (1900) is unable to face the social disgrace of an unwanted pregnancy and dies as a result of a back-street abortion.

It seems then that it is Schnitzler's concern to demonstrate how unliberated these ladies really are, rather than the opposite.

In general Schnitzler does indeed reserve his most sympathetic treatment for those female characters who are not emancipated, but who are presented as the victims of social forces. Prominent examples are afforded by the various 'süße Mädel' who are to be found in so many of his earlier works. But two of his most compassionately drawn female portraits are the heroines of his two major prose works about women, *Frau Berta Garlan* and *Therese*. Berta Garlan is a widow, condemned to bring up her young son within the narrow circle of the small-town relatives of her dead husband, to whose memory she assumes she must remain faithful. Schnitzler compared this fidelity beyond the grave to the oriental custom for a widow to cast herself upon her husband's funeral pyre – an absurd extension of the husband's ownership of the wife.[31] But Berta Garlan is a classic case for a sudden pursuit of illicit sexual adventure. The daughter of a respectable Viennese bourgeois family, she is nevertheless left without means when her father dies, and for economic reasons she drifts into a sexually unexciting, disappointing marriage with a shy, clumsy, middle-aged man. Yet she adapts well to the provincial community, is seemingly happy with the role of wife and mother, and after her husband's early death remains contentedly in the town.

The catalyst for the disturbance of Berta's physical and emotional serenity is the appearance on the scene of Emil Lindbach, the 'great love' of her youth. Lindbach has since become a famous musician, and her memories of him are stirred by a reference to him in a newspaper. Schnitzler then explores with great delicacy a gradual reawakening within Berta of sexual feelings, culminating in her bitter realization that she has been cheated of happiness. This is because she did not surrender to Lindbach's advances during their earlier courtship, but 'saved' herself for a husband she did not love. During this long third-person interior monologue Schnitzler's narrative perspective appears to identify with Berta's own, and her situation is presented with sympathy and understanding:

> Unter den Händen war ihr das Dasein zerronnen, und sie war durstig und arm . . . Was sollte sie nun tun? Sie, die Tage, Nächte, Monate, Jahre ohne Erwartung, ohne Angst sich in der

Zukunft hatte dehnen sehen, schauerte nun vor der Leere des Abends, der vor ihr lag.

(ES I, 429)

(Her life had passed without her realizing it, and she was thirsty and poor . . . What should she do? She had watched without expectations or fear as the days, nights, months and years had stretched out into the future, but now she dreaded the emptiness of the evening before her.)

The decision to rectify the situation by writing to Lindbach and becoming his mistress is not taken lightly, but it eventually takes on the nature of a dramatic mission. It is also an act of emancipation from the restrictions of her narrow life, and she arrives in Vienna (where Lindbach lives) with a sense of freedom and self-fulfilment.

Berta's surrender to Lindbach (or 'conquest' of him) amounts to one single brief encounter in his flat. But afterwards she undergoes a complex reaction process. Morally she feels no remorse or sense of sin. Rather does she feel pride in her new identity as his mistress, even in her own performance in bed (she has discovered a hitherto unsuspected 'gift'). She is excited that she has been admitted into the privileged circles of the sexually active, and entertains optimistic thoughts of a relationship with him beyond the moral conventions of society, 'no matter what people might say'. The spell is finally broken by Lindbach's patronizing proposal that she should visit him for a night every four to six weeks. Berta feels degraded, but Schnitzler broadens the theme beyond her disgust at this blatant exploitation. Berta's friend Frau Rupius, who has herself been visiting a lover in Vienna, becomes pregnant, has an abortion, and dies. Berta's fears that she might pay for the one hour of love in the same fashion are not borne out, but she nevertheless draws a moral conclusion, namely that the pleasure she enjoyed was culpable precisely because she was not indulging for the purpose of procreation. The 'pleasure in his arms' had nothing to do with the longing for a child. Thus Berta retreats into the conventional view of the female sexual role. Schnitzler has been criticized for this unduly moralistic ending.[32] But this is to disregard the full implications of Berta's conclusion. For in a moment of insight, beyond her normally rather naive view of life, Berta goes on to grasp a social truth:

Und sie ahnte das ungeheure Unrecht in der Welt, daß die
Sehnsucht nach Wonne ebenso in die Frau gelegt wird, als in
den Mann, und daß es bei den Frauen Sünde wird, wenn die
Sehnsucht nach Wonne nicht zugleich die Sehnsucht nach dem
Kinde ist.

(ES I, 513)

(And she sensed the monstrous injustice in the world, that
women have a desire for pleasure as much as men, and that it is
a sin if a woman's desire for pleasure is not accompanied by a
desire for a child.)

Schnitzler is not associating himself with Berta's self-condemnation
for her pursuit of pleasure. He is not retreating into moralistic
judgement of her sexual escapade. He is exposing explicitly a social
injustice and the conventional double standard that condemns
women for attempting to grasp the pleasure that is freely available
to the male.

The story of Berta Garlan has several features in common with
that of Frau Beate (*Frau Beate und ihr Sohn*). Both are widows, and
in both Schnitzler explores the gradual reawakening of sexual
feelings after a period of abstinence. Essentially, then, both stories
are psychological studies, pursued both at the conscious and subconscious levels. The culmination of Berta's development is her
recognition that with Lindbach she sought not a reawakening of
their youthful love, but the basic physical satisfaction of a sexual
relationship. This has already been made clear to the reader
through Schnitzler's subtle exploration of half-conscious thoughts
and day-dreams, the occasional merging in her mind's eye of the
image of the young Lindbach with that of her attractive young
nephew, a dream highly charged with Freudian symbolism and a
confusing array of male figures. But as with Frau Beate, Schnitzler
sets Berta's progress towards self-awareness within a particular
social context, namely that of the supposedly respectable bourgeois
society of the small country town. In addition, however, an
important structural element in the story is the image presented of
Vienna itself, which initially offers a contrast to the peaceful life of
the small-town community. For Berta this little town has provided
a sanctuary from the big city where she suffered the unpleasant
experience of her father's bankruptcy, and she remembers Vienna
only as a noisy, uncertain and unpleasant place. But as her interest
in Lindbach increases it becomes the city of excitement and

adventure, she returns there as to her true home, animated by the noise and bustle of the life of the capital. After her humiliation and disillusionment there, she returns to the small town as to a haven of morality. Yet Berta is to learn (from Frau Rupius) that the good citizens of the provincial town are just as 'depraved' as those who seek sexual adventure in the capital, and that the world of the small-town community is a reflection of the 'wicked city'.

In *Frau Berta Garlan* Schnitzler puts a particular slant on his analysis of bourgeois sexual mores. One affair singled out as an example is that between Berta's sister-in-law Albertine and Herr Klingermann, the local libertine. Albertine's husband has found out about the affair, but instead of ejecting her from the house, has exploited the situation to condemn her to a life of drudgery, little better than that of a servant, whilst he may pursue his extra-marital affairs with impunity. From this particular situation Frau Rupius draws the general conclusion that all men are unscrupulous scoundrels, an indictment echoed by Berta herself following her treatment by Lindbach. The depiction of men as the more culpable sex and as the beneficiaries of the sexual scene is extended further into the overall texture of the story. Berta's cousin Agathe is married to a minor official in Vienna, living in a dingy flat in a narrow street in one of the less attractive parts of the inner city. The work of housewife and mother has caused her to age prematurely, and her life, like that of Albertine in the country, is one of drudgery, whilst her unsympathetic husband can relax over a game of billiards in the coffee-house. Meanwhile Frau Rupius's bitterness towards men is seemingly influenced by the sequel to her affair in Vienna – she has to undergo the abortion whilst her lover is free to make his way about the city without remorse, in pursuit of further pleasure. Berta's experience at the hands of Lindbach, and the conclusion that she draws regarding the iniquitous injustices suffered by women, can thus be understood within this overall context of sexual inequality.

Schnitzler's other major work written from the perspective of the heroine is *Therese, Chronik eines Frauenlebens* (Chronicle of a Woman's Life, 1928). Her story is one of the great stories of ill fortune in German literature, and her life comes across as a heroic struggle for existence, dignity and independence in defiance of the problems arising from her social position. Therese is born into a respectable bourgeois home, but the family goes downhill financially and morally, and Therese makes a clean break to seek an independent life in Vienna. There she suffers the fate of the unattached female seeking employment as governess or child-minder, moving from post to post, from which she can be dismissed at will, exposed to the advances of the masters of the household, and at the mercy of the vengeance of their wives. Frequently she has to escape from unsatisfactory conditions. She leaves because she goes hungry, because she is ill-treated, because her wages are in arrears, because the work is physically too demanding. Therese is exploited and has few rights other than to seek the next vacancy to come along. As with Berta Garlan Schnitzler presents her problems with sympathy through the medium of third-person interior monologue:

> Das erbärmliche Dasein, das sie führte, als ein Geschöpf, das nie sich selber gehörte, das keine Heimat hatte, das heute nicht wußte, wo es morgen sein Haupt hinlegen sollte – was hatte solch ein Geschöpf für Anrecht auf ein Menschen-, auf ein Frauenglück?
>
> (ES II, 737)

(In her miserable existence as a creature that never had any life of her own, that had no real home, did not know from one day to the next where she would lay her head – what claim did such a creature have to some happiness as a human being, as a woman?)

The only release would be through marriage, but Schnitzler suggests that the marriages available to her would only represent a form of bondage, little better than a domesticized form of prostitution. At one stage she is even reduced to considering prostitution itself as an alternative easy option.

Therese's problems are indeed accentuated rather than relieved through her relationships with men. Quite early in the novel she discovers her own sensual nature that is to plague her for the rest of her life. Initially she is on her guard against the possible results of a false step: she must avoid taking a lover, she must not become pregnant, above all she must not trust any man. But within weeks her liaison with an army officer robs her of her social reputation and the possibilities of a respectable bourgeois marriage. Then in Vienna she takes a succession of lovers: a brief sordid encounter with a young lieutenant, with whom she exchanges scarcely ten words of conversation; a purely physical affair with a bank clerk; a liaison with a middle-aged government official who picks her up in a railway compartment, and so on. The series culminates in an expedition *à quatre* along the banks of the Danube, in which she and a friend, cast in the role of available 'süße Mädel', serve simply to gratify the sexual appetites of two young rakes in the seclusion of the woods. But her most disastrous affair is that with the artist Kasimir Tobias. The relationship proceeds in cheap inns, the bill frequently paid by Therese herself. She gives him money, and he then disappears without trace when she reveals she is pregnant. Years later she is to discover the full extent of his deception – he had been married all the time. Because of her pregnancy Therese has to investigate the possibilities of a back-street abortion. This she rejects, but when she gives birth to her child, she does so alone, in deprived circumstances. Her problems do not cease here. Because of her need to earn her living she has to have her child brought up by foster-parents. She feels guilt at neglecting him, and eventually the chickens come home to roost: the boy develops early criminal tendencies, he defies her, deceives her, steals from her, physically attacks her, becomes involved in criminal activity, serves time in prison, and eventually murders her. Therese, initially victim of the father, is eventually the victim of the son.

Schnitzler's treatment of Berta Garlan and Therese is certainly suggestive of a writer aware of the injustices suffered by women, and who perceived them as the most devastatingly and critically victimized members of his culture. Those viewing his works from a feminist angle may also point to his apparently critical treatment of male characters who through their condescending or contemptuous attitudes advertise themselves as male chauvinists. The tendency has been perceived in the philanderer Anatol, the pompous husband of *Reigen*,[33] and is particularly evident in the manner of Theodor of *Liebelei*. As he and Fritz discuss the way of the world he will not let Mizi and Christine in on their conversation, which is far too important for 'children'. He even mocks Mizi's exhausting work as a shop-girl and has no sympathy for her personal domestic problems. He is seen in his worst light in Act Three when news is broken to Christine of Fritz's death, and in the face of her distress he blames Mizi for 'bothering' him with this extra inconvenience. But none of this compares with the aggression of Lieutenant Gustl, perhaps the most notorious of Schnitzler's chauvinist figures. In this celebrated story (*Leutnant Gustl*, 1900), Schnitzler explores the consciousness of the typical army officer, his attitude to women constituting a major element of the portrait. Like Anatol, Gustl is a collector of females, but is devoid of all false romanticism and aestheticism. The sexual act affords him the only true pleasure in life, but the identity and personality of the partner are wholly immaterial. He roughly accepts what is readily available from shop-girls and peasant girls, and is unwilling to make any effort necessary to establish the atmosphere for a genuine affair:

> aber die Frau Mannheimer, die hübsche, blonde . . . mit der war was zu machen . . . , bei der hätt' ich Chance gehabt . . . aber faul darf man halt nicht sein . . . da heißt's: Cour machen, Blumen schicken, vernünftig reden . . . das geht nicht so, daß man sagt: 'Komm' morgen nachmittag zu mir in die Kasern'!
> (ES I, 352)

> (but that Frau Mannheimer, the pretty blonde one . . . it would have been worth trying something with her . . . , I'd have had a real chance . . . but you have to work for it . . . you have to court her, send flowers, talk to her . . . you can't just simply say: Come to my room in the barracks tomorrow!)

But for many Gustl is at his most infuriating as he reflects upon the advantages of marriage, and of having a pretty little wife 'available' in the house to serve his various requirements, the ultimate reduction of woman to her utilitarian function as a legally provided sex object.

Despite Schnitzler's occasional concern with emancipated figures, female victims and chauvinistic males, it is important not to attach too much significance to the emancipation theme in his works as a whole. Occasionally feminist issues are touched on peripherally, when Schnitzler's main concern is with psychological, rather than with specific social questions. In the novel *Doktor Gräsler, Badearzt* (Spa Doctor, 1917) he provides a sensitive and moving treatment of a lonely melancholy bachelor who fights shy of marriage to an intelligent, much younger woman, who takes the bold and 'emancipated' step of proposing marriage to him in a letter. Gräsler has been much maligned by critics for his indecisiveness and egocentricity,[34] but Schnitzler explores his motives in detail, and his reasons are psychologically convincing. Sabine will marry him, she writes, despite his vanity, despite his lack of warmth, despite his pedantry, his indifference towards his patients, despite the fact that she does not love him. It is hardly surprising that Gräsler should shy away in alarm from a marriage that may prove disastrous.

A somewhat harsher portrait of the bachelor type is to be found in the character of the artist Julian Fichtner in the play *Der einsame Weg* (The Lonely Road, 1903). In the past Julian had a secret affair with Gabriele, the fiancée of his friend Wegrat; but he abandoned her, and left her carrying his child. She married the unsuspecting Wegrat, and the child, the boy Felix, has meanwhile been brought up as Wegrat's own son. Now Julian wishes to reclaim Felix as his son, and reveals to Felix their real relationship. We are then given actual details of his brief affair with Felix's mother, which took place when he visited Gabriele's village with his friend Wegrat, whom she was shortly to marry. Julian stayed, he and Gabriele became involved in a 'sinful, treacherous affair', and planned secretly to elope a week before her wedding. But on the night before the departure, Julian looked at the country road disappearing into a future of freedom and adventure, and longed to spend his life 'free of all responsibilities and duties'. So he deserted Gabriele without a qualm of conscience; indeed had she committed suicide as a result this would simply have confirmed his own self-esteem.

Julian's behaviour is presented as selfish and unscrupulous, providing a typical example of the Schnitzler erotic adventurer.[35] The egotistical nature of his attitude is perhaps best illustrated by his attempt to justify (to Felix!) the abandonment of Gabriele on the grounds that the period of travel following was the richest and most delightful of his life. But now he comes across as a discontented, homeless man, regretfully conscious of his longing for some form of domestic happiness, yet suspecting that he has forfeited his most attractive opportunity. In the process of growing older Julian has discovered that his independent bachelor-life has turned into an intolerable loneliness, and now he regards Felix as his last hope, claiming to love him, and desiring nothing more than that Felix should become aware of his love and be close to him. To some extent Julian's desire for a positive human relationship with his son presents him in a more favourable light. It is even possible to sympathize with him when Felix rejects him, and he leaves the stage to continue down his lonely road. Yet his love for Felix is essentially a selfish and possessive one, and he has to accept the bitter truth that although he may have fathered Felix, he has, through his subsequent behaviour, deprived himself of all rights to him as a son. Schnitzler's portrait of Julian represents a harsh condemnation of the egocentric bachelor figure, though he depicts his later anguish with sympathy and understanding, and Julian leaves the play a pathetic, rather than a villainous man.

An even more ambivalent picture of a related bachelor character is to be found in the novel *Der Weg ins Freie* (The Road into the Open, 1908). This is a wide-ranging work with a large canvas, covering a number of social and political themes, but at its heart is a problematic male-female relationship. The central character is a young composer, Georg von Wergenthin, who embarks on a love-affair with a singer, Anna Rosner. Anna becomes pregnant, the question of marriage arises, but Georg avoids it, first taking her off to Italy, and eventually installing her in a villa outside Vienna, where she is to have the child. The child is stillborn, whereupon Georg leaves Anna, to take up a position away from Vienna as a conductor. Georg's initial decision, to live unmarried with Anna during the early stages of her pregnancy, classifies their relationship as a 'free union', flying in the face of the outmoded prejudices of society. But Georg is not treated positively by Schnitzler as a socially progressive type. His decision not to marry Anna is presented negatively, as an evasion of responsibilities and commitment, as a desire to preserve his freedom and independence and to devote himself to the pursuit of his art.

As a character Georg is unattractive. He is vain, self-centred, and apparently lacking in the capacity for lasting involvement. He has the temperament and the roving eye of the philanderer. None of these qualities in itself makes Georg into a chauvinist type. Nevertheless there are aspects of the affair, and of his attitude, which feminists would find objectionable. Primarily he dictates the terms of the relationship. The superior aristocratic gentleman indulges in an affair with the socially inferior bourgeois girl, and eventually leaves her in the lurch. He makes the arrangements for her discreet and convenient removal from Vienna for the birth, condescending to visit her from time to time. The only obligations which he feels towards the child are financial. In other words he may be seen as a typical beneficiary of the sexual double standard. For her part Anna is presented as the victim. She is bitter over the loss of her social respectability, she accepts the principle of the free union only with resignation, waiting patiently, but in vain, for the offer of marriage, which others certainly expect Georg to make.

Here then is potential feminist material. But Schnitzler does not really treat it as such. Most notably the affair is not presented from the viewpoint of the female victim. Instead Schnitzler adopts Georg's own perspective through the medium of third-person inner monologue, so that for long passages of the novel we are in Georg's mind, just as we are in the minds of Berta Garlan and Therese. Consequently the question of his feelings towards marriage appears to be handled with honesty and understanding:

> Wär es nicht sogar das Bequemste, wenn ich sie heiratete? . . . Aber er sah sich plötzlich in einem sehr bürgerlichen Heim beim Abendessen sitzen, zwischen Frau und Kind. Und aus dieser geträumten Familienszene wehte es ihm entgegen wie ein Hauch von sorgenvoller Langeweile. Ah, es war noch zu früh dazu, er war noch zu jung.
> (ES I, 839–40)

> (Would it not be easiest if I married her? . . . But suddenly he saw himself in a bourgeois home, sitting at supper between wife and child. And the atmosphere of this imaginary family scene wafted over him, with all its cares and boredom. It was too early for it, he was still too young.)

This does not of course mean that we have an uncritically sympathetic treatment of the male figure. It has indeed been shown that even through the passages of interior monologue the overall presentation of Georg is a critical one.[36] For example, the reader can see through his attempts at self-vindication in leaving Anna so soon after the tragedy. Nevertheless Schnitzler's sensitive presentation of Georg's emotions carries the reader's imagination along with it to a considerable extent, and one occasionally senses a definite closeness to the character. We (in contrast to his friend Else) are party to his brief but genuine anguish immediately following the stillbirth:

> Und ihn bedauerte Else gar nicht. Sie ahnte wohl nicht einmal, wie der Tod des Kindes ihn erschüttert hatte. Wie konnte sie es ahnen! Was wußte sie von der Stunde, da der Garten seine Farben, der Himmel sein Licht für ihn verloren hatte?
> (ES I, 940)

> (And he was not sorry for Else at all. She probably did not even guess at the extent to which the death of the child had upset

him. How could she guess! What did she know about the moment when the garden had lost its colours, the sky its lightness?)

We enter his thoughts as he wrestles with his conscience, and with his conflicting feelings of love, and desire for freedom. The parting from Anna is fraught with emotion, and there is an honesty about his feelings as he wanders aimlessly through the streets in a mixture of pain and relief:

> Und er eilte umher, planlos, durch leere Straßen, wie in einem leichten Rausch von Schmerz und Freiheit . . . er erschien sich wie in einer fremden Stadt: einsam, ein wenig stolz auf seine Einsamkeit und ein wenig durchschauert von seinem Stolz.
> (ES I, 952)

(And he rushed about, aimlessly, through empty streets, as though intoxicated with pain and a sense of freedom . . . he seemed to be in an alien city: lonely, a little proud of his loneliness and a little horrified at this pride.)

At such moments Georg appears suddenly to stand outside the flow of his emotions and to recoil in horror from his own faults and temperament.

Schnitzler's ability to enter the minds of his characters, and to present the situation from their viewpoint, remains one of his most appealing strengths as a writer, and in Georg von Wergenthin he offers a penetrating exploration of a temperament for which he clearly had considerable understanding. As he analyses the death-throes of the relationship between Georg and Anna, we are in an area of complex psychology which relativizes or blurs moral or social judgements. Consequently a straight condemnation of Georg from a feminist angle would appear to oversimplify the case, and miss the ambivalence of the figure.

Schnitzler's sensitive treatment of Georg receives an added spice when one takes into account an apparent link between Georg's experience with Anna and Schnitzler's relationship with Marie Reinhard, a bourgeois girl who sacrificed her reputation by becoming Schnitzler's mistress in 1895. This in the fond hope that he would marry her. He did not, but they lived together in a flat in Vienna. Like Anna Rosner, Marie became pregnant. This did not greatly disturb Schnitzler. He said he would quite like a child, but no wife.[37] Pressure was put on him by her parents, but he grew impatient, and planned to have the child adopted. The child, like that of Georg and Anna, was stillborn. Schnitzler realized that he owed it to Marie to marry her, but by then felt the relationship was over. Two years later Marie died of a perforated appendix; her sister pursued Schnitzler with letters full of accusations, blaming his conduct both for the stillbirth and for Marie's death. The parallels between the respective experiences of Schnitzler and his character Georg do not necessarily signify that Georg is a self-portrait.[38] But the links between author and character are rather more than superficial and circumstantial. Schnitzler admitted that the novel contained much of his innermost self, and it is apparent that he did share characteristics with his character – the venerable Marie von Ebner-Eschenbach declared that she disliked Georg as much as she disliked Schnitzler himself.[39] If Schnitzler has written something of his own experience and personality into the fictional character, then this may account for his ambivalent treatment of him: he is to some extent involved in Georg's fate, yet in hindsight is passing judgement upon him (and perhaps upon himself).

The relationship between experience and imaginative literature is a complex area. Nevertheless the publication of Schnitzler's autobiography *Jugend in Wien* in 1968, of volumes of correspondence, and more recently of the diaries, has yielded an insight into Schnitzler's life and attitudes which is fascinating in the light of the content and the general tenor of his literary work. It is apparent, for example, that in his younger days at least he led a life very similar to that led by male chauvinist types whom he treats critically in his works. Passages from *Jugend in Wien* convey the contempt of the upper bourgeois male for the girls of the Vorstadt. Numerous 'süße Mädel' were passed around among his colleagues, he indulged in brief, trivial affairs with girls he can no longer remember, his declarations of love were 'half-conscious lies'.[40] Despite his surface charm the autobiography suggests at times a vain, irresponsible and even callous man, occasionally indifferent to the distress that he caused to others. He possessed a remarkable ability to engage in a number of affairs at the same time without the knowledge of the other parties. His diary entries about affairs with others were written whilst one mistress, Jeanette Heger, sat opposite him in blissful ignorance and sewed.[41] Twice there is evidence that he cynically abandoned girls careless enough to become pregnant.[42] References to women are frequently degrading, as creatures over whom he passes his critical eye. Several times he admits to an affinity to the philanderer Anatol.[43]

The Schnitzler who emerges from the autobiographical writings is perhaps a somewhat unexpected personality, given his sympathetic presentation of female characters in so many of his works. Indeed *Frau Berta Garlan* offers a particularly intriguing example of the transformation of experience into literature, the character Berta having been based on Franziska Reich, the sweetheart of Schnitzler's own youth. Franziska had eventually been married off to the chairman of an insurance company. He died, and in 1899 she wrote to the now famous Doctor Schnitzler, just as Berta writes to the violinist Emil Lindbach. Like Berta and Emil they met in an art gallery (the Secession), Franziska chatted away, got on Schnitzler's nerves, he took her to dinner, then to the Hotel Victoria, and then his physical urges got the better of him.[44] Two days later he wrote to her and told her he would never see her again. These bald facts suggest that Schnitzler took advantage of her in an unseemly and ungentlemanly fashion; but Schnitzler the writer rewrote the experience in reverse, to present his own actions critically from the perpective of the exploited female. His adoption of the viewpoint of his victim represents an extreme externalization of his own behaviour. Further evidence of a discrepancy between Schnitzler the man and Schnitzler the enlightened writer is suggested by his self-confessed predisposition towards jealousy. Whilst he moved with ease between the favours of Jeanette Heger and the actress Marie Glümer, he became aggressively jealous at references to Marie's former lovers. He took a new mistress when Marie went to Germany, but on discovering that Marie in turn had been unfaithful to him there, he reacted irrationally, displaying an attitude clearly indicative of a temperamental inability to overcome the prejudices implanted in him by the conventional double standard. Likewise his reactions to the infidelities of the actress Adele Sandrock, whilst reserving his right to pursue his own, have prompted the conclusion that in his private life Schnitzler observed the social norms and prejudices of his age.[45] This is also borne out in his refusal to marry Marie Glümer (who had had lovers previously), because of the social stigma attached to her.

The portrait of Schnitzler sketched briefly above is that of the younger, pre-1900 Schnitzler, but his temperamental problems were to pursue him into his marriage to the singer Olga

Gussmann, as he recognized in principle the validity of his wife's professional aspirations, but was unable to come to terms with them emotionally. Her desire for recognition in her own right, rather than merely as his wife, led to serious arguments from the very beginning of the marriage, and to their eventual divorce.[46] Schnitzler may have moved in feminist circles and paid lip-service to their views, but in his private life he found it difficult to live up to them. In highlighting evidence of Schnitzler's personality problems to suggest an apparent inability to behave in a manner commensurate with his insight into social prejudices, there is obviously a risk of presenting a one-sided view of Schnitzler the man. Schnitzler was clearly a sensitive and complex person, difficult to live with, jealous of his freedom and independence, and consequently impossible to 'possess'. That he enjoyed, and needed, a large number of relationships with women is, however, clear from the frequent references in his diaries to female acquaintances, and from various volumes of correspondence. One has only to read the recently published correspondence of the elderly Schnitzler with the young Hedy Kempny to appreciate his capacity for a close and sympathetic relationship.[47] It has, however, become apparent from the publication of autobiographical material, that there is a close affinity between the content of his creative writings and his personal experiences, and that he was an active participant in the life of the city whose sexual mores, prejudices and hypocrisies he so tellingly exposes.[48] In his literary works self-criticism and social criticism clearly overlap.

Schnitzler's presentation of the sexual life of Viennese society may be seen as part of a tradition of writing on this theme. As early as 1874 the novelist Leopold von Sacher-Masoch published a titillating account of the depravities and perversions of aristocratic ladies in *Die Messalinen Wiens*. By the turn of the century a widespread interest in sexuality had been stimulated in part by the writings of Freud and the work of the psychologist Krafft-Ebing. In addition a flourishing pornography circulated secretly about the city. The most notorious example was the novel *Josefine Mutzenbacher. Die Lebensgeschichte einer wienerischen Dirne* (Memoirs of a Viennese Whore), which was written anonymously, but allegedly by Schnitzler's friend Felix Salten,[49] and which describes in explicit detail what Schnitzler could only express in the dotted lines of *Reigen*. It is indeed important to note that it is never Schnitzler's concern to titillate or excite the reader with suggestive accounts of sexual behaviour. Despite his own highly active and enthusiastic sex life,[50] his presentation of sexual relationships is essentially a cynical one. Physical satisfaction is sought, but as the count in *Reigen* discovers, does not afford lasting or uplifting pleasure. Moreover the relationships that he presents are generally casual affairs, they frequently involve deception and exploitation, and there are few instances of genuine 'love' in his works (Christine of *Liebelei* is the outstanding exception). Schnitzler's view of sexuality contrasts markedly with that of Karl Kraus, for whom the sexual experience could be spiritually, as well as physically uplifting. Kraus sensed a spiritual void underlying Schnitzler's works, and an absence of emotional and existential enrichment in the relationships he presents.[51] At the same time Kraus himself recognized that the repressive moral code of bourgeois propriety was responsible for the secret and mindless pursuit of sexual gratification prevalent in Vienna, so he was certainly aware that Schnitzler's less idealistic view had its basis in the reality of the life of the city. Despite the cynicism of Schnitzler's view, it must also be stressed that his works are by no means devoid of emotional appeal. In particular his sensitive and sympathetic treatment of female characters is suggestive of his awareness that the villain of the situation was the social code, rather than human nature. In this respect he may be contrasted with another leading intellectual figure of the day, the notorious Otto Weininger, who took his life at the age of twenty-three, allegedly because of his distress at the irreconcilable gulf between sexual desire and the strictness of the moral code.[52] For Weininger the code was rationally based, and it was man's inability to control his rational self that led to sexual misbehaviour. In particular he claimed that the sexual impulse was stronger in the female than in the male, and that the evil sensuality inherent in woman was responsible for the licentiousness prevalent in society, a one-sided view totally out of line with Schnitzler's more balanced presentation.

Schnitzler was not of course the only Viennese writer of the period to treat the sexual issue. The theme is raised, perhaps most entertainingly, in Hermann Bahr's comedy *Das Konzert* (1909). Here Bahr focuses on the marital problems experienced by the virtuoso pianist Gustav Heink and his wife Marie. Heink is the typical egotistical, chauvinistic husband, expecting his wife to remain faithfully available at home to wait upon his every whim, whilst he pursues his glamorous life as a musical celebrity, and indulges in brief affairs with his numerous admiring female pupils. The situation is disturbed when Heink disappears for a weekend at his country cottage with a young married woman, and this information is conveyed to her husband Franz Jura. But Jura is a man of unconventional views and an unusually tolerant disposition, his opinion being that if Heink and Delfine (Jura's wife) are in love, they should be free to marry. To test the strength of their relationship Jura confronts Heink at the cottage, with the proposal that the two couples should exchange partners, namely that Heink should marry Delfine, and that Jura should marry Marie. Jura comes across as a controversial and 'modern' figure, advocating that the marital contract is not permanently binding, and that it is perfectly possible for a woman to transfer her affections from one man to another. Bahr's play raises explicitly, through the views of an outstanding individual, fundamental issues relating to the double standard, such as infidelity, divorce and the position of the wife in relation to the husband. In this respect his technique differs essentially from Schnitzler's, for Schnitzler is generally content to depict the sexual scene through a thorough analysis of sexual relationships, in which psychological issues are to the fore. There is little room for lengthy thematic discussion. For example, the principles of Theodor, Christine and Katharina Binder are conveyed in short isolated statements of attitude, and social issues are usually embedded implicitly in the texture of individual relationships.

Schnitzler's treatment of the sexual issue must also be viewed within a larger European context of a widespread revolt against conventional sexual attitudes at the turn of the century. In late-Victorian Britain, for example, a growing number of writers attacked the double standard, and some questioned the institution of marriage itself. The concept of the 'free union' and the figure of the 'new woman' surfaced in several novels, for example in Grant Allen's *The Woman Who Did* (1895) and Thomas Hardy's *Jude the Obscure* (1896). George Gissing's *The Odd Women* (1893) presents the most sympathetic treatment of women's problems.[53] In Germany the Naturalist writers such as Gerhard Hauptmann and Richard Dehmel were generally sympathetic to the emancipation cause, Hermann Sudermann and Heinrich Mann treated the theme of the 'fallen woman', and Frank Wedekind in particular attacked conventional sexual morality. In his advocacy of sexual liberation Wedekind champions the truly liberated woman as the one who recognizes the power of her sexuality, and uses it to rise above all moral codes and conventions.[54] Wedekind's sexually liberated woman is just one of the stock female figures that fascinated *fin-de-siècle* writers and included the 'femme fatale', the 'femme fragile', the 'demi-vierge', the 'femme enfant' and Schnitzler's 'süßes Mädel'.[55]

Because so many of Schnitzler's works present 'free' sexual activity, it is clearly tempting to proclaim him too as one of the champions of sexual liberation. Nevertheless it is important to bear in mind the essentially cynical view of sexual relationships that emerges from his works, and to recognize also that his main concern is to explore relationships within the social context of a strict moral code. Beneath the façade of bourgeois respectability natural urges assert themselves, but because of the dominance of an unnatural code, the result is often hypocrisy, deception and frustration. In his exposure of the stifling effects of the bourgeois moral code Schnitzler comes close to Wedekind. Likewise his sympathetic treatment of female characters as the victims of outmoded conventions and of social barriers, aligns him to some extent with the contemporary German novelist Theodor Fontane. In *Effi Briest* (1895), for example, Fontane depicts the disastrous consequences of an arranged marriage, and the fate of the adulteress at the hands of the harsh and rigid code of Prussian morality. In an earlier novel *Irrungen Wirrungen* (1888) he presents a relationship between a bourgeois girl and a Prussian aristocrat who lacks the strength of will to flout convention and marry for love. The social divisions that Schnitzler exposes in Vienna are paralleled in Fontane's Berlin.

Schnitzler was not the only Viennese writer of the time to present sexual relationships in terms of the social divisions of the city, and in this respect his technique bears comparison with that of Altenberg. The latter's sketch *Siebzehn bis dreißig*, for example, depicts an attractive young cashier at a fashionable hairdresser's. She exudes the optimism of youth ('My whole life lies before me, do you realize that?') and the narrator assumes she will be seduced by a count, or even a prince. Instead she marries the owner of a café, who goes bankrupt, and she is then exploited as mistress, nursemaid or housekeeper by a succession of wealthy young gentlemen, until she has to recognize that life has passed her by. The narrator makes no comment on the course of her life from seventeen to thirty, but the social point is carried implicitly in the bald facts of the succinct account. Schnitzler's exposure of the reality of sexual urges and practices behind the bourgeois moral façade was also by no means unique. Even the highly respectable Ferdinand von Saar dared to reveal a tendency towards immorality beneath the surface primness of a girl from a good bourgeois family. This is Else Schebesta, the heroine of *Geschichte eines Wiener Kindes*, who lives with her widowed mother in a fine new house in Wieden. Evidence that Else is a girl of easy virtue is provided when she attempts to entice the narrator to a dancing establishment of doubtful reputation, which she admits to frequenting every Saturday evening. Here, the narrator knows, bachelors of all ages can expect to pick up women of the demi-monde, and also girls such as Else, who have gone there in search of pleasure without the knowledge of their parents.

The picture of sexual life in Vienna which emerges from the literary works of Schnitzler and other sexually conscious authors, has done much to promote the legend of light, casual sexual relationships pursued despite the strictures of a harsh moral code. It would be fallacious to argue, however, that Vienna in this respect was unique. For example it has been suggested that Schnitzler's celebrated 'süßes Mädel' is a uniquely Viennese phenomenon,[56] yet Schnitzler found plenty of the same available in Berlin, and a particularly co-operative example in London.[57] It is possible that the dominance of the sexual theme in Schnitzler's works has created an exaggerated and distorted picture of the city. Even though Schnitzler drew for his material on his own personal experiences and on those of his immediate circles, it must be borne in mind that he belonged to a small class of young officers and sons of the upper bourgeoisie. The sexual freedom that they enjoyed was not necessarily shared by the vast majority of fine upstanding citizens: Schnitzler's own father, for example, heartily disapproved of his son's philanderings, and when faced with Arthur's sexual precociousness, could only advise him 'to abstain'.[58] That the moral code was as strict as Schnitzler implies was certainly true. Its violation in the form of extra-marital sexual activity at all levels of Viennese society was a fact, as indeed in other European cities; but such activity may not have been as widespread in Vienna as its superabundance in Schnitzler's works might suggest. Nevertheless it is appropriate to conclude this chapter with the words of Frederic Morton: 'In Vienna propriety was not bleak compulsion, but velvet stagecraft. Propriety acted less to inhibit sex, than to stimulate erotic games.'[59] Such 'games' are acted out with regularity in Schnitzler's works.

5

THE BOURGEOISIE

The social world presented in Schnitzler's works is predominantly that of the bourgeoisie, occasionally the 'Kleine Welt' of the lower middle classes of the suburbs, but mainly the 'Große Welt' of the upper bourgeoisie, the cultured professional families and the wealthy industrialists of the inner city. Schnitzler had an intimate personal knowledge of both of these two major social groups. By birth and upbringing he belonged to the latter sphere, but his social life, and particularly his sexual activities, meant that he frequently, though somewhat furtively, moved with comparative ease between the two areas. Thus although the divisions between the two groups were real, and in many ways insuperable, it was possible to cross the social divide, a situation reflected in many of Schnitzler's early stories and plays. We have already seen that in *Anatol* and *Liebelei* these divisions are expressed within a forum of sexual relationships which transcend the social barriers. A similar context is to be found in two further plays of the 1890s, *Das Märchen* and *Das Vermächtnis*, but each develops into a more thorough and wide-ranging analysis of bourgeois attitudes and prejudices.

Das Märchen (1891) is so called because it presents an attack on the fallacy, or 'tall story', that a 'fallen woman' has, by definition, deprived herself of the possibility of a respectable bourgeois marriage. It is set in the unassuming bourgeois household of the Theren family. The father has apparently died, and Frau Theren has been left to bring up her two daughters, Klara and Fanny. The family is not well off financially, there are no servants, and the three women enjoy a rather modest standard of living. But Klara's career as a piano teacher, and particularly Fanny's as an actress, have given them access to the company of the young bourgeois intelligentsia, writers, artists and doctors. Not all of these are from the upper ranks of bourgeois society, but the Witte brothers are from the professional classes, are wealthy and elegantly dressed. The Theren family are in the habit of receiving these young gentlemen to afternoon tea and cakes in a very modest version of a cultural salon, thus creating a kind of 'neutral' social circle that cuts across the class barriers within the wider sphere of the bourgeoisie. In effect the Theren sisters have raised their social status, but it is stressed that the possibilities of their achieving ultimate respectability through marriage into the upper circles are limited. It is just feasible that a successful and famous actress (as Fanny becomes) might win for herself a rich husband. Consequently poor *Mädel* from the Vorstadt (like the naive Emmy Werner) fondly imagine that entry into the classless world of the theatre may enable them to 'catch' a prince or a baron, or to marry a 'Kavalier'. But for the majority these are idle dreams. Klara, for example, recognizes that the exclusive circles in which the Witte brothers move, will remain for ever closed to Emmy and herself, and is settling for a marriage to a middle-aged minor official, Adalbert Wandel, whom she does not love. Thereby she will achieve a degree of respectability and status, in effect promotion to the middle ranks of the bourgeoisie, though in Fanny's opinion she is simply 'selling' herself for material security. The rather questionable social status of the 'circle' which gathers in the Theren household is indicated by the attitudes taken by August Witte and the pretentious young student Emerich Berger. For Witte it is certainly not 'die noble Welt' (he notes with distaste that the artist Robert Well is really quite shabbily dressed), but on the other other hand not the real Vorstadt either, and he is left in some puzzlement as to 'what sort of circle it actually is'. As for Berger, he has come along for one purpose only, and assumes that Fanny and Klara are both sexually available ('one is in the theatre, the other plays the piano, there must be a chance of getting something going there').

In this situation Schnitzler focuses on the relationship between Fanny and the writer Fedor Denner. This is complicated by the fact that Fanny has one particular disadvantage, namely that she has previously been the mistress of two men, first her former fiancé, and then Friedrich Witte. As such she encounters the moral prejudices of the bourgeoisie against the woman with a 'questionable reputation', prejudices that the apparently enlightened and classless artists and writers have brought with them from their respective social backgrounds. In effect Fanny recognizes that she is 'not the sort of girl that one can marry', and the play develops into a study of bourgeois moral attitudes. Initially Denner, who knows only of her previous relationship with Witte, is the voice of progress and tolerance. He attacks the established prejudices that create such an artificial and irrevocable distinction between the 'respectable woman' and the so-called 'Gefallene', who has surrendered to her natural feelings and has allowed herself to be seduced by the man she loves. But on learning that her past is rather more shady than he had imagined, Denner rapidly retreats from his enlightened position. And when the question arises of marriage to Fanny (which, given her success and fame, would now be *socially* acceptable), he abandons his former image altogether.

Denner's problem is essentially a psychological one. He recoils from the realization that, as her husband, he would be dismissed by others as the lover who allowed himself to be 'caught'; from the prospect of meeting socially her former lover (Friedrich Witte), and seeing the sneer on his face; from the endless stream of flowers and garlands from admiring barons.[1] But because they are set within the wider social context of bourgeois moral attitudes, Denner's psychological difficulties serve to illustrate the mentality of a man who cannot escape deeply rooted prejudices, and to confirm the durability of the double standards operating in the social circles in which he moves. Even in the Vorstadt moral attitudes have hardened. Adalbert Wandel feels that the sexual issues raised by Denner undermine the order of society. His own marriage to Klara must epitomize the ideal of a genuine bourgeois marriage, and he is determined to remove her from the contaminating influence of Fanny and her now less than respectable family. Higher up the scale Doctor Leo Mildner counsels Denner that he cannot marry into this lowly household, but must seek a girl from a 'good family', with an untarnished reputation. The extreme viewpoint is presented by Friedrich Witte, whose objections to the Theren household are social, as well as moral. For him all girls of the Vorstadt are tarred with the same brush, whether they are seamstresses or actresses; and he has chosen his wife from his own exclusive circle.

Das Märchen presents a more complex and fluid social scene than that suggested by the strict divisions presented in *Anatol* and

Liebelei. For such as Witte these frontiers are sacrosanct, but they may apparently be transcended by those with cultural or artistic aspirations. Yet this very fluidity may produce its own problems, of a moral kind. By aspiring beyond the limits of her own class to enter the emancipated world of the theatre, Fanny has put herself morally beyond the pale, in the eyes both of the representative of Vorstadt propriety, and of those who are still the prisoners of inborn bourgeois moral prejudices.

A more devastating and direct attack on the values and hypocrisy of the upper middle classes is presented in *Das Vermächtnis* (The Legacy, 1898). Again, as with Fedor Denner of *Das Märchen*, members of the bourgeoisie are the spokesmen for enlightened views, and in turn their enlightenment collapses, in this case in the face of social pressures. The situation presented in *Das Vermächtnis* has obvious parallels with *Liebelei*, but here the attitudes of the upper-middle-class Losatti family are examined in detail – in *Liebelei* the emphasis is on the love relationship, and Fritz's family remains unseen in the background.

The Losattis are a respectable family from the professional classes, inhabiting an elegant apartment on the Ring. The father, Adolf Losatti, is Professor of Economics at the University, and liberal member of parliament. His daughter Franziska is virtually engaged to Ferdinand Schmidt, a young doctor with a highly promising career ahead of him; his son Hugo is a doctor of law, and is serving his year of voluntary service as an officer in a cavalry regiment. The family is plunged into sudden grief and crisis when Hugo is thrown from his horse in a riding accident in the Prater, and is brought home with severe concussion – to die. But before his death, during brief periods of consciousness, Hugo reveals to his astonished family that he has a four-year-old child and a mistress, Toni Weber, a girl of humble origins. Mother and child are housed in a flat in a side-street only a short distance from the Losatti home. He charges them with the duty of taking Toni and the child in after his death, and of accepting them as full members of the family.

Schnitzler's concern is now with the reactions of this respectable, but supposedly enlightened bourgeois family, to the very difficult task which is thrust upon it. Toni and the child are indeed accepted into the family home, but the welcome is not entirely spontaneous. Only the daughter Franziska responds with genuine, uncomplicated affection both to the child and to Toni herself. For whereas Hugo's mother, Frau Losatti, is instinctively attracted to her grandchild, she is at heart resentful of the part Toni has played in depriving her of her son's company and confidence. Out of a sense of duty to her dead son she nevertheless goes through the motions of being pleasant and attentive to Toni's needs, even eventually bringing herself to embrace her as her daughter. Equally ambivalent is the reaction of the father Adolf, whose tolerance is stretched to the limits as he is torn between his duty to fulfil his son's wish, and his own social prejudices. Initially he cannot cope with the situation, refusing to take seriously the possibility of Hugo's death, and seeing only the social drawbacks of the proposal to fetch Toni, primarily because of the need to 'protect' his daughter from the contaminating presence of a mistress and child from the lower orders. His consequent proposal to introduce Toni as a nurse to Hugo is rendered even more fatuous when Franziska reveals that she had suspected all along the existence of Hugo's 'family', and when she is the one who responds most naturally and warmly to their arrival. The barriers of respectability erected to shelter young ladies from 'unpleasant' realities are shown to be artificial and ineffectual.

Once Losatti perceives that there is no way of avoiding the problem, he fetches Toni himself. But again social considerations are in the forefront of his mind, for he is well aware that if he were to send the maid, the result would be unwanted gossip in the kitchen. He then plays, somewhat ham-fistedly, the role of the generous and adoring grandfather, and to Toni that of the condescending, 'forgiving' father – though he tends to call her 'the mother', or even, pejoratively, 'die Person' rather than by her own name! Losatti styles himself as the champion of liberal ideals, and is proud to present an image of enlightenment and tolerance against the narrow-minded prejudices of his fellow citizens. Yet he is always conscious of the social dangers of his family's action, and is concerned that the 'slap in the face' that they are giving society should not cause them to be socially ostracized. He is dubious that his daughter Franziska should be seen out alone with Toni, and is anxious to secure her engagement to Doctor Schmidt as soon as possible: clearly he would prefer to shut Toni away like a skeleton in the cupboard. Meanwhile it has become clear that the real reason for Losatti's 'generous gesture' is his recognition that he must comply with his son's dying wish. He is aware that he is thereby breaking the social rules, but it is out of a sense of duty, not in the spirit of genuinely humane principles. Indeed he indicates that it requires a special effort of tolerance to treat the child as though it were his legitimate grandchild, and his reluctance and reservations contrast markedly with his declared intention to fight social attitudes and prejudices. The other members of the family well realize that he would not have acted in such an enlightened fashion had Hugo lived!

The hollowness of Losatti's liberal pose is exposed fully by the next turn of events — the death of Toni's sickly child. It is at this point that the poisonous attitude of Doctor Schmidt begins to take effect. Schmidt is the play's unequivocal representative of middle-class protective values, and he clings to them all the more aggressively because he has himself risen by dint of effort and intelligence from the lower ranks of society. Having successfully climbed the ladder and become accepted into the portals of bourgeois professional society, he is all too conscious of his new status, and jealously guards the standards which set him above his own kind. Thus from the beginning he is inhumanly hostile to Toni, and resentful that she should have been admitted to see the dying Hugo. (He holds precisely the attitudes that do not permit Christine to attend the funeral of Fritz in *Liebelei*). Then, when Toni has been taken into the family, he shows all the snobbery of the parvenu, objecting that Hugo's mistress should be permitted to sit at the table of a respectable bourgeois family, and should endanger the purity of soul of his intended Franziska. For Schmidt Toni comes from 'another world', in which the moral laws that uphold the order of bourgeois life are no longer valid.

After the child's death Schmidt decides to force the issue, urging them to recognize that Toni no longer has any ties with the family. Now he finds a readier listener in Losatti himself, especially when he points out the embarrassment the family will suffer when Toni begins to receive male admirers. Losatti agrees that the best course will be to make arrangements for her financial support elsewhere. In this proposal, which conveniently removes her and salves Losatti's conscience, Schnitzler exposes the superficiality and hypocrisy of his liberal pose. Respectability and convenience are being purchased with money. And its cowardice is also revealed, for it is the smug Schmidt who is given the task of informing Toni that she is no longer welcome in the house.

Not all members of the family share Losatti's deep-rooted prejudices. Notably Franziska remains faithful to Toni to the end, and when Toni's suicide note is discovered she reacts angrily to their inhuman treatment of the girl who had been so close to her dead brother. She also bitterly attacks her fiancé for his inhumanity and narrow-minded bigotry. Earlier Emma Winter, the widowed sister-in-law of Frau Losatti and close friend of the family, has also been able to treat Toni as a human being rather than as an embarrassment, and through her gentle but pointed interjections, she produces an ironic commentary on the attitudes of the Losatti parents. She is openly contemptuous of Adolf's magnanimous 'forgiveness' of Toni for her 'sins', and attacks Schmidt for his snobbery and for the inflexibility of his class-consciousness:

> Wie ein Kind von Fabelländern reden Sie von dieser 'anderen Welt'. Als wenn's irgend welche Grenzen dieser Art gäbe! . . . Hier 'die Tugend' – und dort 'das Laster'. So einfach ist das Leben nicht, mein guter Doktor. Die Grenzen wären ja sehr bequem für Sie – nur existieren sie nicht. (DW I, 437)

> (You speak of this 'other world' as a child talking about fairyland. As though there really were frontiers of this kind – on this side 'virtue', on the other 'vice'. But life is not as simple as that, my dear doctor. These barriers would be very convenient for you – unfortunately they don't exist.)

Emma's words amount to a condemnation of the class divisions as artificial and unnaturally rigid. But her most savage accusation is made against Losatti. This is in connection with her own relationship with Hugo, which was close, close enough indeed for Hugo to have confided in her about the existence of Toni and the child. She knows that Losatti has assumed all along – wrongly she insists – that she and Hugo were lovers. For her this assumption effectively sums up a man who cannot conceive of a close personal relationship without reading sexual implications into it. But more than this, his continued tolerance of her in his household in the light of this false assumption only serves to heighten the contrast of his shameful treatment of Toni. For if Emma *had* been Hugo's mistress, then Toni would have been angelic by comparison! His removal of Toni is a matter of social convenience only. It has nothing to do with morality *per se*. Schnitzler here exposes with great clarity the double standards of the members of the bourgeoisie, who tolerate the sexual adventures of their own sons (and even those of their mature womenfolk, if they are pursued with discretion), but who keep at arm's length the lower-class girls who serve to gratify the young men's sexual desires. Towards the end of the play Losatti reiterates to Franziska his strongly held conception of a closed upper-middle-class sphere, demonstrating that he has learned nothing from his experiences:

> Mein gutes Kind, du kennst die Welt nicht. Als junger Mensch wird man in sonderbare Abenteuer hineingezogen. Sprechen wir es endlich aus. Wäre unser Hugo am Leben geblieben, er hätte dieses Verhältnis sicher selbst gelöst. Er hätte eine Frau genommen aus unserem Kreise – aus der anständigen Gesellschaft, zu der wir gehören, wie es schließlich fast alle jungen Männer tun, die ihre Eltern lieb haben und in der Welt und mit der Welt leben wollen.
>
> (DW I, 461)
>
> (My dear child, you know nothing of the world. When one is young, one gets involved in all sorts of adventures. Let us not beat about the bush. If Hugo had lived, he would certainly have ended this relationship himself. He would have married a girl from our own respectable circles, from the society that we belong to, as all young men do in the end, who love their parents and wish to be part of our own world.)

In *Das Vermächtnis* bourgeois standards and conventions are presented as a deep-rooted set of prejudices which have become the basis of the attitude and behaviour of the bourgeois father-figure. His display of liberal, enlightened generosity towards Toni is shown to be no more than a façade, belied throughout by his reluctance and concern, and then abandoned when the child dies. Losatti is indeed a hollow man.

After the turn of the century Schnitzler became less concerned with the prejudices arising out of the social divisions of the city, and began to concentrate on the themes of family and marital relationships within the sphere of upper bourgeois society. To some extent this shift in interest reflects developments in his private affairs, for it was during this period that he married Olga Gussmann and settled down to a family life of his own. Two major plays which illustrate this trend are *Der einsame Weg* (The Lonely Road, 1903) and *Das weite Land* (The Vast Domain, 1910).

Der einsame Weg is essentially a domestic play, set mainly in the modest garden of a professional bourgeois family, with its dignified manners and conversation, and slightly oppressive atmosphere. The mood is predominantly reflective and nostalgic, as characters pursue their memories on gentle autumn days, thus suggesting a perfect impression of 'melancholic, backward-looking Vienna'.[2] The close links between the cultured bourgeoisie and the world of art are represented through the acquaintance of the Wegrat family with the artist Julian Fichtner and the playwright Stephan von Sala. At the same time the loneliness of these two figures (signalled in the play's title) suggests the spiritual isolation, as well as the aloofness, of the artist figure. By contrast members of the Wegrat family are treated more sympathetically, an indication to some that the value affirmed in the play is the bourgeois life-style of the family itself.[3]

Dramatically, as well as thematically, *Der einsame Weg* is a complex play possessing two interlocking lines of action. Schnitzler's first concern is with the lonely, ageing bachelor, the painter Julian Fichtner, and the revelation that Felix Wegrat is his own natural son, conceived during his brief affair with Gabriele, now the wife of Professor Wegrat, Director of the Academy of Fine Arts.[4] The initial problem centres on the conflict within Felix between the interests of the natural father (Julian), who wishes to reclaim Felix as his son, and those of the still ignorant foster-father, Professor Wegrat. As the play proceeds, however, interest shifts to the other artist figure, Stephan von Sala and his affair with the daughter of the Wegrat family, Johanna, which ends tragically with Johanna's suicide. But eventually Schnitzler returns to his original preoccupation by developing the character of Wegrat, and interest is now added to the final stages of the drama through the more positive, deliberate choice by Felix in favour of his foster-father, which provides the play with a thought-provoking and ambivalent conclusion.

Despite the late shift in emphasis to Felix and Wegrat, Julian and Sala still dominate the play, and the full significance of Felix's choice can be appreciated only when viewed within the context of the attitudes and behaviour of the two artist figures. Initially Schnitzler focuses on Julian, his selfish and unscrupulous desertion of Gabriele Wegrat, followed by the years of independent travel, more latterly on the belated longing for domestic happiness. Sala is a more complex and enigmatic character. He is courteous, reflective and apparently the well-meaning friend of both Julian and the Wegrat family, yet in the field of human relationships his attitudes transcend those of Julian. For the latter's self-imposed exile from Vienna and his friends is more than matched by Sala's aloofness and detachment, and his utter denial of the value of relationships within the family, and of friendship itself. In effect he has elevated Julian's former evasion of commitment and involvement into an actual philosophy of life. During the course of the play we are given several indications that Sala is suffering from a terminal illness, which may help to explain his behaviour. He has begun to 'distance' himself from people, an attitude which is perhaps best symbolized by his retirement to his elegant villa outside Vienna in the seclusion of the wooded countryside. As he nears death, Sala has cultivated his loneliness and distance from others. In this respect he differs markedly from Julian who, as he enters the final phase of his life, is hoping to end his lonely wandering existence by settling in Salzburg close to his son Felix. In response to Julian's revelation of an emotional need, the cynical Sala offers him little sympathy or comfort, and sneers at his dependence on the affection of another human being. In Sala Schnitzler has created a man who is detached in a disturbingly inhuman way from the world of what could be called 'normal' human emotions.

Running parallel with the two principal male characters, and offering similar points of comparison and contrast, are the two main female characters, Irene Herms and Johanna Wegrat. Dramatically and in attitude the former is associated more closely with Julian, and her twenty-five years in the theatre in Vienna, during which she formed no lasting attachment, offer a parallel to Julian's years of restless wandering. Just as the ageing Julian can no longer enjoy the independent bachelor life, Irene's time as a glamorous actress is past, and she has retired to the country to live with her sister's family. Irene is seemingly content, but her situation is not entirely satisfactory. Her main regret is that she has had no child of her own, and she will consequently always feel unfulfilled, biologically and emotionally. Her natural paradise in the country is but a sterile substitute for the natural fulfilment which has been denied her. While not strictly alone, she too is experiencing her own version of the lonely road. Both Julian and Irene long for a happiness the value and very existence of which is denied by the more independent Sala, namely the happiness to be found in a domestic environment. When Irene returns to Vienna she indulges in nostalgic memories not of her bohemian days as an actress, but of her childhood there (she even visits her old home and weeps in the presence of the new tenants). Like Julian she looks back on pleasant evenings spent in the garden of the Wegrat home. But like Julian too, she could now find complete fulfilment only in the most fundamental of all relationships, that between parent and child.

The other main female character, Johanna Wegrat is temperamentally closer to Sala. Like Sala she has recently begun to live a more detached, independent life. She has no friends, and her love for her mother has waned since the latter's illness. Similarly, after her mother's death, she feels unable to offer her father emotional support, even admitting to a feeling of hostility towards people who have a genuine claim upon her sympathies. In her gradual estrangement from her family, Johanna reveals a harsh independent streak which finds its parallel in Sala's attitude to friendship and family relationships, and in some ways it is appropriate that she should eventually accompany Sala down the lonely road to death.[5]

The characters of Sala and Johanna set in sharp relief the attitudes displayed by Johanna's brother Felix, particularly concerning his relationship with his natural father Julian Fichtner and his foster-father Professor Wegrat. Felix is an officer in the Imperial Army, is often away from home, and early on there is a hint that he shares his sister's desire to escape from an orderly bourgeois existence. After his mother's death he too begins to feel slightly estranged from his home, and when the possibility arises of an archaeological expedition to the Middle East, he finds the prospect attractive. At the same time he recognizes that he would be leaving people behind whom he might possibly hurt by his departure. In the same vein he also reminds Johanna of her own duty to their father, and expresses his hopes that she will not hurt Wegrat in any way. Later in the play, when Johanna in fact disappears, he informs his father that he is cancelling his plans for the journey, and throughout the closing scenes Felix and Wegrat become ever more considerate of each other's interests and well-being, until the climax of this development is reached in the final moments of the play.

The process whereby Felix grows closer to his foster-father has its origins, paradoxically, in his discovery that Julian is his real father, and in the revelation of Julian's betrayal of Felix's mother. In contrast to Johanna, Felix appears to have had a close relationship with his mother, and on their last evening together he felt particular affection for her. But he does not respond with similar affection to Julian. His overriding feeling is one of outrage at his mother's unhappiness and suffering as a result of Julian's behaviour. More significantly he feels more drawn towards his foster-father than to Julian himself, and his appreciation of Wegrat's nature and character increases, rather than the reverse. Until this point Wegrat has enjoyed only a supporting role in the play, upstaged by the dominating figures of Sala and Fichtner. From the start he comes across as a modest, generous-hearted man, contrasting his own limited abilities as a mere academic administrator with the genius of the true artist, Fichtner. He is also a man of greater sensitivity than Sala, and looks back sentimentally and with natural sadness over his own past. Yet he does have something of Sala's resigned acceptance of his own lonely position in life. The death of his wife has left him with a sense of loneliness, and he also recognizes the reality that in the course of time children grow apart from their parents, who should never attempt to claim ownership over them. This realistic attitude is expressed most impressively when Wegrat, in a moment of supreme unselfishness, attempts to persuade Felix to continue with his plans for the journey, even after Wegrat himself has been left totally destitute by Johanna's disappearance. Felix's reaction is to round angrily on Julian, to express his disgust that such a noble and generous-hearted man should have been so deceived:

> Und dieser Mann wurde belogen – sein Leben lang – von uns allen . . . Hier hat man die Lüge ins Ewige getrieben. Darüber kann ich nicht weg. Und die das getan hat, war meine Mutter, – der sie dahin gebracht hat, waren Sie, – und die Lüge bin ich selbst, solange ich für einen gelte, der ich nicht bin.
>
> (DW I, 832)

> (And this man was deceived – all his life – by all of us . . . The lie has been perpetuated into eternity. I can't get over that. And the one who did it was my mother, – and the one who drove her to it was you, – and I myself am the lie, so long as I am regarded as someone who I am not.)

Earlier the 'Lüge' has been viewed more positively by the family doctor, on the grounds that it has preserved peace in this household for many years, and in a sense Felix eventually agrees, however appalled he is at the original deception. For as the play reaches its climax he too persists in the 'lie', as he kisses the hand of Wegrat as that of his true father:

> FELIX Vater! *Er ergreift die Hand Wegrats und küßt sie.* Mein Vater!
> JULIAN *ist langsam gegangen.*
> WEGRAT Müssen solche Dinge geschehen, daß mir dieses Wort klingt, als hört' ich's zum erstenmal?
>
> (DW I, 836)

> (FELIX Father! *He seizes Wegrat's hand, and kisses it.* My father!
> JULIAN *has walked slowly away.*
> WEGRAT Do such things have to happen for me to sense that I am hearing this word for the first time?)

Wegrat assumes that it is simply Johanna's death that has brought father and son closer together, but essentially Wegrat 'wins' Felix through his own unselfish refusal to demand for himself Felix's love and attention.

Wegrat's unselfishness stands therefore in contrast to the love for Felix exhibited by Julian. For despite Julian's protestations to Sala that he desires a genuinely human relationship with Felix as father and son, his love is essentially a selfish, even a possessive one. Julian needs Felix for the sake of his own happiness, and thus feels he has a genuine claim upon him. But although we may sympathize with Julian in his need, Sala is nevertheless correct in his observation that Julian has in fact no right to 'possess' Felix. Julian may have fathered Felix, but through his subsequent behaviour he deprived himself of all rights to Felix as a son, which Wegrat, on the other hand, has indeed earned through his own unselfish behaviour and attitude.

Felix's choice in favour of the foster-father over the natural father is arguably a radical, or 'modern' decision, for technically it represents a rejection of the traditional values of birthright and ties of blood, and a revolutionary revision of the concept of true paternity.[6] The generous and unselfish love displayed by Wegrat betokens the real father, the selfish, possessive claims of Julian are rejected. But within the context of the situation as presented in Schnitzler's play, Felix's action has a more specific dramatic function, for it ensures that in the short term at least, neither Felix nor Wegrat will be condemned to suffer the kind of loneliness experienced by other characters. It also establishes a bond between parent and child, the kind of relationship sought so desperately by both Irene Herms and Julian himself. As such it appears to belie Wegrat's own remarks on the inevitability of a growing estrangement between parents and children, and Sala's similar conviction that loneliness is the inevitable fate of all, even within the family situation. More generally it affirms the values of love, friendship and interdependence which are denied by Sala, and in its establishment of a positive, living human relationship, points a positive contrast to Sala's own self-centred detachment and aloofness.

Felix's positive response to Wegrat also offers a final contrast to Johanna's gradual alienation from her family, and appears to contradict the desire expressed earlier by Johanna, and more hesitantly by Felix himself, to break away from the ordered bourgeois existence of the Wegrat household. It is indeed tempting to view Felix's choice as a decision to remain within the family circle in which he has been brought up, and consequently as an affirmation of the bourgeois way of life,[7] for the father-son relationship asserted is that which has existed within a bourgeois family context. But one of the most striking aspects of the final moments of the play is Wegrat's own puzzled reaction to Felix's demonstration of love. The still unwitting Wegrat intuitively senses a fresh note of sincerity in Felix's voice, suggesting that the relationship which is being established is something new. Though there have been indications of a close relationship between Felix and his mother, Wegrat himself has been conscious of the growing estrangement between himself and his children, so that Felix's words and gesture of affection come as a welcome surprise. It is possible that Felix's expression of love for Wegrat as his true father reflects Schnitzler's own hopes for a fruitful family life and the end of his own lonely road. His friends Richard Beer-Hofmann, Hermann Bahr and Hugo von Hofmannsthal also married at about this time, rejecting what had previously been a deliberately chosen bachelor life of freedom and non-commitment. But there is also a strong suggestion that Schnitzler had his own parental home in mind when he was planning the presentation of the Wegrat family. From his autobiography and diary entries it is clear that he had a cool relationship with his parents, who were mostly concerned with their own problems and interests, and took little part in the inner development of their children.[8] Perhaps it is not without significance, then, that *Der einsame Weg* closes with the establishment of a father-son relationship based not on the automatic ties of blood, but more positively on the newly found values of genuine love and affection. Whilst it is true that Felix's action does indeed appear to embody a decision to remain within a bourgeois family environment, it need not necessarily be taken as an affirmation of bourgeois family life *per se*. Rather is it an assertion of a sincere and meaningful human relationship, which is presented as something *novel* within a professional bourgeois family.

Das weite Land (The Vast Domain, 1910) is another full-length major drama with a variety of characters drawn from the upper bourgeoisie, which focuses on the themes of family and marital relationships. As the title implies (the 'domain' referred to is that of the human soul, with its infinite possibilities), psychological problems are very much to the fore in this play, but they are examined within the context of relationships between individuals who belong to a particular social group. Friedrich Hofreiter is one of Schnitzler's most powerful and charismatic figures, a manufacturer of electrical products, full of drive and initiative, as he directs his energies into the development of new products and the extension of his factory and workforce. Extremely wealthy, he has moved out of the centre of Vienna to a villa in Baden with a large garden in luxurious surroundings, though he has an office and flat at his factory in the city, and he often stays late in Vienna, where he dines in splendour with acquaintances at the Hotel Imperial. His is a world of bankers and motor cars, though in true bourgeois fashion he also cultivates artistic circles, and has, for example, been closely acquainted with the virtuoso pianist Alexei Korsakow (who, until his death shortly before the play begins, actually resided at the Imperial). Hofmeister is also a very 'modern' man of the world in the new era of industrial expansion. He is interested in world affairs, reads English newspapers, has plans for a business trip to America, where he will take the opportunity of travelling right across to San Francisco. Physically energetic, he is a keen tennis player and mountaineer.

In the main, Schnitzler concentrates on the negative effects of Hofreiter's personality and attitudes. As an ambitious man of the world he sails through life at his own pace and with his own concerns in mind, driven on by internal demonic forces. Consequently he seems inconsiderate of the interests of others, and appears to use people as functions and services, without really taking the trouble to get to know them. Particularly within the sphere of his own family, relationships are strained, and there is a distance between husband, wife and son. Here, as usual, Schnitzler's interest is of a psychological nature, as he concentrates on the private world of the individual family. But, as in *Der einsame Weg*, the general theme of the façade of family ties surfaces frequently in a number of contexts. On a human level, Hofreiter's relationship with his young son is not a close one, and he has plans to despatch the boy to England for a few years, where he will be educated in the useful arts of golf and rowing. As for the marriage itself, the atmosphere between Hofreiter and his wife Genia is tense and edgy, and his suspicions over her relationship with the pianist Alexei Korsakow are but a catalyst for his growing insecurity concerning her attitude to Hofreiter himself. Meanwhile as a true chauvinist husband he proceeds to ride roughshod over her feelings as a housewife – having invited his friend Doctor Mauer to dinner, over the preparations for which she has presided with some care, he impulsively and tactlessly insists on dragging both Mauer and Genia off to the Kurpark where they may all dine in more convivial company.

The root cause of the strain which has developed in the relationship between Hofreiter and Genia is Hofreiter's sexual infidelity. He has just had an affair with Adele Natter, the wife of his banker, and is now displaying a blatant interest in the young Erna Wahl, the daughter of a friend of Genia's. Rather like Gustav Heink of Hermann Bahr's *Konzert* Hofreiter needs the company and adulation of women, to bolster his self-esteem and his youthful, energetic image. Genia responds, like Marie Heink, with apparent indifference, being more concerned for her husband's welfare (at the hands of a potentially vindictive Natter), than constricted with jealousy. Adele herself is moved by Genia's generosity and tolerance, and warns Hofreiter that he does not deserve such a perfect wife. Yet Genia has not always remained so impassive in response to Hofreiter's aberrations; indeed she confesses that in the past she has been taken to the brink of leaving him altogether, of suicide even, and she once considered taking her revenge through an affair of her own.

This then is the background to the incident which provides the play with its opening crisis, and which places the marriage under even greater strain, namely the suicide of the pianist Alexei

Korsakow. Since Korsakow's death, Genia's behaviour has given Hofreiter cause to suspect a liaison between the two, but when he presses her to confess, she insists that Korsakow never became her lover. However, she adds that this was 'unfortunate', for she has since received a letter from Korsakow, written before his suicide, in which he has explained that he is taking his life precisely because Genia has, 'despite everything', refused to become his mistress. Hofreiter's reaction to this revelation is understandably complex. Even more suspicious of her true feelings towards Korsakow (and to himself), he is nevertheless alienated by her virtue, that has led to the death of his dear friend. Far from kneeling before her in adulation of her steadfastness and fidelity, he finds her behaviour frighteningly inhuman, and feels she is using Korsakow's suicide as a weapon against him. In this frame of mind he takes off for a holiday in the Dolomites, for a breath of fresh air (and the charms of Erna Wahl).

Ostensibly Hofreiter's reaction may seem an unconventional one – he is repelled by his wife's fidelity, rather than the opposite. When he presses her for the truth about Korsakow he even goes so far as to admit that she would have had a perfect right to an affair, given his own behaviour, and suggests that they should in future be more open with one another. For example, he would have told her of his affair with Adele had she questioned him directly about it. Later he is to tell Mauer that a woman is not to be judged by the strictures of the moral code alone. A woman of easy virtue may make an excellent wife and mother, better indeed than many a so-called 'anständige Frau'. Seen in this light, Hofreiter comes across as an unusually enlightened and 'modern' husband. But as with so many of Schnitzler's characters, his enlightenment is only skin-deep, and we are soon to find that he pays only lip-service to these sentiments. Genia's response to Hofreiter's censure and departure is to take a lover of her own, not out of revenge (as was once her previous intention), but in an effort to win Hofreiter back. Her choice is a deliberate one, namely Otto Aigner, a young naval officer, who is about to be posted abroad, and it is her intention to tell Hofreiter of the affair once Otto has left. Genia almost succeeds in her objective. Not because the discovery of her infidelity arouses in Hofreiter feelings of pain, jealousy or love. But simply because he enjoys a sense of freedom as a result, relieved of the burden of guilt for his own affairs, and convinced that they are now closer as human beings. In a way it is as though she has done penance for Korsakow's death, and in a very sensible and enlightened fashion. Hofreiter's apparently enlightened and tolerant response to her infidelity is then a matter of psychology rather than principle. The man's self-esteem will simply not allow him to be morally humiliated by a superior wife. Unfortunately Genia's plan ultimately misfires, not because of her infidelity itself, but because of the *manner* of Hofreiter's discovery of it. Here too his personal vanity is a significant factor.

When Hofreiter returns from the Dolomites he does so unannounced, and at an unexpected time – in the early hours of the morning. Just in time to witness young Otto Aigner climbing out of Genia's bedroom window. Hofreiter's response (next day) is to call Otto a coward, thereby provoking him into a duel, in which Otto is subsequently killed. Hofreiter's recourse to this old-fashioned, but still widely practised remedy[9] is wholly out of tune with the tolerant and enlightened front that he has previously maintained. Yet it is not born of a sense of outraged honour in the conventional sense. Nor is it the result of hatred, rage, jealousy or love, as Genia well knows. It is simply a response to the realization that he is being made a fool of in his own house, which is further aggravated by the impudent, triumphant expression that he perceives on Otto's face. The duel is a farce, a hollow sham. It has nothing to do with principle, morality or deep emotions, but is the result of hurt pride and a fit of pique. At the same time the duel has a serious outcome, out of all proportion to the casualness of the affair that provoked it, and to the sheer pettiness of Hofreiter's reaction.

The tragic outcome of the duel stands in stark contrast to the general air of indifference, casual non-commitment and even frivolity that prevails for the most part in this social tragi-comedy. So often relationships are entered into without genuine or lasting emotional involvement, and just as easily dispensed with. The conclusion of the affair between Hofreiter and Adele Natter appears to have left no scars on either party, and both may now resume 'normal relationships'. Adele moves on to a meaningless affair with an amiable young officer, Demeter Stanzides, who already has a mistress in the theatre (whom he refers to discreetly as an 'acquaintance'). Hofreiter spends a night at the Hotel Völser Weiher with Erna Wahl, but leaves the hotel immediately so as not to compromise her and to enable her to continue with life as though nothing had happened. He attributes their sudden 'love' to a moment of passion brought on by the intoxicating atmosphere of the mountains, and certainly the intensity of his feelings evaporates as soon as normal life is resumed. The play presents, then, a rather less blatant version of the eternal *Reigen* of sexual relationships, the most promiscuous participant being the proprietor of the Hotel Völser Weiher, Doctor von Aigner, who left his wife and family years ago, and is rumoured to have fathered children all over the Tirol. Though the play is essentially a study of individual human relationships, these are enacted within a clearly defined social milieu characterized by polite conversation, which for the most part excludes serious discussion and the voicing of sincere and deeply felt emotions, against the background of games of tennis, mountaineering expeditions and weekend hotel parties. This is essentially a society at play, playing at life and at superficial and short-lived emotional attachments.

Occasionally the prevailing atmosphere of nonchalance and levity is jarred by an unwonted note of serious involvement. Aigner himself reveals that he and his wife were united by a bond of love so uncompromising in its demands and expectations, that his initial (inexplicable) act of infidelity was sufficient to blow the whole marriage apart; Erna Wahl claims that her love for Hofreiter is so powerful that she 'belongs to him for ever'; Herr Natter is so 'helplessly in love' with his wife that (in contrast to Frau Aigner) he has to tolerate her frequent infidelities. Yet these emotions are felt to be 'foreign' in the half-hearted atmosphere of this society.[10] Hofreiter is baffled by the story of the Aigner marriage. Genia finds Frau Aigner's attitude uncompromisingly intolerant and unjust, and cannot believe in Erna's commitment to Hofreiter, for life has become so much more 'easy-going' in recent years. As for the unfortunate Natter, he cannot himself comprehend the emotions which have bound him to his wife ('I love her . . . in spite of everything – ! It's awful, isn't it?').

The character who 'fits in' least with the general air of frivolity is the earnest friend of the Hofreiter family, Doctor Franz Mauer. True, he has a mistress in the city (presumably some shop-girl or actress), but because he harbours serious intentions in the direction of Erna Wahl, he has broken with her as a demonstration of good faith. Erna herself is impressed by this unexpected display of 'moral decency'. But Mauer's chief function in the play is to provide the voice of explicit critical commentary on the superficiality of the game of life that he sees played out around him. Mauer is the moralist, who condemns the half-heartedness of a society that has lost all belief in itself:

> Aber dies Ineinander von Zurückhaltung und Frechheit, von feiger Eifersucht und erlogenem Gleichmut – von rasender Leidenschaft und leerer Lust, wie ich es hier sehe – das find' ich trübselig und grauenhaft – . . . Der Freiheit, die sich hier brüstet, der fehlt es am Glauben an sich selbst.
>
> (DW II, 307–8)

(But this mixture of restraint and shamelessness, of cowardly jealousy and feigned indifference, of wild passion and empty pleasure-seeking, that I see about me – I find it all depressing, horrible . . . – The freedom that everybody boasts about so much, is lacking in all belief in itself.)

The listener at the time, whose affair with Otto Aigner has actually provoked Mauer's remarks, is Genia Hofreiter. Earlier in the play Genia has herself displayed an admirably high standard of personal behaviour in her refusal to become Korsakow's mistress. This was due not to a sense of propriety or morality, and certainly not to any feelings of loyalty towards her husband. Rather was it based on a desire to preserve her own sense of self-respect and personal integrity, a feeling which itself sets her apart from the more frivolous members of her circle of acquaintances, and which her husband for one cannot understand. Genia's irresponsible affair with Otto represents, then, a radical betrayal of her personal principles and standards. Certainly she is conscious that she has thereby joined the ranks of the deceptive society, putting on an act before all and sundry, before Herr Natter, Frau Wahl, even her housemaid – and at night she lets her lover in through her bedroom window, just like all 'the rest'.

Apart from Mauer, Genia is the one character who possesses a degree of insight into the behaviour of a society whose members preserve a façade of respectability (that all recognize to *be* a façade), but who indulge nevertheless, without scruple or hesitation, in the social whirl of illicit affairs. She too senses the full horror of Otto Aigner's death as a result of Hofreiter's duel, and she rounds on her husband as a murderer and villain. The duel is but an empty gesture, the hollow remnant of a now meaningless institution, typifying a society that plays out its code of honour as casually as it indulges in the game of love. If Otto pays for the duel with his life, it is Genia's moral tragedy, as a character of integrity and sense of decency, that the duel was itself provoked by her own indiscretion and betrayal of her principles.

Although it focuses on the relatively limited theme of the sexual norms of a particular group of characters, *Das weite Land* captures through the very tone of its dialogue and the breadth of its canvas, the distinctive atmosphere of a particular social milieu. Through the sexual immorality of the bourgeoisie one senses an all-pervading corruption. In some of his shorter dramas, however, Schnitzler concentrates on a far more limited sphere of reference, and relationships are dissected at a purely psychological level. Consequently the sense of 'social comment' is far less apparent. A case in point is offered by the one-act playlet *Stunde des Erkennens* from the trilogy *Komödie der Worte* (1914), which is essentially a study of a relationship at a psychological level, with no explicit wider social implication. Nevertheless it is set within the framework of the world of the professional bourgeoisie, and offers an individual example of a bourgeois marriage that has maintained the veneer of harmony and respectability, and concealed the potentially destructive feelings of resentment and jealousy smouldering beneath the surface.

The portrait of bourgeois society presented in this chapter has been taken from Schnitzler's four great dramas of the bourgeoisie. This reflects his widely recognized tendency to focus in his plays on social relationships, and in his shorter prose works on the individual psyche.[11] To some extent, however, this is a misleading generalization, for many of his prose works are set within a clearly defined social milieu (pertinent examples are *Frau Berta Garlan* and *Frau Beate und ihr Sohn*), and even shorter works such as *Die Toten schweigen* have obvious social implications. The *fullest* account of bourgeois life, simply because of the multitude of bourgeois households described, is to be found in the late novel *Therese*, published in 1928, but still set in the pre-war period. Through the various families with whom Therese is employed as governess (at least twenty-six during the course of the novel) Schnitzler presents a catalogue of bourgeois life in Vienna at various levels. In almost all cases, the most telling comment on the life-style or attitudes of her employers is provided by the reason for Therese's dismissal, or voluntary departure from her employment.

Many of Therese's periods of work are so short-lived that we gain only a fleeting glimpse of the life of the household. Her early posts are with families from the *Kleinbürgertum*. She begins in the house of a minor official with four children, but the apartment is miserable and noisy, the children hungry, and the parents ill-tempered and malicious. Therese has to supplement her food with her own money. In her next position with a widow with two children she is treated as a servant, in the next the house is dirty, in another, with the family of a commercial traveller, the wife receives a lover in the afternoons, and Therese is dismissed when she discovers this. Eventually Therese obtains a position with the family of Doctor Gustav Eppich, a wealthy lawyer with liberal views, who lives in one of the elegant houses of the Ringstrasse. In July the family goes to a villa in Ischl for the summer holidays, there are walks, rowing parties and party games with other children and governesses. Therese is treated politely and with consideration as a member of the family, until she has the misfortune to become pregnant. Whereupon the liberal pose of tolerance and enlightenment vanishes. Therese is told she must leave at once, 'for the sake of the girls', who are told that Therese's mother is ill in Salzburg. The whole charade is played out right to the moment of her departure. After the birth of the child Therese works for three years for the family of a Doctor Regan. The family is comfortably off, the parents kind, the children well-behaved, the atmosphere pleasant. There are musical evenings playing Haydn and Mozart quartets, and Therese performs piano duets with the eight-year-old boy. This is an orderly, cultured and sophisticated bourgeois existence. Suddenly, without warning, though with some embarrassment, Therese is dismissed because they have decided to take a French governess instead. Therese now perceives their kindness as a front, and is convinced that they have been deceiving her all along. She leaves with a bad taste in her mouth.

It is now Therese's misfortune to experience the ugliest and most repulsive aspects of bourgeois life. In one household a young husband and wife quarrel shamelessly at table without consideration for her or for their children, yet when they entertain guests they behave in genteel fashion as a happily married couple; in another household, which is apparently quite prosperous, the child is neglected; in another the husband makes brutal advances to Therese whilst his wife and children are in the next room; a bank manager with four children is heavily in debt, but he and his wife still pursue their extravagant social life as though nothing is wrong, whilst omitting to pay Therese her wages; a woman who has been deserted by her husband and has to work long hours in an office job, cannot afford a doctor for her sick child. There are quarrelsome families, families living in dirty conditions, a family with insufficient food because the husband gambles, unhappy marriages with wayward husbands, and wives who berate them with obscene language.

Such scenes present an image of Viennese society rarely seen either in literary works or the personal reminiscences of any authors writing about turn-of-the-century Vienna, and they will certainly come as a surprise to readers who are familiar only with the mannered tone and dignified atmosphere of Schnitzler's earlier bourgeois plays. The later novel reveals aspects of bourgeois life far removed from the world of *Der einsame Weg* and *Das weite Land*. Admittedly there are common aspects: infidelity, strained family relationships, hypocrisy, all familiar elements in the bourgeois façade. But in *Therese* Schnitzler goes much further than in earlier works in taking the lid off the seamy side of bourgeois life, to present a startlingly frank portrait of the realities beneath the veneer of decorum and politeness so characteristic of his society. It is with Schnitzler's detailed analysis of the social façade that we shall be concerned in the following chapter.

6

THE SOCIAL FAÇADE

Schnitzler's portrayal of the façade of bourgeois life is clarified and enlivened considerably by his detailed analysis of characters' behaviour in individual scenes and encounters. Frequently it is clear that characters are indulging in role-play, concealing beneath a façade of outward behaviour their true feelings, which may be glimpsed only through involuntary gestures or remarks, or through the insight occasionally afforded into their thought processes. Instances of role-playing, or conscious posing, are to be found in the private sphere of inter-personal relations, as well as on the public stage of social life.

In Schnitzler's dramas characters' gestures, movements and facial expressions are often conveyed in detail in the stage directions, which clarify their true feelings, and so make a vital contribution to an understanding of the dialogue which is taking place.[1] In the *Reigen* scene between the young man and the married woman, for example, both characters act out an elaborate game against a sordid web of lies and deception, but spontaneous reactions indicated by stage directions such as 'pleased', 'worried', 'sighs deeply', momentarily interrupt the role-play of the characters, and intensify the irony of the conversation taking place. From the very beginning the young man pretends that the hired flat (in the Schwindgasse) is his own, whereas the lady must be aware that he lives in the Porzellangasse way beyond the other side of the inner city. She goes along with the pretence simply to mask the purpose of their encounter. For her part, she has explained her absence from home with the excuse of a visit to her sister, who must in turn be a trustworthy party to the arrangement. But the prominent feature of the scene is the manner in which she sustains a seemly show of reluctance and innocent vexation at the situation into which she has allowed herself to be manipulated. At the same time she exhibits a skilful seduction strategy of her own to ensure that she gets exactly what she came for. A succession of protestations that she will stay for only 'five minutes', reproaches that he is breaking his promise 'to be good', are interspersed with clear signals of encouragement, and a number of positive gestures and actions which are part of the tactics of the experienced seductress. References to the warm, stuffy atmosphere prompt him to help her remove her coat, hat and veil. Here she plays the passive victim ('she acquiesces'), and allows him to sit with her and kiss her hands. As he grows in confidence and begins to cover her face 'with passionate kisses', she calls a halt, permitting him one final kiss, only to offer further encouragement by responding to the kiss with even greater passion. As for the young man himself, his attempts at persuasion rely almost exclusively, and rather naively, on fervent protestations of love and adoration, but these too are seen to be no more than a sham. His behaviour at one stage is described as 'mechanical', and after her departure he coolly and proudly contemplates his achievement at 'having an affair with a respectable woman', an indication that it is ambition, and not love, that has played the decisive role. Throughout the scene neither character can admit to the other the truth of his or her intentions. The young man deliberately conceals his motives behind a mask of false emotion; the young wife's posing is determined by the requirements of her social position.

A façade of a very different, and more public nature is displayed in Schnitzler's next play *Das Vermächtnis* by the father, Adolf Losatti. From our examination of this play in the previous chapter we have seen that Losatti, as a representative of the liberal intelligentsia, makes a token display of tolerance and enlightenment when he agrees to take his son's (socially inferior) mistress and child into his household.[2] That his enlightenment is only skin-deep, and totally at variance with his real feelings, is indicated from the outset by his initial spontaneous reaction to the revelation of Toni's existence, and to Hugo's request. Losatti's gestures betray his sense of outrage and instinctive horror at such a suggestion (he makes a 'violent movement', 'shakes his head in disbelief'), and are clearly in tune with the social prejudices of his time and of his class. By Act Two Toni and the child have already been accepted into the family, but Losatti's behaviour again suggests that his agreement to this step is not wholly sincere.

True, he plays the role of the doting, generous grandfather, bringing numerous gifts, but Schnitzler suggests through the stage directions that his enthusiasm is forced — and therefore false:

> Na, was macht das Bubi? Was macht das süße kleine Bubi? . . . *Liebkosung, übertrieben* Was hab' ich da dem Bubi mitgebracht?
> (DW I, 429)

(Well, what's the little lad doing? What's the sweet little lad doing? . . . *With an exaggerated caress* Look what I've brought for the little lad.)

Likewise, in no sense is Losatti's response to Toni genuine — his grandiloquent gesture at the close of Act Two is all too illustrative of his conscious posing:

> ADOLF Nennen Sie mich immerhin Vater. – Jawohl, Vater nennen Sie mich!
> TONI *küßt ihm die Hand.*
> ADOLF Nicht so, mein Kind! *Schließt sie in seine Arme* Hier ist Ihr Platz! *Winkt Betty zu sich, in der deutlichen Absicht, eine Gruppe zu arrangieren.*
> (DW I, 444)

(ADOLF Anyway, call me Father. – Yes, do call me Father!
TONI *kisses his hand.*
ADOLF Not like that, my child! *Takes her into his arms* This is where you belong! *Signals to Betty to come over to his side, with the clear intention of forming a group.*)

This studied gesture is wholly contrary to the prejudices and reluctance that Losatti has otherwise shown, and its superficiality and insincerity are soon revealed by his rapid acquiescence in the views of Doctor Schmidt after the child's death.

One of the most striking features of Schnitzler's society is the ability to maintain a façade of behaviour which is either at variance with the feelings of the character concerned, or is inappropriate to the circumstances. The result is often a sustained piece of ironic writing, as scenes are acted out by characters performing as marionettes a role imposed on them by social convention or the requirements of good taste. The following exchange from *Das weite Land* has a chilling irony about it.

During the closing stages of the play, as the duel is being

fought out between Friedrich Hofreiter and Otto von Aigner, Genia Hofreiter, who is in a state of alarm and anxiety, is visited by Otto's mother, Frau Meinhold. Apparently the latter knows nothing of the duel. Genia's agitation is conveyed in the stage directions. As Frau Meinhold is announced she 'gives a start', but she pulls herself together 'with extreme self-control', and the two converse on the superficial level of polite social gossip. The façade is partly broken as Frau Meinhold reveals her knowledge of the affair between Genia and Otto, and Genia is unable to sustain her composure any longer. She suddenly breaks out in uncontrollable sobs, and her head sinks down onto the table. But Frau Meinhold assumes that Genia's distress is caused by the fact that Otto is about to go abroad, and there is still no mention of the duel. The tension reaches a peak as Hofreiter arrives, but is unable to break the news of Otto's death to the desperate Genia because of Frau Meinhold's presence. And he too has to act out the social niceties, with greater success than Genia. Once again the stage directions give a precise account of the degree of self-control that he achieves and of the dramatic effect that it is intended to produce:

FRIEDRICH *lächelt starr ohne zu nicken. Zu Frau Meinhold in seiner lachend boshaften Art, die nun wie eine Maske wirkt* Küss' die Hand, gnädige Frau. *Er nimmt ihre dargebotene Hand mit einem kaum bemerklichen Zögern* Wie geht's?
(DW II, 316)

(FRIEDRICH *smiles stiffly, but without nodding. Then to Frau Meinhold, in his laughing, mocking manner, which now has the effect of a mask* Greetings, dear lady. *He takes her hand, that she has offered him, with almost imperceptible hesitation* How are you?)

And for fully ten minutes he sustains a polite conversation about his morning walk, Frau Meinhold's estranged husband (the father of the boy he has just shot), his recent holiday, even future visits. After her departure he reveals to Genia that Otto is dead. To Genia his apparently unconcerned performance to Frau Meinhold, which, it must be conceded, he carries off with such brilliant aplomb, is a gruesome display of cold inhumanity. The dialogue has proceeded in the most unusual of circumstances, and in a highly charged atmosphere of dramatic irony, yet in its intensity it highlights a tendency to avoid embarrassing truths and to gloss over unpleasantries with a veneer of superficial charm. Hofreiter's cowardly social hypocrisy has produced one of Schnitzler's most devastating scenes.

Schnitzler's use of stage directions in his dramas to convey the attitudes and feelings of his characters, and so penetrate the façade of their public behaviour, is paralleled in his prose works by a meticulous attention to gestures, facial expressions and other aspects of outward behaviour. Two scenes from *Spiel im Morgengrauen* illustrate how the portrayal of characters' behaviour may clarify a relationship and reveal the true feelings of the participants. The scenes in question are between Willi Kasda and Leopoldine, a former flower-girl, but now a wealthy woman. From our previous examination of their relationship, we have seen that Kasda attempts to exploit their former love relationship to rescue himself from financial embarrassment.[3] He first visits her at her home, but she behaves in a formal, polite manner, showing no sign of recognition. When he seeks to resume their romantic association by kissing her hand, she withdraws it hastily, and when he desperately requests a loan she makes discouraging businesslike remarks about security and tied-up assets. But the possibility that a degree of personal involvement still lurks beneath this frosty exterior, is suggested by his perception of a sympathetic expression in her eyes, a regretful shake of the head, even a flirtatious tone of voice. The impression is confirmed by her sudden, unexpected acknowledgement of recognition and seemingly spontaneous transfer into the familiar mode of speech. Kasda's hopes are further raised when she now permits him to kiss her hand, and promises to send word to him concerning the results of her attempts to raise the money.

Even more encouraging is the arrival that evening at his quarters in the Alser barracks of Leopoldine herself. Such a compromising visit by a respectable married lady to a young lieutenant can be for only one particular purpose, and Leopoldine quickly adopts the role of the reluctant, and eventually compliant lover. But throughout this scene there is no mention of the loan, and Kasda is simply left to assume that the prospects of sexual success carry with them the promise of financial reward. Next morning, however, there is still no reference to money by either party. Kasda plays the role of the affectionate lover, stretching out his arms longingly in an attempt to embrace her and persuade her to stay. Leopoldine resumes her businesslike, detached manner, and is firm in her intention to leave for an important engagement. That Kasda's show of affection is simply an attempt to acquire the money, is suggested by the anxiety in his voice as he bids her to stay, then by the panic in his eyes as he scans the room for signs of a package discreetly left for him. But her eyes convey only mockery, even a sadistic pleasure in his discomfort. At last, as she leaves, she tosses him a single one thousand florin note, a fraction of the amount he needs. Her gesture of contempt and the icy look in her eyes indicate that her purpose in sleeping with him was to teach him a lesson for his insulting payment to her of ten florins after their night of love on the previous occasion. For Leopoldine had slept with him then not for money, but for love. Leopoldine conveys her meaning by looking for a second time into Kasda's eyes, and as he begins to understand the grave injustice he has done her, her eyes communicate to him the same childlike sparkle which he remembers from their first night together. Unfortunately Leopoldine's expression of the love she still has for Kasda is quickly forgotten, for Kasda's thoughts are dominated by the manner of her carefully planned lesson to him. Instead of arousing in Kasda an appreciation of her love for him, her action repels him. He first feels disgust, anger and bitterness at the insinuation that he was willing to 'sell' himself for money. Then his bitterness turns to shame and a sense of humiliation, as he acknowledges the truth of her accusation. Leopoldine's lesson has misfired, for she has veiled her true motives and the reality of her love, glimpsed all too briefly in the momentary expression of her eyes. Instead of genuine communication between the two there is the gulf of a tragic misunderstanding, and when Leopoldine does send him the money, it is too late, for Kasda is dead.

In the situation just described Schnitzler is operating in the field of private human relations, and does not appear to be making a 'social point'. In the late short story *Der Sekundant* (1932), he again presents a detailed exploration of the gestures and outward behaviour of two characters involved in a sexual relationship, but this then develops into a study of social role-play.

The story begins with a duel, in which a married man Loiberger is killed, but the focus of attention shifts to the relationship between Eißler, Loiberger's second, and Loiberger's wife Agathe. It is Eißler's unwelcome task to break the news of Loiberger's death to the unsuspecting Agathe, but when he calls on her he is initially distracted by the look in her eyes. It is 'questioning', 'promising', 'alluring', and he recalls various signs and signals that she has previously given him of her willingness to have an affair with him. Moreover he is convinced that her undisguised joy at what she takes to be a most daring visit during her husband's absence, suggests a desire to exploit the occasion for their mutual pleasure. Throughout lunch this impression is confirmed by the tone of her voice and pointed glances, so that after their meal they proceed naturally to the satisfaction of their physical desires. Following this, Eißler falls asleep and his dreams suggest his feelings of guilt at sleeping with the wife of his dead friend, and also that he has no feelings of genuine attachment to Agathe. Emotionally he is as indifferent towards her as is she towards him.

When he awakes he is now too cowardly to reveal the outrageous circumstances in which they have made love, and she, still unaware of the truth and fearful of discovery, is keen to get him out of the house as quickly as possible. At first this seems also to be an honest attempt to terminate an encounter which has involved no profound emotional attachment. But then, unexpectedly, comes her claim that she loves him. Since she has previously displayed only physical desire, and shown that she is quite capable of never seeing him again, her expressions of love are obviously a pretence, a succession of platitudes:

> Ich liebe dich sehr. Ich habe es nicht gewußt, wie sehr ich dich liebe. Du mußt es ja nicht glauben. Aber warum sollte ich es dir sagen, wenn es nicht so wäre. Du sollst es nur wissen, ehe du gehst.
>
> (ES II, 897)

> (I love you so much. I didn't realize how much I love you. You don't have to believe me. But why would I tell you if it were not true. I just wanted you to know before you go.)

Agathe is simply going through the conventions of a confession of feelings in order to put a gloss of emotional involvement over her sexual fulfilment.[4] This is confirmed when Eißler, who knows that her husband is dead and that they are free to pursue their 'love' if they so wish, suggests that they should go away together. Agathe turns pale, urges him to be 'sensible' and to put away such childish thoughts, in effect to return to the roles they occupy in society. This she does when she eventually learns the truth of her husband's death, for she takes the news calmly, and with apparent fortitude.

Only a quick initial glance displays horror at Eißler's deception, but she also communicates understanding, forgiveness and possibly even gratitude that his silence permitted her to exploit the occasion for her own pleasure. But she still remains emotionally indifferent towards Eißler, and years later, when they meet again, her innocent facial expression betrays no recollection of the afternoon they spent together. In effect Agathe has resumed the façade of indifference and social respectability, ignoring the reality of their previous encounter.

Another narrative work which includes a study of the façade of respectability is *Frau Beate und ihr Sohn*, but here the attempt of the central character to maintain an innocent and virtuous outward appearance founders altogether, as her sexual urges become dominant. In the early stages of the story Beate is herself unaware of her own awakening desires, and she successfully preserves her façade. This is illustrated by her visit to Fortunata, a former actress of questionable social reputation, who has married a baron, and whom Beate suspects of initiating a sexual relationship with Beate's own young son Hugo. It is Beate's intention to confront Fortunata with her suspicions, and to discourage her before Hugo loses his innocence. When Beate arrives at Fortunata's villa both women pretend that her visit is a simple social call. Fortunata plays the role of polite hostess, and Beate that of the equally polite visitor, though Schnitzler conveys from the beginning that the relationship is one of mutual hostility. When Beate is announced Fortunata's face stiffens momentarily, before it melts into a smile, as she greets Beate warmly and with apparent sincerity. As Fortunata talks, Beate registers that her words are being carefully chosen, and behind Beate's own mask of politeness she identifies Fortunata in her private thoughts as a 'hussy'. Only when Hugo is mentioned is there any sign of genuine communication, and then only in a facial expression. Momentarily Beate loses control, and looks at her with undisguised hostility, but Fortunata's eyes respond with wicked amusement. Eventually Beate is able to speak frankly of the purpose of her visit, and it is at this stage that the social behaviour of the two women diverges. Fortunata begins to speak openly of her sexual reputation, and mockingly suggests that had *she* a son she would recommend Beate herself to him! Beate refuses to pursue the conversation on this level, which she finds shameless and undignified, for she cannot abandon her façade of middle-class respectability to discuss sexual matters so openly.

Immediately after she leaves she realizes that she could have responded to Fortunata by offering her as a substitute for Hugo the latter's handsome friend Fritz, but at the time she was incapable of descending to such frivolity.

That Beate's prim, respectable front is just a façade, however, is clear from a subsequent social occasion, and from developments which occur in her own relationship with Fritz. When she goes on a picnic expedition into the hills with a number of acquaintances, it becomes apparent that the feelings and attitudes that she attempts to convey at the conscious level, contrast markedly with what she communicates unconsciously by involuntary gesture. During the picnic three of the men display a sexual interest in her, young Doctor Bertram, the older bank manager Welponer, and Fritz. Bertram invites her to take her place beside him on his coat, which he spreads out enticingly on the grass; he is not put off by her refusal, and feasts his eyes upon her as she stretches out on her own rug; he even dares to invite her to take tea with him in his rooms. Outwardly Beate is discouraging, and behaves in a cool and distant manner. Yet his aspirations and assumptions are not entirely without foundation. During the course of the afternoon Beate comes to acknowledge his sexual interest in her, and senses his eyes upon her body. At one stage she briefly sleeps, and her first involuntary action upon waking is to look for the smoke of his cigarette: he is indeed there watching her closely. As she gets up and straightens her dress, she suddenly realizes that she is looking down upon him in an encouraging way. Similarly, when Beate detects an enraptured look on Fritz's face as he stares at her, there is no indication that she consciously offers encouragement, but she later catches herself behaving in a sexually provocative manner:

> Fritz sah zu Beate auf mit glühenden Wangen, sie lächelte ihm entgegen. Bertram, sich erhebend, ließ einen Blick zum Himmel aufsteigen und dann in kleinen Fünkchen über sie niedergehen. Was habt ihr nur alle? dachte sie. Und was hab' ich? Denn plötzlich merkte sie, daß sie die Linien ihres Körpers wie lockend spielen ließ.
>
> (ES II, 71)

(Fritz looked up at Beate with glowing cheeks, she smiled at him. As he got up, Bertram looked up towards the sky, and then his eyes sparkled as he gazed down at her. What is the matter with you all? she thought. And what is the matter with me? For suddenly she noticed that she was displaying the contours of her body in a most enticing fashion.)

Thus Beate gradually becomes aware that the non-verbal communication between herself and the men around her has not been one-sided, and that their bold behaviour has been in response to her own encouragement. The façade of respectability adopted by Beate in the early stages of the story has been gradually destroyed by her unconscious display of latent sexual urges.

Schnitzler's attention to gesture and outward appearance to clarify the true feelings of a character, is frequently reinforced by an even more effective device, namely the first-hand rendering of the thought processes of the character concerned. The employment of this technique is clearly in tune with Schnitzler's interest in psychology, for it enables him to explore the individual consciousness down to the very last detail. Yet perhaps the most interesting achievement of Schnitzler's probings of characters' mental processes is their side-effect, namely the revelation to the reader of the hidden truths behind insincere role-playing in interpersonal relationships, and behind the façade of politeness adopted during social encounters and public behaviour.

In many of his stories Schnitzler provides brief glimpses of characters' thought processes simply to clarify feelings or intentions, which would otherwise remain obscured behind the cloak of conversation. In the short story *Die Toten schweigen* (The Dead Keep Quiet, 1897), a young man (Franz) begs his mistress, a married woman (Emma), to leave her husband and elope with him. Circumstances would seem to point to the seriousness of Franz's proposal. As he waits for Emma to meet him in a wind-swept and dark side-street, he experiences tension and dissatisfaction with the situation; when she arrives he complains that otherwise they meet only socially, in public. So he now offers her an ultimatum: either she leave her husband for him, or their relationship should end. Apparently this is not the first time that he has expressed dissatisfaction, but he has never presented her with such a clear-cut choice, and she now accepts that this is her 'dismissal'. The question remains, however, as to whether his suggestion that they should reveal their relationship publicly, is a serious one. Clearly such a declaration would amount to a dramatic break with social convention, and would require a degree of courage and freedom of thought that Emma simply does not possess. Why then does he make such an impossible proposal? The answer is suggested in a brief elucidation of his thoughts as he waits impatiently for her arrival at the beginning of the story:

> Noch eine halbe Stunde, sagte er zu sich, dann kann ich gehen. Ach – ich wollte beinahe, es wäre so weit.
>
> (ES I, 296)
>
> (Another half hour, he said to himself, and then I can go. Oh, I almost wish the time was up.)

Franz's reluctance to continue the relationship is already visible in this half-wish that she might not turn up at all. The ultimatum that he delivers to her, the answer to which he must anticipate, is simply to provide him with an excuse to leave her.

Schnitzler allows the reader just one brief glimpse into Franz's thoughts, otherwise the narrative consists only of the setting of the scene and the conversation between the lovers, which is presented very much as it would be in a drama. But in the second half of the story he alters his technique dramatically. The lovers take a ride in a coach, there is an accident, and Franz is killed. Now Schnitzler's sole preoccupation is with Emma's reaction, and the story turns into a full exploration of her thoughts and feelings via the medium of narrated monologue. Faced with the stark reality of her lover's death, her immediate reaction is not one of shock or sorrow. Her first priority is to get away from the scene undiscovered, so that she may resume her role as wife and mother as though nothing had happened.

> Sie muß ja nach Haus, sie hat ein Kind, sie hat einen Mann, sie wäre verloren, wenn man sie dort bei ihrem toten Geliebten gefunden hätte.
>
> (ES I, 306)
>
> (She must go home, she has a child, she has a husband, it would have been the end of her if she had been discovered there with her dead lover.)

Briefly she is aware of the immorality of her flight, and is visited by a sense of shame at her 'cowardly' and 'wicked' desertion of Franz. But she can justify her behaviour to herself in terms of her duty to her family:

> Sie ist ein Weib – und sie hat ein Kind und einen Gatten. – Sie hat Recht gehabt, – es ist ihre Pflicht – ja ihre Pflicht.
>
> (ES I, 308)
>
> (She is married – and she has a child and a husband. - She was right, – it is her duty – yes, her duty.)

Emma displays no emotion in response to Franz's death, her behaviour is due entirely to her cowardly fear of the consequences of being 'found out'. Her dominant concern is for her own welfare, and Schnitzler conveys vividly her relief at her return to the anonymity of the crowded inner city, and then to the security of the domestic haven. Her only desire is for safety. Everything else (including Franz's death) is a matter of indifference to her. When Emma reaches home, however, her problems are far from over, for she comes face to face with her husband, from whom she must now conceal her anxiety. Once more Schnitzler takes us directly into Emma's thought processes, which are hidden from her husband, and therefore 'behind' the outer façade she is attempting to project. Here again the focus is on her continued preoccupation with her fears of discovery, that Franz might still be alive and betray her identity to the doctors treating him. As she imagines the scene, her anxiety breaks down her mask of composure and she gives an involuntary scream. For the time being she avoids giving an explanation, and succeeds in restoring her façade of unconcern, taking her husband's hands, drawing him towards her, feigning happiness and affection. But again the mask slips as her thoughts return to Franz and the possibilities of betrayal. As she reassures herself that he is dead she involuntarily voices her thoughts out loud:

> er ist tot ... er ist ganz gewiß tot ... und die Toten schweigen. 'Warum sagst du das?' hörte sie plötzlich die Stimme ihres Mannes. Sie erschrickt tief. 'Was hab' ich denn gesagt?'
>
> (ES I, 311)
>
> (he is dead, he is definitely dead ... and the dead keep quiet. 'Why did you say that?' she suddenly heard her husband say. She is utterly shocked. 'What did I say then?')

As he proceeds to repeat what she has said, Emma realizes that she cannot sustain for ever a series of mechanical responses and poses, and that peace of mind will come only through an honest confession of the truth:

> Und während sie mit ihrem Jungen langsam durch die Tür schreitet, immer die Augen ihres Gatten auf sich gerichtet fühlend, kommt eine große Ruhe über sie, als würde vieles wieder gut.
>
> (ES I, 312)
>
> (And as she walks slowly out of the room with her little boy, still feeling her husband's eyes upon her, a feeling of great peace comes over her, as though everything were going to be all right again.)

Although Schnitzler provides no clear-cut indication of the effect that her confession will have on their marriage, the open ending suggests the possibility at least that it may lead to a more open and fruitful relationship.

Essentially Schnitzler's exploration of Emma's thought processes is a psychological study of a developing anxiety neurosis that eventually can find relief only through confession. But it is not without its social and moral implications. Most immediately Emma's fears of social disgrace, that so dominate her consciousness following the accident, represent a self-centred reaction to the death of her lover, which demonstrates all too clearly the superficiality of her feelings towards him. Thereafter the façade of normality and unconcern which she attempts to sustain, comes across as a callous and inhuman mask, concealing her 'betrayal' of the dead man. Yet although Emma is essentially, and from the beginning, driven on by fear, her thoughts from time to time indicate that she is not without a sense of morality and an awareness of her own cowardice and wrongdoing. And in this connection the most interesting aspect of Schnitzler's study of Emma is her progression to a point at which she is no longer able to sustain her façade. This she reaches when she is visited by her basest thought, expressing her subconscious wish that Franz is indeed safely dead, the thought that provides the story with its title words. Ultimately there seems to be a level of immorality beneath which she can sink no further, for no sooner has the thought (or 'wish') crossed her mind than she is prompted, involuntarily, to betray it: 'The dead keep quiet.' This is then followed by her conscious recognition that a full confession to the man whom she has been deceiving for years might be for the best. Most immediately Emma's confession is prompted by a psychological need to alleviate her state of anxiety, but eventually the psychological need coincides with a deep-rooted moral urge.[5]

One of Schnitzler's most celebrated social façades is that adopted by the young hero of the short story *Leutnant Gustl* (1900), a work noted primarily for Schnitzler's skilful use of the sustained inner monologue. This affords the reader immediate access into Gustl's thought processes, and because there is no intervention by a narrator figure, we are obliged to rely solely on the inner monologue for an understanding of events. Nevertheless Schnitzler's successful combination within the monologue of spontaneous mental activity and external experiences, enables the reader to recognize Gustl's social façade for what it is.

In the opening section of the story, during which Gustl is attending a concert, Gustl is primarily preoccupied with the image that he is projecting to the world at large. For example, when he wishes to look at his watch to ascertain how much longer the concert will last, he has to consider first whether this is acceptable behaviour ('I must look at my watch . . . but that is probably not done at such a serious concert'). For the most part he shows little interest in the music, and even when he does consciously force himself to take note of what is happening, his responses are governed entirely by the requirements of social manners and conventions. The contrast between his true feelings and the façade which he consciously projects is also evident when he speaks to others. As he leaves the concert and waits to collect his coat he cannot conceal his impatience with the cloakroom attendant:

> Sie, zweihundertvierundzwanzig! Da hängt er! Na, hab'n Sie keine Augen? Da hängt er! Na, Gott sei Dank!
>
> (ES I, 343)

> (You, two hundred and twenty-four! It's hanging just there! Haven't you any eyes in your head? There it is! Ah, thank God!)

But even these sarcastic and peremptory remarks are more polite than his thoughts: 'When on earth is the idiot going to take my number?' Between the impolite thought and its communication in speech a split second has elapsed, sufficient to temper his feelings a little, and enable him to express the thought in a slightly less offensive manner.

The concert episode is crowned by a confrontation between Gustl and a baker from the coffee-house which he frequents with his colleagues. Once again the inner monologue indicates Gustl's true feelings, and points to his attempt to act the role of the socially superior army officer. Gustl is impatient with the baker, who is blocking his way, but the baker tells Gustl to be patient and wait his turn. In keeping with the façade that he must present at this challenge to his social position, Gustl demands that the baker allow him to pass. Here Gustl is not behaving with measured politeness, but is asserting himself with the aggression required of an officer when confronted by a civilian who does not acknowledge his superiority. But when the baker persists in his defiance, Gustl finally loses his temper and thoughtlessly blurts out: 'You, shut your trap!' Immediately he is aware that he has broken his façade by using language in public unsuitable for an officer and gentleman: 'I shouldn't have said that, I was too coarse.' As the confrontation continues, the baker firmly grips Gustl's sword, asserting his physical superiority over the effete lieutenant. At this the latter's rage turns to fear, as the baker's words indicate:

> Aber ich will Ihnen die Karriere nicht verderben . . . Also schön brav sein! . . . So, hab'n S' keine Angst, 's hat niemand was gehört.
>
> (ES I, 344)

> (But I won't spoil your career . . . So just behave yourself! . . . Right, don't be frightened, nobody heard anything.)

Gustl's anxiety that the baker will cause a scandal by publicly revealing his physical defeat, must be obvious from his involuntary facial expression. Schnitzler has thus created a particularly stressful situation in which the façade of superiority and self-confidence, which he is expected to present through his position in society, is impossible to sustain.

Throughout the night following this episode Gustl has to come to terms with the consequences: the necessity for his suicide because of the dishonour he has suffered. This remains the position until Gustl goes to the coffee-house for an early breakfast. During his conversation with the waiter who serves him, he learns that the baker is dead, and registers that he may escape the consequences of their altercation after all. Here Gustl successfully preserves his self-control by displaying a decent concern at the baker's fate. When he is told that the baker has had a stroke, he realizes that he must not show too much enthusiasm, and consciously controls his voice:

> 'Was?' . . . ich darf nicht so schreien . . . nein, ich darf mir nichts anmerken lassen . . . ich muß ihn noch einmal fragen . . . 'Wen hat der Schlag getroffen?' – Famos, famos! – ganz harmlos hab' ich das gesagt!
>
> (ES I, 364–5)

> ('What?' . . . I must not shout so much . . . no, I mustn't let him see anything . . . I must ask him again . . . 'Who has had a stroke?' – Splendid, splendid! – I said that quite innocently!)

Throughout this episode the monologue indicates just how excited he is, but also the care he takes over the crucial question of the baker's death:

> ich muß fragen, ob er tot ist . . . aber ganz ruhig, denn was geht mich der Bäckermeister an – ich muß in die Zeitung schau'n, während ich den Kellner frag' . . .
>
> (ES I, 365)

> (I must ask if he is dead . . . but quite calmly, for what do I care about the baker – I must look at the paper as I ask the waiter . . .)

When he receives the desired confirmation, his thoughts reveal that he wishes to jump on the billiard table with delight, yet by exercising maximum control over himself he is able to communicate deep regret.

In the sections of *Leutnant Gustl* where inter-personal communication occurs, Gustl's emotions are generally at odds with the image that he presents to society at large. Only his confrontation with the baker temporarily destroys his façade, but this is an unusually stressful situation. In normal circumstances the young lieutenant is able to present to society the image of the superior, self-confident, and occasionally aggressive officer; yet it is also apparent that beneath the surface is a very 'ordinary' human being. The façade of the army officer is essentially as hollow – and unnatural – as that of the liberal poseur, the progressive bourgeois industrialist, the primly respectable widow, the secret adulteress. Politeness and decorum are inevitable ingredients in the social life of a civilized society, and it is arguable that the Viennese social façade was no more artificial or hypocritical than elsewhere. But Schnitzler's characters behave so often like marionettes, performing roles imposed upon them by social convention and the requirements of good taste, that one is left with the impression that the veneer of superficial charm and cowardly hypocrisy, the façade of politeness and prim respectability adopted during social encounters, are major features of his society.

7

SOCIAL GROUPS

THE ARMY AND THE CODE OF HONOUR

Though Schnitzler's world is largely that of the professional bourgeoisie, other identifiable social groups with which he came to be associated also feature in his literary works. In particular he was well acquainted with the intellectual and cultural circles of the city. But one of the major institutions of the empire to find a place in so many of his stories and plays is the army. As a military cadet, and then as a medical officer in the reserve, Schnitzler had first-hand experience of army life. In any case, because of the prominent position occupied by the officers of the Imperial Army in the social fabric of Vienna, it is not surprising that army officers are present in such considerable numbers in Schnitzler's works. The Austrian Empire had a large and expensive standing army, and its officers enjoyed a privileged position within society, forming a highly conspicuous element in the day-to-day official and social life of the capital. They were seen on parades, at balls and dances, theatres and concerts, in the coffee-houses and restaurants. With their brilliant uniforms they made up a truly representative part of the ostentatious display of gay Vienna.

The number of officers and ordinary soldiers in the standing army was augmented by a considerable reserve. This was fed by a three-year conscription system, though university students were allowed to serve for just one year as officer-cadets, known as 'Einjährig-Freiwillige'. At the end of his year's service the young cadet was commissioned as a woefully prepared second lieutenant of the reserve, and received promotion to the rank of first lieutenant on attending the annual exercises. The title of Leutnant der Reserve carried a great deal of social kudos, and its holder was entitled to wear the uniform even when not on active duty. Schnitzler himself served his year as a cadet in 1882–3 in the military hospital in Vienna, was commissioned as a medical officer of the reserve, and testifies in his autobiography to the glamour of the life, and in particular to the fascination which he exercised over women through the power of his uniform.[1] The reaction in *Liebelei* of Mizi to the photograph of Fritz resplendent in his magnificence as a handsome young officer provides a typical example of this effect.

Though he enjoyed the elegant life-style afforded him by his rank, Schnitzler's reaction to his experiences as a cadet and to the behaviour and attitudes of his colleagues, was essentially negative. Several diary entries testify to his detestation of everything connected with the military organization, and his lack of commitment to the duties of a cadet is indicated in a very cynical account in his autobiography of army manoeuvres, from which he and his companions simply deserted.[2] His antipathy towards militarism is also expressed in the highly critical picture he presents in his works of army life, of the temperament of the typical officer and of the code of conduct expected of him. The play *Freiwild* (1896), for example, takes place in a provincial spa not far from Vienna, where a cavalry regiment is stationed. The officers appear to lead a life of idle pleasure, drinking, gambling and flirting with the actresses of the local provincial theatre, the 'fair game' referred to in the play's title. There are references to late moonlight parties, open-air concerts, tennis parties with the local bourgeoisie, whom the officers treat with disdain. The prime offender is Karinski, a cavalry officer with an aggressive temperament, who has previously been pursued for gambling debts, and has recently been charged with assaulting a civilian in a restaurant. During the course of the play Karinski behaves in a highly offensive manner to the heroine Anna Riedel, a virtuous and serious-minded bourgeois girl, who is in her first post as an actress with the local company. Schnitzler was also very much aware that the life of the career officer was not always as glamorous as it was popularly held to be, particularly if he did not enjoy the advantages of a substantial private income with which to supplement his pay. In *Spiel im Morgengrauen* Lieutenant Willi Kasda lives in modest, penny-pinching circumstances because the regular allowance paid him by his uncle has ceased. He has had to cut down his visits to coffee-houses and expenses on cigarettes, and has ceased spending money on women altogether. He has to rely on visits to rich acquaintances for the occasional free meal, and has his eye on the daughter of a wealthy industrialist for the dowry she might bring him. His former colleague Otto Bogner has had to leave the army because of gambling debts, and now cuts a sorry figure as the fallen officer, pale and shabbily dressed, and reduced to tears as he relates his experiences. An equally pathetic case is that of Lieutenant Colonel Hubert Fabiani, the father in *Therese*, who retires from the army at the age of sixty, and suddenly finds himself deprived of the regular habits, security and dignity of the officer life. He tries to recapture his identity by holding forth on political and military matters in local inns, where he often appears in full uniform, suffers from delusions of grandeur, and is eventually confined to a lunatic asylum.

Schnitzler's hostility towards military life was expressed most forcefully in his criticism of the code of honour and the associated practice of duelling, which, though technically illegal according to the Civil Law, was still widely indulged by regular officers and by officers of the reserve. In effect the code of honour had jurisdiction over most male members of the upper bourgeoisie. For Schnitzler the obligation to duel, particularly for civilians, was the most conspicuous and obnoxious symptom of militarism in society, and his attitude is conveyed in a number of major works, from the early play *Freiwild* to the posthumously published *Der Sekundant*.[3] These feature a variety of duels, which afford considerable insight into the conventions of the practice.

In *Freiwild* the possibility of a duel arises through the behaviour of Lieutenant Karinski, whose position in the cavalry regiment is very much in question due to his gambling debts, and who is therefore desperate to find a means of demonstrating that he is a man of honour. The method he chooses is to goad the central character, Paul Rönning, into insulting him. Rönning is normally a courteous and mild-mannered man, who has recently been ill and has during his convalescence struck up a close, but wholly innocent friendship with the actress Anna Riedel. Meanwhile Karinski is also attracted towards Anna, and publicly, and in Rönning's presence, announces his intention of visiting her in order to invite her to dinner. When he returns to his colleagues with the news that Anna would not even admit him, Rönning shows his amusement at this expected rebuff. Karinski now attempts to provoke Rönning. First he demands to know the cause of Rönning's amusement. Rönning is evasive. Then Karinski suggests that perhaps Anna locked her door to him because she had company (with the implication that her guest was male). Rönning still refuses to rise to the bait, but responds that she was presumably protecting herself from Karinski's 'advances'. Karinski now seizes his chance, and takes offence that his invitation to dinner issued to some 'tart from the theatre' should be tantamount to 'making advances'. At this blatant insult to Anna's honour Rönning strikes him in the face.

The rules of the code of honour now decree that Karinski has the right to demand a duel with Rönning, who in turn has the obligation to 'give satisfaction'. Karinski has been doubly insulted, first by the insinuation that his invitation to Anna represented a (sexual) advance, secondly by the physical blow, so that a duel is the only means for him to restore his lost honour. The situation is patently absurd. It has been deliberately engineered by Karinski who wished Rönning to insult him. If anyone's honour has been injured it has been Anna's. Karinski's interest in Anna was indeed sexual, so that Rönning's so-called 'insult' was but a statement of the truth! The duel is simply a means for Karinski to deny an unpleasant truth. Furthermore, because Karinski is (technically) the insulted party, he has choice of weapons and the right, should he choose pistols, to shoot first!

The absurdity of the situation is stressed further by Rönning's response to the challenge, and the ensuing consequences. Rönning is a civilian, a man of private means, with no profession or responsibilities, and possessing an independent disposition and intelligent mind. His reaction is to reject Karinski's proposal out of hand. As far as he is concerned Karinski has behaved like an oaf, and has been treated as such. To have 'insulted' Karinski in this fashion does not constitute a willingness on his own part to stand up and have himself shot dead. The circumstances and probable consequences of the duel are out of all proportion to the incident that has provoked it, and defy all sense of logic: Karinski actually deserved the blow he received, but Rönning does not deserve to die for delivering it! Yet Rönning is told that he and his fellow civilians are as much bound by the code as the regular officers:

Wir leben innerhalb eines Kreises, in dem diese Anschauungen maßgebend sind, und es ist nicht möglich, sich darüber hinwegzusetzen. Du darfst es so wenig wie ein anderer.

(DW I, 299)

(We are part of a society in which these views are sacrosanct, and it is impossible to ignore them. You cannot do this, any more than anyone else.)

The code governs all social interaction. The moment that Rönning responded in anger to Karinski's provocation, he was placing himself within its demands. Indeed, as soon as Karinski asked him why he was smiling in satisfaction at Anna's rejection of Karinski, Rönning should have offered a duel! His refusal of Karinski's proposal is 'impossible', and he is thereby making himself a social outcast. Moreover Karinski himself will remain 'dishonoured', and will be forced to resign his commission. Thus Karinski's only solution will be to pursue Rönning and force him to give satisfaction. If this fails his only face-saving alternative is to kill Rönning, and then to commit suicide.

The possibility of a physical threat from Karinski places Rönning in a dilemma. Anna Riedel urges him to flee, but Rönning argues that to do so would be to acknowledge the validity of the code; yet if he remains he must fight Karinski in order to protect himself. Rönning's answer is to confront Karinski openly, insisting on his right to go away or remain as he pleases. Karinski's response is to shoot Rönning dead.[4] Karinski has salvaged his honour, but to retain it he must now commit suicide. Schnitzler was clearly aware that the defeat and death of Rönning, the representative of humanity and common sense, at the hands of unscrupulous prejudice, would shock the audience into an awareness of the inhuman brutality of the code.[5] That Karinski must likewise pay for his actions with his own life only heightens the absurdity of this outmoded, but still prevailing convention. Because of the provocative nature of the play's theme and implications, *Freiwild* was not felt suitable for performance at the Burgtheater, but instead had its première in Berlin. A brief run in the Carltheater in Vienna in 1898 aroused fierce hostility from military circles (Rönning was dismissed as a first-class coward),[6] and only in 1905, when the general feeling in Vienna had itself become more hostile to duelling, did the play enjoy success at the Deutsches Volkstheater.

Schnitzler's basic hostility to the inhumanity and brutality of the code of honour was accompanied by a contempt for the sheer pettiness of some of its aspects, which may seem almost comic to the objective outsider, but could still have absurdly violent consequences.[7] An incident from the novel *Der Weg ins Freie* will illustrate the point. It concerns a confrontation between young Oskar Ehrenberg and his father. The Ehrenbergs are Jews and wealthy members of the upper bourgeoisie, but the father clings to his Jewish identity and disapproves of his family's social aspirations. In particular he is hostile to the snobbish pretensions of Oskar, who is attempting to assimilate into high society. The conflict comes to a head when Oskar, in an attempt to impress some young aristocrats, raises his hat like a good Catholic, as he passes the Michaelerkirche. His father regards this as treachery to the Jewish faith and boxes Oskar's ears. According to the code Oskar is dishonoured by this public assault, but as a son is not permitted to challenge his father to a duel, and so cannot expiate the shame. Thus he will be excluded from 'high circles' and will lose his rank as a lieutenant in the reserve. The narrative voice during this incident is that of Therese Golowski, who takes an ironic line on the father–son confrontation, and hopes that the episode will show Oskar what a fool he has been to aspire to a social group with such ridiculous principles. The episode has a grotesque sequel. To salvage his honour Oskar attempts suicide, but succeeds only in blinding himself in the right eye. For Heinrich Bermann the whole sequence of events takes on the nature of a tragi-comedy: old Ehrenberg's original assault on his son was a brutality, Oskar's suicide attempt stupidity, its failure clumsiness. Perhaps the ultimate absurdity is that the botched attempt was itself sufficient for Oskar to retain his honour and rank!

One of the social and political issues of the day which had side-effects on the operation of the code of honour was the growing feeling of anti-Semitism in Vienna at the turn of the century. Though duels between non-Jews and Jews were quite common by the 1890s, the so-called *Waidhofener Beschluß* of 1896 put an end to them amongst students by declaring Jews to be 'satisfaktionsunfähig' (ineligible to give satisfaction).[8] This sinister development was followed by attempts amongst the military to deprive Jewish officers of the 'privilege' of being permitted to duel.

Schnitzler touches on the issue in his treatment of an incident in *Der Weg ins Freie*. It concerns young Leo Golowski, who has suffered from various anti-Semitic inconveniences during his year as a volunteer, particularly at the hands of Lieutenant Sefranek. At the conclusion of his year Leo accosts Sefranek, threatens him physically, and in the ensuing duel shoots him dead. Leo is arrested, and the legal authorities are to try him for murder. Attempts are made by Leo's lawyer to get the trial quashed, but initially these fail. It is assumed by Leo's Jewish friend Berthold Stauber that the legal authorities are coming under pressure from influential parties, who wish to prevent Jews from seizing an advantage over Christians through the medium of the duel. Had Leo fallen and Sefranek been arrested, the official attitude would have been entirely different. In other words Schnitzler uses the incident initially to highlight the Jewish question. But he then shelves the issue by refusing to take the matter to its ultimate conclusion – Leo is eventually pardoned by the emperor before he comes to trial. In effect this deprives the Jews of exploiting the incident as providing evidence of anti-Semitism in official places, but Therese Golowski takes the opportunity to renew her attack on the duelling system *per se*: as far as she is concerned the release of Leo simply demonstrates that the code of honour is itself corrupt, and amounts to a legal sanction to commit murder, condoned by a militaristic state.

In *Der Weg ins Freie* Schnitzler's criticism of the code of honour is implied implicitly in his depiction of the kind of situation which can arise because of the code's very existence. Criticism is also voiced through the opinions of a number of characters, who are representative of the numerous groups hostile at the time to elitist and militaristic practices. In Schnitzler's most celebrated treatment of the army mentality, the short story *Leutnant Gustl*, he succeeds very cleverly in indicating to the reader exactly what he thinks of the code through his exposure of the thoughts and feelings of a lieutenant, who is depicted, initially at least, as one of the code's most enthusiastic representatives. Here there is no narrative comment, and no direct criticism from other characters, only the voice of Gustl himself. Yet through the medium of Gustl's internal monologue Schnitzler both ridicules Gustl's failure to uphold the code to the last degree, and at the same time conveys his hostility to a code that places such unnatural and inhuman demands upon those who come within its orbit.

In the early stages of the story Gustl is presented as the guardian of the honour and dignity of the Imperial Army. As he sits at the concert his mind wanders to the previous evening and his encounter in the coffee-house with a lawyer (a socialist), who has dared to suggest in public that not all imperial officers have joined the army solely to defend the fatherland. Gustl has taken this as a personal insult, tantamount to a suggestion that he became a cadet simply because he had been ejected from school and had no other alternative. His response has been to challenge the lawyer to a duel. Gustl can claim that he is thereby defending his honour as an officer. The colonel of his regiment has confirmed that he has behaved 'correctly', and he is likely to enhance his reputation as a result. Yet his subsequent thoughts during the course of the evening reveal to the reader that he has indeed joined the army as a regular officer simply because he is fitted to do little else. Like Karinski's challenge to Paul Rönning in *Freiwild*, Gustl's duel is a response to a valid accusation. Its function is to enable him to deny ('legally' and 'officially') an unpleasant truth. In this instance it requires little courage on Gustl's part to invoke the code of honour. As the injured party he has choice of weapons, namely sabres, and as a regular officer in practice he has the upper hand. Hence his confidence, and the reader is left to infer the iniquity of a system which permits ignorance and brute force to prevail over intelligence and insight.

In this situation Gustl behaves enthusiastically and confidently within the terms of the code simply because he has the physical advantage. During his encounter with the baker in the foyer of the theatre, however, this is not the case. The baker compromises Gustl's position in three ways. First he refuses to give way in the queue and responds in kind to Gustl's verbal challenge; secondly he prevents Gustl from drawing his sword through sheer physical strength; thirdly he threatens to break his sword into pieces, but then promises not to ruin Gustl's career by so doing. Gustl's problem is that he has been humiliated by a *Kleinbürger*, a civilian beneath his social station, but it takes him some time before he appreciates the awful consequences. Gustl knows that according to the code he should have drawn his sword and carved the baker to pieces, and recognizes that if his failure to do this had been observed by others he would have had to commit suicide on the spot. But even after the baker's departure he realizes the incident is not closed, and that his honour is still compromised. He cannot challenge the baker to a duel, because the baker is not high enough up the social scale; he cannot pursue the baker and kill him, for he should have done that at the time of the incident;[9] he cannot beg the baker to keep silent, for this will only compound his dishonour; if he goes and asks his colonel's advice he will undoubtedly have to resign. But it is only when he remembers that next day he is due to fight his duel with the lawyer, that he recognizes the full implications: the dishonour he has allowed himself to suffer has rendered him 'satisfaktionsunfähig'; whether or not others are aware of this, his own knowledge of his condition requires him to commit suicide.

During the course of Gustl's wanderings through the night, Schnitzler shows us that when this ultimate sacrifice is required of him, his lieutenant's devotion to the code is but a hollow sham. Most obviously this is revealed through Gustl's joyous reaction to the baker's fortuitous death. Previously he had stated quite categorically that even if the baker did die that night, it was his own awareness of his dishonour that was the decisive factor. Now he feels that the removal of the baker conveniently relieves him of his obligation. Indeed, had he not learnt of the baker's death, he would have shot himself 'in vain'! In the interests of escaping with his life he has thus abandoned altogether his own principles. When the story was first published in the *Neue Freie Presse* in 1900, it was fiercely attacked in military circles, and Schnitzler, as an officer in the reserve, was actually summoned before a military tribunal.[10] It was felt that in presenting a situation in which a lieutenant in effect takes the coward's way out, Schnitzler had insulted the honour of his station and called into question the reputation for courage, discipline and loyalty of the average officer of the Imperial Army. It is true that basically Gustl is exposed as a coward. But in their outrage over the final outcome it is possible that the authorities overlooked a potentially even more explosive implication of the narrative, namely that the reader is encouraged to be pleased at Gustl's lucky escape. It is the code itself that is presented as the greater evil, more evil certainly than its imperfect, but very human representative.

As Gustl walks through the city streets preparing himself for the final act, the uncontrolled inner ramblings of his mind betray, on a human level, a basic lack of sympathy with the code, the implications of which he himself does not grasp, but which the reader is easily able to perceive. Gustl senses, for example, how absurd it is that such a petty incident should require the sacrifice of a young life:

> es ist ja zu dumm, zu dumm! – Deswegen soll ein Kerl wie ich, so ein junger, fescher Mensch . . . Ja, nachher möchten's gewiß alle sagen: das hätt' er doch nicht tun müssen, wegen so einer Dummheit; es ist doch schad'!
>
> (ES I, 347)
>
> (it's too stupid, too stupid! – that all because of that, a chap like me, so young and attractive, should have to . . . Yes, afterwards I'm sure they'll all want to say: he shouldn't have had to do that for such a silly mistake; it's a real shame!)

Several times a more sentimental Gustl becomes visible when he realizes the effect that his death will have on others: his mistress Steffi will weep; his sister Klara, who has had little luck in life, will be unhappy at now losing her only brother; Anna, the girl from home who loved him dearly, will be distressed at his early death; as for the effect on his mother, that does not bear thinking about. Occasionally a softer, more human side to Gustl is seen beneath the brash and aggressive exterior: he longs to confide in another human being, he admits he is afraid of the step into the unknown, that he is on the brink of tears as he contemplates writing to his sister. The letter itself is that of a gentle, caring and penitent man:

> Du mußt mir verzeihen, liebe Schwester, und bitte, tröste auch die lieben Eltern. Ich weiß, daß ich euch allen manche Sorge gemacht habe und manchen Schmerz bereitet; aber glaube mir, ich habe euch alle immer sehr lieb gehabt, und ich hoffe, du wirst noch einmal glücklich werden, meine liebe Klara, und deinen unglücklichen Bruder nicht ganz vergessen.
>
> (ES I, 363)
>
> (You must forgive me, dear sister, and please, comfort our dear parents too. I know that I have caused you all a deal of worry, and at times have hurt you too; but believe me, I have always loved you all dearly, and I hope you will be happy once again, my dear Klara, and not forget your unhappy brother altogether.)

Apart from these suggestions of a man emotionally out of tune with what is demanded of him, Schnitzler also gives several indications that, deep down, Gustl does not really believe in the institution of the code itself and what it stands for. He even begins to sense this on a conscious level as he searches desperately for an alternative to suicide: 'Gustl, can it be that you don't really believe in it any more?' But generally his attitude is conveyed unconsciously through the disparaging references to the code that he involuntarily allows to invade his thoughts. As he contemplates emigration to America as a means of escape, he recalls the case of a dishonoured count who recently made his fortune there, and can now jeer at the 'whole caboodle'. Gustl is aware of the injustice of a situation that allows the baker to live on with impunity, whilst he must die a wretched death, and he has to force himself to obey a code that he actually describes as a 'load of old rubbish'. But Gustl is at best only vaguely conscious of his rejection of the code, and it is only a temporary condition. Having escaped from his terrifying obligation, he can now reassume his outward display of self-confidence and aggression, and he contemplates with relish the prospect of the appointed duel, and of making mincemeat of his opponent.

Schnitzler's cynical presentation of Lieutenant Gustl's superficial and selective observation of the code of honour is balanced by the deeply ingrained sense of personal honour displayed by Lieutenant Willi Kasda of *Spiel im Morgengrauen*. Kasda is no paragon of virtue, particularly in his relationships with the opposite sex, but at heart he is a decent and generous man, and when his former friend, the now disgraced Lieutenant Bogner, comes to him begging for financial assistance, Kasda resolves to help him. Unfortunately the means he chooses to raise money for Bogner is to gamble, initially with caution and within his own financial limits, but when the fever grips him uncontrollably at the gambling table Kasda finds himself indebted to the sum of eleven thousand florins. Kasda recognizes that his failure to settle his debt would mean dishonourable resignation from the army (as in the case of Bogner himself), and because he cannot contemplate this, the thought of suicide crosses his mind. But Kasda's sense of honour does not yet require him to take his life, and he attempts to rescue the situation by begging for money, first from his uncle, and then from his uncle's wife (and his own former mistress), Leopoldine.[11] Only after his humiliating experience with the latter, which culminates in his deeply shameful realization that he has been prepared to prostitute himself in order to obtain money and the restoration of his honour, does Kasda take the final step. Kasda cannot live with the knowledge that he has attempted to purchase his honour as an officer with the price of his honour as a man. His tragic suicide, which results from a profound sense of personal dignity, is a far more admirable sacrifice than the meaningless loss of life caused by the mechanics of an inhuman code.

Despite the growing opposition within certain Viennese circles to a code whose associated practices were recognized as outmoded and essentially barbaric, it still exercised a powerful influence on the attitudes and behaviour of officers, and of civilians too. In *Der Sekundant* Schnitzler's narrator looks back with nostalgia, though also with considerable irony, from a position in the late 1920s to the duels of the pre-war era. He acknowledges that the duel was often fought over a triviality, such as honour, a woman's virtue, a sister's reputation, but that the institution invested social life with a certain dignity and style. Whether or not one accepts the word 'triviality' as an appropriate label for the issues to which he refers, his attitude highlights the apparent disparity between the kind of incident that tended to provoke duels, and the serious consequences to which it might lead. Duels were a matter of life and death. Petty insults, public humiliation, even the discovery of a wife's adultery, might not always seem to be.

The comments by the narrator of *Der Sekundant* also suggest that the majority of duels involving civilians were fought over sexual indiscretions. This was particularly true of the bourgeoisie, who regarded duels as an aristocratic (rather than strictly military) convention.[12] To some extent adulterous relationships were quietly tolerated, so long as they were pursued with discretion, but once discovered, or flaunted in public, the code of practice was as rigid and automatic as in military circles. In *Der Sekundant* the cause of the duel is an affair between Loiberger and the wife of a cavalry officer stationed some distance from his home. The officer is informed of the affair in an anonymous letter, his challenge to Loiberger swiftly follows, and is immediately accepted. Loiberger and his second respond like marionettes, going silently through the 'usual formalities' that precede and follow the duel itself. A similar impression is provided by the duel in *Liebelei*, which becomes inevitable once the husband discovers Fritz's letters to his wife. His statement to Fritz that his wife has left her veil at Fritz's apartment is but a pretext to provoke the duel, and Fritz knows exactly what is 'expected of him'. Schnitzler's attitude to this now pointless duel (the relationship between Fritz and the married lady is now effectively over) is suggested by the sombre effect that it has on the atmosphere of the play, and by the shadow which it casts over the new relationship between Fritz and Christine.

The sheer complexity of the code and its implications for the lives and reputations of respectable bourgeois citizens may be appreciated from an episode in *Das Weite Land*, the drama whose events culminate in the fatal duel between the industrialist Friedrich Hofreiter and the naval officer Otto von Aigner. But even before this incident and the bizarre circumstances that led to it, the subject of duels, imaginary and fictitious, potential but unrealized, has arisen to disturb the frivolity of bourgeois life. The root cause is the affair that is now over between Hofreiter and the wife of his banker Herr Natter. The affair was not exactly common knowledge, but both Genia Hofreiter and Natter himself knew about it, and Genia certainly fears that Natter, for all his bonhomie and charm, might be the man to seek honourable retribution. She reckons without the seemingly irrational love that Natter has for his errant wife. Natter would not risk compromising her in public by challenging Hofreiter, for he would be forced to renounce her. His 'revenge' takes another form. Believing, like others, that Genia Hofreiter has had a close relationship with the pianist Alexei Korsakow (who has recently committed suicide), Natter spreads a rumour that Korsakow's suicide was the result of an American duel with Hofreiter. An American duel was popular amongst civilians unskilled with the pistol or sabre, for it could be 'fought out' in the form of a game (for example, billiards), the loser being honour bound to commit suicide. The implication of Natter's rumour is that Hofreiter challenged Korsakow, who duly lost the game. Natter knows that Hofreiter cannot respond with a challenge in kind, for he is disqualified through his affair with Natter's wife (Hofreiter is the guilty, Natter the 'insulted' party); moreover Hofreiter cannot disclose the proof to the contrary (Korsakow's suicide note, revealing that Genia rejected him), for this would compromise Genia and make Hofreiter look ridiculous. Hofreiter is thus left with a much damaged social reputation. The whole sequence is a complex mass of calculated gestures, all carefully gauged by the terms of the code, which is here being exploited to serve one man's pathetic revenge.[13]

Schnitzler's hostility to the more bizarre, as well as the brutal, aspects of the code of honour was clearly one that he shared with many of his more enlightened contemporaries. Often he expressed his attitude through the comments of characters representing the various protesting groups, such as Therese Golowski or Heinrich Bermann in *Der Weg ins Freie*. In this novel too, an Englishman Ralph Skelton voices his criticism of the duel within the context of a general assessment of circumstances in Austria. For Skelton it is characteristic of a prevailing lack of sincerity in Austrian society that duels are fought between people who feel no hatred for each other, just as love affairs are pursued without expectations of mutual fidelity. In other words the duel is yet another ingredient in the façade of Austrian social life.

Schnitzler's criticisms of the duel and of the code of honour are voiced in *Der Weg ins Freie* by characters who are technically 'outsiders', a Jewess, a Jewish writer, a foreigner. Apart from the momentary, half-conscious utterances of Lieutenant Gustl, Schnitzler's works contain no explicit condemnation of the code from the inner ranks. In view of the reception which greeted *Freiwild* and *Leutnant Gustl*, it is not surprising that Schnitzler should have avoided such risky material, and it is apparent that he lacked the advantage of hindsight and the freedom enjoyed by later writers, such as Joseph Roth. In Roth's *Radetzkymarsch*, for example, which contains a detailed and fiercely critical analysis of army life and protocol, a duel takes place in grotesquely absurd circumstances. The young hero Carl Joseph is rumoured to be having an affair with the wife of the regimental doctor, Demant. This Carl Joseph denies, and the rumour is patently untrue. But Carl Joseph has been seen escorting Frau Demant home from the theatre in suspicious circumstances, which prompts Count Tattenbach, who is drunk at the time, to publicly warn Demant about his wife's conduct. As a result Demant is honour bound to challenge not Carl Joseph, but Tattenbach, and in the ensuing duel is killed. Carl Joseph, who comes out of the affair with no credit or honour at all, has to transfer to another regiment. Before the duel takes place, Roth includes a scene between Carl Joseph and Demant, in which the latter questions the values of the code in no uncertain terms, and urges Carl Joseph to leave the Imperial Army altogether:

'Diese Dummheit! Diese Ehre, die in der blöden Troddel da am Säbel hängt. Man kann eine Frau nicht nach Haus' begleiten! Siehst du, wie dumm das ist? Blödsinn!' schrie er plötzlich, 'infamer Blödsinn!'[14]

('This stupidity! This honour, which is attached to that ridiculous tassel on the sabre. One cannot even escort a woman home! Don't you see how stupid that is? What nonsense', he suddenly cried, 'what infamous nonsense!')

Later Carl Joseph is in fact forced to resign from the army in particularly shameful and dishonourable circumstances, when he fails to respond with appropriate belligerence to a fellow officer who casts aspersions on his patriotism and loyalty.

Roth's devastating account of an army whose officers are only half-heartedly going through the motions of a code of practice in which they no longer believe, has no direct parallel in Schnitzler's works. Likewise Roth's exposure of the weaknesses of the unwieldy, ungovernable empire, his portrayal of the monotony of garrison life on the eastern frontier that led to gambling and drinking amongst the officers, constitutes a much more detailed treatment of army life, through which the wider political implications are clearly visible. The moral degradation in the army reflects that in the government of the empire as a whole. Nevertheless Schnitzler's exposure of the absurdity and futility of the code at all levels at which it operates, provides a striking anticipation of some aspects of Roth's analysis. Schnitzler's harsh criticism of the principles governing the behaviour of army officers contrasts markedly with the romanticized portrayal of cavalry life of some of the popular literature of the time, for example Baron Torresani's novel *Aus der schönen wilden Leutnantszeit* (1889) and its sequel *Schwarzgelbe Reitergeschichten*, which tended to idealize the army and depicted its officers as dashing, handsome and brave. Yet even these works were tinged with nostalgia for a more glorious past, a tacit admission of decline.[15] Schnitzler was not alone in his criticism, which reflected a widespread contempt in more progressive circles for the army and its outmoded ideals and practices. This contempt achieved its most effective expression in the army scenes of Karl Kraus's *Die letzten Tage der Menschheit*, in which Kraus picks out the very negative characteristics of the military that Schnitzler had condemned before him. The young officers of the Ringstraße at the beginning of the play have no awareness of the political implications of Sarajevo, and are more concerned with the social whirl of dinner engagements, drinking parties and sexual conquests. As the war proceeds and harsh reality catches up with the illusion, Kraus exposes the brutality and incompetence of officers, which had been perceived by some in the pre-war era, but which manifested itself most destructively during the death throes of the empire.

THE ARISTOCRACY

Because the social classes represented in Schnitzler's works are predominantly from the world that he himself knew best, those groups at the extreme ends of the social scale, namely the higher aristocracy and the proletariat, rarely feature. The aristocratic figures who occasionally make an appearance tend to be isolated individuals, of psychological rather than of social interest (an example is the central character of the story *Das Schicksal des Freiherrn von Leisenbohg*, 1903), or are members of the lower aristocracy, or *Briefadel*, already tending towards a position on the fringes of the bourgeoisie. For example, the father of the von Wergenthin brothers in *Der Weg ins Freie* was a baron who married the daughter of a civil servant. But he had no country estate, and the family divided its time between rented apartments in the inner city and a nomadic existence in hotels in the south, using up a considerable portion of its modest inheritance. Now the brothers are having to give up their apartment opposite the Stadtpark, and whilst Felicien can still command a privileged position in the foreign service, Georg is having to seek employment as an orchestral conductor.

Occasionally Schnitzler makes brief allusions to the moral degeneracy of the aristocracy. In *Spiel im Morgengrauen* there is a reference to a young lady from an aristocratic family, who, after two years of marriage, is found working in a high-class brothel, a so-called salon where the sexual services of respectable ladies are available at highly inflated prices. The decadence of the aristocracy is also suggested in *Traumnovelle* through the speculation that the sexual orgies of the secret society are held by aristocratic gentlemen, possibly even archdukes of the imperial family. This notion is supported by the reference to a young lady who was betrothed to an Italian prince, but who took poison before her wedding (either because her participation had been discovered, or as 'punishment' for betraying the society). Likewise Fridolin is convinced that the lady who helps him escape from the house is a Baroness D. who has paid with her life in a similar fashion. The decline of the aristocracy, both moral, social and financial, is represented in the figure of the mother in the novel *Therese*. Therese's mother comes from the minor nobility, but after being widowed, she sinks into moral degradation, taking lovers and writing trivial novels. She ends her life in a miserable little room rented in one of the less desirable outer suburbs (in a house on the Hernalser Hauptstraße), leaving Therese a few insignificant personal possessions and a number of debts. One of Therese's positions as governess is actually with an aristocratic family, that of a high-ranking civil servant, whose wife is a baroness. But their life-style is scarcely elegant. Mother and child are sent on holiday to a poor-quality guest-house in Styria, a shabbily dressed Hungarian noble takes lunch with them, and they have to be generally sparing with their meals. Back in Vienna the house seems more like a prison to Therese, and she eventually leaves when she feels insulted by the meanness of the family's Christmas present to her. One of Schnitzler's more curious creations is the count in *Reigen*, who leads a seemingly empty and monotonous life with his garrison on the Hungarian plain, with occasional visits to Vienna and his mistress, Fräulein Birken. Life for him is a series of automatic conventions that fill the void, and he adheres to a rigid timetable that governs his sex life as well as his eating habits. But as the actress perceives, he is essentially an impostor, who conceals his vital urges behind a façade of cynical philosophizing, and she has little difficulty in seducing him on the spot, forcing him to admit that his stated 'Programm' for the day was but a pose.

Schnitzler's only extended treatment of aristocratic family life and attitudes is to be found in the comedy *Komtesse Mizzi oder der Familientag* (The Family Reunion, 1907), though here too he presents an eccentric, rather than a 'normal' family. The setting is an eighteenth-century villa on the outskirts of the city, formerly a hunting lodge of the Empress Maria Theresa, and now the home of Count Arpad Pazmandy. The count has retired from the army, and now lives an isolated life with his daughter Mizzi, protected from the inconveniences and prying eyes of the modern expanding city, with its detested politicians and journalists. Their life together is a parody of the parasitic aristocratic existence, as they go about their amateur leisure pursuits of riding and painting. Since the count's wife died some twenty years ago his main preoccupation has been his mistress Lolo, a former ballet dancer, whom he used to visit regularly at her flat in the Mayerhofgasse. But Lolo, who is now thirty-eight, is about to make a respectable bourgeois marriage, and the count is left to rue his lonely and futile existence, enlivened only by the occasional visit from his friend Prince Ravenstein, and game of dominoes with his daughter. But his relationship with Mizzi is not a close one. He knows little about her, and is certainly unaware that some years ago she had a love affair with Ravenstein, by whom she had a child (he vaguely remembers that at a time when she inexplicably went a little 'hysterical', she temporarily disappeared from home). Of limited intelligence, the count is comically oblivious of the realities of life which are proceeding almost under his very nose, and finds it difficult to cope with unexpected revelations. He is, for example, so flabbergasted when Ravenstein discloses the existence of the child, his son Philipp, that it is perhaps fortunate that he never learns that Mizzi is the mother (or that she now has a new lover, the professor who comes to give her painting lessons!). Mizzi's secret life casts an ironic light upon her father's ridiculous attempts to shield her from 'unpleasantries', such as the news that Ravenstein has an illegitimate child, or a social encounter with Lolo.

During the course of the play interest shifts to the more serious theme of the relationship between Mizzi and Prince Ravenstein. At the time of Mizzi's pregnancy his wife was still alive, but Mizzi was prepared to fly in the face of convention by living with Ravenstein as his mistress. She was thwarted by his cowardice, the child was born in secret and taken away from her eight days afterwards. Mizzi remains bitter about her experience, which has killed her love for the prince (she has so far rejected his proposals of marriage following the death of his wife), and stifled any maternal feelings she might have for her son. Prince Ravenstein himself is presented as a shallow character, an aristocratic ex-diplomat, complete with French accent, who has failed in his attempt to make his mark as a politician, and now sits as a silent and ineffectual member of the Herrenhaus. Mizzi's rejection of the prince is paralleled in the play by Lolo's rejection of a desperate proposal of marriage from the count. By marrying a small businessman (the estimable Wasner, who runs a fleet of hackney-carriages), Lolo is in effect turning her back on the aristocracy and asserting the values of bourgeois solidity and stability. Mizzi, who is intelligent and independent-minded, a very 'modern' woman and the opposite pole to her father in fact, establishes an immediate bond of sympathy with Lolo. Her relationship with the professor also provides an indication that her own inclinations, both intellectual and temperamental, lie in the direction of the bourgeoisie. Schnitzler's treatment of the aristocracy is essentially satirical, radically different in tone from Hofmannsthal's idealization of Austrian aristocratic values in *Der Schwierige*. Indeed Schnitzler became estranged from Hofmannsthal in later life partly because of the latter's adoption of an aristocratic life-style.[16] It is significant that in a play that satirizes the nobility, it is the bourgeoisie, specifically the *Kleinbürgertum*, represented in the figure of Wasner, and the professional classes, represented by the professor, that should appear in a more favourable light. We therefore have a feeling of regret that ultimately Mizzi remains a prisoner of her aristocratic background. The professor is married, her relationship with him doomed by convention, and she is taken away to accompany her father and the prince on a holiday to Ostend. The aristocrats are in symbolic retreat, leaving the city in the hands of the bourgeoisie.

THE LOWER CLASSES

Schnitzler's knowledge of the life of the working classes inhabiting the new industrial areas of the outer suburbs was strictly limited, and it rarely intrudes into his works. His more humble characters are generally drawn from the lower middle classes, the *Kleinbürgertum* of the inner suburbs such as the Josefstadt and Mariahilf. But even within this relatively prosperous class Schnitzler exposes the drabness of life and deprivations suffered, particularly in comparison with the glamour of the fashionable districts.

In *Liebelei* we are given an idyllic picture of a room in the Vorstadt with views over the roofs to the Kahlenberg. Christine's diligence, her cultural awareness – even her modest little library – are contrasted favourably with the indolence and ignorance of the young gentleman and officer of the reserve. But Christine's father is well aware of the narrowness of their existence, and is saddened that his daughter must spend her days at home sewing and copying music. The life led by the 'süße Mädel' of the Vorstadt is also described in *Reigen* when she tells of her efforts to help her mother run a large family, its income apparently supplemented with the wages of her elder sister, who works in a flower shop, and those of her brother, who is a barber. The material want that a family might suffer when deprived of the income of the bread-winner is conveyed in *Freiwild*, for Anna Riedel has sought work as an actress because her family is now poverty-stricken following the death of her father. Mingling with the *Kleinbürgertum* of the Vorstadt are the artisans, such as the decorator of the early story *Reichtum* (Wealth, 1889). His working hours are spent painting walls and ceilings, his evenings drinking in the local beer-house; his wife is sickly and takes in sewing; his son wears patched clothes and is continually hungry; their meals are sparse, their rooms in a wretched state of deterioration. On the fringes of bourgeois society are the artists, some of whom could themselves live in depressing circumstances. In *Der Weg ins Freie* the novelist Nürnberger has quarters in a run-down area in the Innenstadt, in a narrow gloomy street leading down to the Donaukanal. His rooms look out on to the grey walls of the old houses opposite, with small dusty windows; a gutter between two houses is full of rubbish, broken bottles, scraps of waste paper and rotting plants.

In many of his works Schnitzler gives us occasional glimpses of a darker, more miserable existence, beyond the prosperous, comfortable world of the upper bourgeoisie. In *Der Weg ins Freie* the young socialist Therese Golowski embarks on a pilgrimage to investigate the conditions of the poorest and most wretched inhabitants of the city. Dressed as a poor woman she intends to visit soup kitchens, workhouses and the refuges for the homeless, the so-called *Wärmestuben* which provide a little warmth and comfort in the most obscure corners of the 'golden heart' of Vienna. In the drama *Fink und Fliederbusch* (1916) the central character, now a journalist, refers to his humble origins in the Schiffamtsgasse, where the houses are bleak and depressing, the stairways smell of cabbages and potatoes, the women stand around gossiping in overalls covered in cooking fat. In *Traumnovelle* Fridolin crosses the Rathauspark and sees a tramp sleeping rough on a bench, but hesitates to offer him the price of a bed for the night, for there are thousands of such 'poor devils' in the city, and it would be impossible to care for them all. A glimpse then, of an insuperable social problem. In *Spiel im Morgengrauen* Lieutenant Willi Kasda passes through a wretched village between Baden and Vienna, with small, squalid houses. An old man in shirt sleeves is seen watering his garden, a woman in a tattered dress is carrying a can of milk.

Arriving in Vienna Kasda sees the city's early risers, a wild-looking man with sleeves rolled up washing the streets, an old woman cleaning the windows of a café. Lieutenant Gustl also sees street cleaners operating in the early hours of the morning, and a little later the shop-girls, already on their way to start their long working day that will last right through into the evening. These are the workers who service the city as an economic unit. There are others who cater for the pleasures of the wealthy, the prostitutes who operate from dingy rooms with dirty shutters, dilapidated furniture and evil-smelling oil lamps (*Reigen*), or who risk death from sexually transmitted diseases (*Traumnovelle*). There are servant girls who spend long days performing menial tasks, like the *Stubenmädchen* of *Reigen*, who is at the beck and call of the young master of the house, drawing curtains, fetching him drinks, quite apart from the sexual function that she later fulfils for him. Rarely does Schnitzler, either through his narrator figures or dramatic characters, make explicit comments on the social injustices that he sees around him, but the glimpses of them that he affords us in his works are sufficient to remind us of their existence, and of the stark contrast which they make with the comfortable and elegant existence enjoyed by those at the upper levels of society.

The work which provides the most detailed treatment of the 'other side' of Vienna is *Therese*. Technically at least, Therese is a member of the bourgeoisie, but the life she leads as governess, often no better than that of a servant girl, puts her beyond the periphery of a respectable and protected bourgeois existence. She goes hungry, gets worn out by her work, sleeps in a narrow bed by a damp wall, gets called out in the night by crying children, woken early in the morning by gossiping servants. Between jobs she stays in a house in Wieden that smells of oil and cooking fat, and where she sleeps with the landlady and her children in the same wretched room. From three o'clock in the morning the courtyard is filled with the noise of carts, horses and rough voices. When Therese is pregnant she becomes careless with her dress and gradually cuts herself off from her earlier respectable existence. In her search for a room where she will have the child there are references to shrieking children and wife-beating drunkards. But it is through Schnitzler's treatment of the actual birth of her son Franz, and of his subsequent development, that he takes us further into the darker life of the city.

When Franz is born and Therese lies alone in the darkness with her child, she feels no love for him, and her first instinct is to rid herself of the burden by smothering him. The scene is reminiscent of that described in the early short story *Der Sohn*, in which a mother likewise attempts to murder her child, whose subsequent violent behaviour towards her is attributed to the traumatic effects of this immediate post-birth experience.[17] In *Therese* too the possibility is certainly raised that Franz's unconscious recollection of his mother's intended violence is alone responsible for his eventual physical attack upon her. But in this longer novel, Schnitzler adds other determining factors as he builds up a sociological case study of Franz as a juvenile delinquent.[18]

From the very beginning Therese faces considerable difficulties in her task of raising her child. Because of her situation (that of an unmarried governess) she has to have him brought up by foster-parents who are beneath her in social status and level of education. They are peasant farmers, farming their own small-holding, but leading a much less sophisticated life than the bourgeois families of the city for which Therese works, and from which she herself stems. The peasant woman is occasionally aggressive and hostile, and neglects the child, especially when Therese gets behind with her payments. The house is cold and damp, and stinks of tobacco, and the peasant farmer has alcoholic tendencies. But Franz grows attached to the family, becomes a real country lad, and Therese feels increasingly alienated on her visits. In particular his relationship with the daughter Agnes is seen to be far closer than that to his mother, and as the two children grow older takes on a more sensual nature, an anticipation perhaps of Agnes's later career as a prostitute in the city.

Therese's problems become more acute, however, when she removes Franz from the country, and attempts to find suitable accommodation for him with families in Vienna itself. Some are at artisan level, and he picks up bad language, such as Therese has never heard before. His behaviour becomes wild and unruly, and he takes up with a rabble of youngsters, spending evenings wandering the streets looking for trouble. When questioned by his mother he is insolent, and becomes physically violent. If the seeds were sown in the country, the delinquent is moulded in the city, and he joins a gang of youths and girls who go thieving. Now part of the shifting, criminal element of the capital, he is reduced to a thin and bent figure, down at heel, homeless and out of work, until, inevitably, he spends six months in prison. It is after his release that his fatal attack on his mother takes place, after she has refused one of his frequent demands for money. In the light of the general tenor of his earlier works, his interest in depth psychology, and then in the social milieu of the middle classes, Schnitzler's analysis of the socially determinant factors in Franz's development betokens an unexpected interest on his part in the uglier face of society and the darker forces of the city. It is indeed with this later novel of the 1920s that he offers his most striking contrast with his former colleagues of the Jung Wien group. For it is a feature of the Austrian literature of the turn of the century, as also of the decades immediately thereafter, that the 'social question' plays a relatively insignificant role, in comparison, for example, with the works of the German Naturalists and the socialist writers of the Weimar Republic. Despite the concentration in Vienna of all the evils and deprivations associated with a rapidly developing industrialized city, there is little actual literary record of them. The dramatist Anton Wildgans treats such material in his play *Armut* (Poverty, 1914), and in the post-war period Alfons Petzold records in his novel *Das rauhe Leben* (The Harsh Life, 1920) the wretched conditions and social injustices endured in the outer suburbs, which were rife with the 'Viennese disease' of tuberculosis, and alcoholism.[19] But these are isolated examples, which serve only to underline the fact that of the major and enduring writers of his time, Schnitzler was one of the few to tackle in his literary works contemporary social problems.

THE THEATRE

The world of the Viennese theatre formed the social group that was perhaps best known to Schnitzler, and it is hardly surprising that it features in many of his works, ranging from the genteel, elegant world of Burgtheater circles to the cruder atmosphere of the cheap variety theatres of the suburbs and the provinces. The picture that he presents is not always a flattering or positive one, and it is apparent that he viewed theatrical circles with the same critical eye as that with which he contemplated the world of the bourgeoisie.

From the early play *Das Märchen*, we have seen that for lower-middle-class girls of the Vorstadt the theatre offers an avenue of escape into a classless world, affording wealth and a degree of social respectability for the most successful, and the possibility of liaisons with upper-class admirers. The actors of the Burgtheater, for example, had considerable social status, and enjoyed a life-style modelled on the aristocratic salons, to which many of them had access.[20] Such is the case with the actress of *Reigen*, who is 'honoured' by the visit of the count to her luxurious bedroom. She represents a classic example of the successful, independent actress, sexually liberated, self-confident, proud of her reputation, and was allegedly modelled on the star performer of the Burgtheater Adele Sandrock, with whom Schnitzler himself enjoyed a brief liaison.[21] Another of a similar status is Kläre Hell, an opera singer in *Das Schicksal des Freiherrn von Leisenbohg*. Her father was an official in the postal service, and her first love was a young student who had a room in the Alsergrund suburb. But she graduated via a series of lovers, including a singer, a wealthy merchant, a conductor, a count, to become the mistress of Prince Richard Bedenbruck, the most elegant gentleman of the empire. Now she mixes with aristocratic ladies and the wives of wealthy Jewish financiers, and behaves like an archduchess herself to her countless admirers.

Schnitzler's treatment of Kläre is lightly satirical, and he was well aware that the life of the theatre was often shallow and superficial. Irene Herms, for example, the actress figure of *Der Einsame Weg*, has broken off her career to settle down in the country with her sister's family, bitterly conscious that her pursuit of international fame and success has deprived her of the domestic happiness and security of a bourgeois family home. For the less successful, life could be even more unsatisfactory. A particularly pathetic case is described in the novel *Der Weg ins Freie*, in which the sister of the novelist Nürnberger embarks at the age of sixteen on a career in the theatre. She spends ten restless years employed in a succession of companies, in minor roles in poor quality plays. She spends her time dreaming of fame and fortune, but eventually returns home ill and broken, recognizing that her life has constituted no more than a succession of petty, futile adventures in hired rooms and guest-houses in foreign towns. As she approaches her early death she regrets having missed out on the more concrete pleasures of 'real life'.

Schnitzler's most detailed critical exposure of theatrical life is to be found in *Freiwild*, which demonstrates the vulnerability of actors and actresses in a small-town company. Their work is demanding (with frequent changes of repertoire), and wages are low – it is assumed, for example, that actresses in a garrison town will have their living costs supplemented by admiring officers. Indeed the success of the company may depend upon the ability of its actresses to attract custom in this very fashion. Anna Riedel is actually dismissed because she refuses to have affairs with local officers, and is then offered reappointment on half wages to encourage her to be more co-operative.

Schnitzler's sympathy for the small-time actor in the lower ranks of the profession is also conveyed in the story *Der Ehrentag* (The Day of Triumph, 1897). This is essentially a psychological study, but it is set within the context of the theatre world, which is presented as cruel and heartless in its treatment of a sensitive individual. The central character Roland is a minor actor, condemned to play insignificant roles, usually little better than walk-on parts. Unlike his colleagues of a similar status, who are prepared to accept their modest position in the theatre, Roland values his own talents more highly. His personal pride leaves him angry and dissatisfied with his lot as a portrayer of nameless pages, servants and conspirators. Unfortunately Roland's behaviour serves only to advertise his sensitivity, and he becomes the butt of jokes, smirks and cruel remarks on the part of amused colleagues. As a result he develops a paranoid condition, causing him to imagine mockery where it is not intended, and he withdraws into loneliness and the comfort of private drinking. Another tragic victim of the theatre world is the heroine of the story *Das neue Lied* (The New Song 1905), which is set in a popular variety theatre in the suburbs, complete with piano, Hungarian folksingers, clowns and slapstick comedians. But the company depends for its financial survival on the talent of a girl singer Marie, who has gone blind. The song-writer Rebay has written her a poignant song about a blackbird, which refers to the beauty of the spring and to her lost love, neither of which Marie will ever see again. The implication here is that her misfortune is being exploited for profit.

Reminiscent of the cheap suburban theatre of *Das neue Lied* is the second-rate music hall described in *Therese* where the heroine meets again her former lover, the artist Kasimir Tobias. An unattractive middle-aged woman, ridiculously made up and dressed in a short skirt, sings a saucy song about a lieutenant; a clown performs conjuring tricks available in most toy-shops; an old man appears with two performing poodles and so on. All to the accompaniment of a small 'orchestra' consisting of piano, violin, cello and clarinet. In this episode Schnitzler uses the theatre world very much as the social realist, to introduce local colour, and to set the character within his social ambience. But in *Der Ehrentag* and *Das neue Lied* the theatre forms more than just a background to help characterize a personality and his situation. Both these stories end tragically – Roland and Marie commit suicide – and in them the atmosphere and practices of the theatre world are inextricably linked with personal misfortune.

CREATIVE ARTISTS

Schnitzler's picture of the theatre world that he knew so well is predominantly a negative one, ranging from his depiction of arrogant prima donnas of Burgtheater circles, to the more humble and even sordid conditions of the suburban and provincial theatres. His depiction of the world of the arts presents a similarly disenchanting view. Few of the artists and writers who appear in his works have achieved success, and those that have are rarely sympathetically drawn. In sum they form an unattractive group, and represent an unflattering reflection of the literary circles within which he moved from the days of Jung Wien onwards. To some extent this is a surprising feature of his works, and one might have expected to find a more enthusiastic depiction of the significant cultural developments of his age. But Schnitzler clearly possessed an ironical temperament which occasionally bordered on cynicism, and he was as much alive to the deficiencies of his fellow artists, particularly the less talented amongst them, as he was to the bourgeoisie.

An obvious example is the poet of *Reigen*, in whom Schnitzler offers an amusing, satirical caricature of the literary poseur of the 1890s. As a personality he is vain and self-conscious, obsessed with his fame as a writer. To the 'süße Mädel' he acts the role of the superior intellectual, his pretentious phrases contrasting with her more down-to-earth practicality. In anticipation of his seduction of her, he wants the atmosphere and the aesthetic conditions to be exactly right, the semi-dark, the rug, the cognac and the linguistic poses all contributing to his imaginary scene in an 'Indian castle'. Afterwards he is more concerned that she should be impressed with the identity of her lover as 'the great Bibitz', than that she should display any natural affection.

In the drama *Der einsame Weg* Schnitzler focuses on the

selfishness and egoism of the artistic temperament. Both the painter Julian Fichtner and the playwright Stefan von Sala are explored essentially as human beings rather than as 'artists'. Nevertheless their problematic relationships with others are due primarily to temperamental factors, which are inextricably linked with their artistic calling. In the early stages both are depicted as living apart from, or only on the fringes of, the cosy bourgeois world in which the play is enacted. Both are characterized initially by an inclination to travel. When Sala appears he is about to embark on a long journey, and Julian comes across as the archetype of the wandering artist, a restless genius who has never realized his full potential, and whose assertion of personal freedom and independence led to his desertion of Gabriele Wegrat, and eventually to his own unhappiness. Meanwhile Sala, a self-centred and arrogant dramatist, who is singularly unpopular in the theatre world, and remains aloof from society and human relationships, has constructed for himself a beautiful villa in Dornbach, complete with classical pillars, Roman statues at the head of an avenue, marble bench and pool, very much in tune with turn-of-the-century aestheticism.

In the novel *Der Weg ins Freie* Schnitzler introduces a number of artist figures, and provides here a greater degree of insight into the nature of their art, and into their problems of creativity. The central character, Georg von Wergenthin, is himself a composer, and during the course of the novel works at a quintet, composes songs, and embarks on a score for an opera. His librettist is Heinrich Bermann, like Schnitzler himself a writer of satirical social comedies, which arouse hostility in conservative and clerical journals. Bermann has inclinations in the direction of social realism, and during the novel writes a political comedy, researching his material through attending debates in parliament. Wergenthin is also acquainted with the novelist Edmund Nürnberger, whose first novel was set in the early nineteenth century, but which anticipated the atmosphere of his own contemporary Austria. It exposed the values of a hypocritical society, the cult of age and experience for their own sake, the lack of enterprise and vitality, the mindless and cowardly pursuit of the values of humanity and patriotism, now cheapened into the empty phrases of a bankrupt epoch. Nowhere else in Schnitzler's works is there to be found such a harsh judgement upon his own society.

But Schnitzler's interest in his presentation of these three major artist figures of the novel is not centred on the 'content' of their work. His main concern is to expose their limitations and shortcomings, both as artists and as human beings. Georg von Wergenthin, for example, possesses a temperament very much akin to that of Julian Fichtner (though he clearly lacks Fichtner's artistic genius), and this is reflected in the problems that he experiences with composition, and in his personal relations. His desire to remain 'unattached' and free of responsibilities leads to the failure of his relationship with Anna Rosner. Like Fichtner Georg lives a life on the fringe of society. A member of the declining aristocracy, he is no more than a 'guest' in the houses of the upper bourgeoisie. As an aristocrat too, he will never be truly admitted into artistic circles. And deservedly so, for his restlessness and the superficiality of his personality are a serious impediment to any meaningful artistic production. He works half-heartedly at his quintet, but is rarely in the mood for significant progress; he leaves it unfinished to embark on the opera with Bermann, but he never gets beyond a few ideas for individual scenes; whilst at the Prater one evening he hears a melody suitable for oboe or clarinet, a scherzo perhaps for a symphony, but he never develops such melodies and sketches into a full-scale work. Not that he is unaware of his shortcomings. As he extemporizes at the piano in a restaurant to entertain his acquaintances he is conscious of the futility of his work, and Anna frequently attempts to jolt him out of his casual 'playfulness' to more productive activity. He acknowledges that he is no genius, and he strikes others as the typical decadent dilettante, unable to apply himself with any degree of self-discipline to his calling. The quality of his music is also called into question. No Mahler or Schönberg, his compositions are condemned as sentimental and derivative, in the romantic tradition of Mendelssohn. In no sense then is Georg meant to represent a typical composer of the time. But he is a kind of representative figure of the period of aestheticism. He is the artist type who plays at art, essentially no more than a showman. Eventually he finds his true calling as a conductor of other people's music, and he enjoys the atmosphere of the concert-hall and the effect of his elegant appearance in his new role.

Heinrich Bermann is a more complex being than von Wergenthin. More productive as an artist (he completes his political comedy and considerable portions of the libretto for their opera), his main problem lies in the field of human relationships due to his ruminating, gloomy nature, and occasional bouts of depression and emotional deficiency. Anna Rosner condemns him as a cold and brutal egoist. Bermann himself acknowledges the unattractive paradox of his personality: he can be sentimental, yet also heartless; he is sensitive, yet ruthless; he needs company, yet can be moody and cantankerous. The catalyst for Bermann's problem is his relationship with an actress who is unfaithful to him. Bermann is tortured with jealousy and terminates the affair. Full of remorse she begs to be taken back, but Bermann refuses to consider a resumption of the relationship. Like the writer Fedor Denner (of *Das Märchen*) he acknowledges the unreasonable harshness of his attitude, yet is unable to compromise. When she then commits suicide Bermann is briefly distressed, but suffers no permanent feeling of guilt or remorse. Interestingly Edmund Nürnberger perceives a connection between Bermann's emotional inadequacy and his obsession with his art. Like the literary hack condemned in Thomas Mann's *Tonio Kröger* for his lack of genuine feelings, Bermann is too preoccupied with his calling to experience anything more than brief moments of emotional suffering. Even Bermann's political comedy is unconvincing, Nürnberger feels, because the writer has been too objective and not genuinely involved in his subject.

Ultimately neither Bermann nor von Wergenthin has the talent or the commitment of the genuine artist. But what of Nürnberger himself? Having written one novel displaying considerable insight into society's imperfections, he has now become disillusioned with his self-appointed role as a social educator, and is reduced to the ineffectual position of a cynical mocker on the periphery of Viennese society. To some extent Schnitzler shared his character's scepticism, particularly with regard to the treatment of political themes in his writings. Schnitzler rarely expressed himself publicly on any political issues, and recognized the futility of all attempts to change the course of politics through the power of the pen.[22] Nevertheless the various notes on political matters that he left amongst his papers at his death, demonstrate that he was certainly not apolitical,[23] and whilst his dramatic and narrative works do remain predominantly free of political themes, there are a few very notable exceptions. It is with these that the following chapter will be concerned.

8
POLITICS AND THE JEWISH QUESTION

Schnitzler did not advertise himself either in his writings or public pronouncements as a political animal. He was not an enthusiastic supporter of any of the major political movements or causes of his age, and he rarely expressed his views publicly on political issues. Like many of his contemporary intellectuals and fellow artists he took a cynical view of political developments in Austria during the final years of the monarchy. It is therefore hardly surprising that his literary works also remain predominantly free of political themes. In only two of his works are contemporary political issues raised in any significant degree, the novel *Der Weg ins Freie* and the drama *Professor Bernhardi* (1912), and in both his major specific concern is with the Jewish question.[1]

Schnitzler's interest in the problems facing the rapidly increasing Jewish population in Vienna stemmed from his own family origins. His father was a typical Jewish immigrant from Hungary, who had followed the example of so many of his fellow Jews by embracing one of the learned professions, the commonest means used to escape the ghetto and secure social assimilation and advancement. By the 1890s a disproportionate number of lawyers, doctors, academics and productive thinkers in every field were Jewish.[2] It was as a student at the University that Schnitzler first found himself on the receiving end of anti-Semitic prejudices,[3] and he later came across numerous examples in his professional career. As a social issue the Jewish problem receives relatively little attention in his works as a whole. There are brief disparaging comments from Lieutenant Gustl on the number of Jews being accepted as officers of the reserve, or attending the concert ('You can't even enjoy an oratorio in peace any more'), and he quickly recognizes the Jew in his girlfriend's 'sugar-daddy' ('Besides, he must be a Jew! Of course, he's in a bank, and look at his black moustache'). But the truly irrational nature of the wave of racist anti-Semitism sweeping through Vienna is conveyed when such comments are set against the surprise Gustl experiences when he learns that the Mannheimers, whose sumptuous dinners and fat cigars he has enjoyed in the company of the blonde, attractive Frau Mannheimer, are also (assimilated) Jews! In the novel *Therese* Karl Fabiani (Therese's brother) is actively involved in a nationalist student society, changes his name to the German-sounding Faber, and later sits in parliament as a member of Schönerer's Pan-German Nationalist Party. Evidence of his anti-Semitism is seen when he chastises his sister for 'knocking around with some rich old Jew'.

These brief examples of anti-Semitic attitudes do not in themselves constitute any kind of 'treatment' of the issue itself, they simply add an extra dimension to the personality or social position of the character concerned. But in the novel *Der Weg ins Freie* Schnitzler offers a much more wide-ranging and penetrating view of the problems experienced by Jews in Vienna. Initially one is struck by the sheer volume of cases, ranging from the purely domestic (Else Ehrenberg has little hope of marrying Hofrat Wilt, for an alliance with a Jewish family would prejudice his career), to the political (Heinrich Bermann's father, a former member of the Reichsrat, had been forced out of the Liberal Party). Many occur in the professions. As a lawyer, Bermann's father also began to lose clients; Bermann mentions Jewish civil servants who do not gain promotion, university lecturers who cannot get professorships, officer cadets who fail to get their commissions. Even talented Jewish artists are in a disadvantageous position compared, for example, with aristocratic dilettantes. Potentially the most serious case of anti-Semitism involves Leo Golowski, who is arrested after killing Lieutenant Sefranek in a duel. It is unlikely that charges would have been pressed against a non-Jewish officer, but it is feared that the authorities intend to use Leo as an example. The reality of the threat against him is underlined by a reference in the text to an actual incident which took place in Bohemia in 1899, when a Jewish apprentice Leopold Kilsner was convicted of the murder of a nineteen-year-old seamstress. The prosecutor implied that he had committed a ritual murder to obtain Christian blood for matzoh, and the case, which coincided with the Dreyfus affair in France, intimidated Jews throughout Austria. In Schnitzler's much less gruesome fictional parallel Leo is eventually pardoned before he comes to trial, but the concern of his friend Berthold Stauber is illustrative of the anxiety felt by many Jews over the gathering pace of anti-Semitism in official circles, as well as in society at large. The trend is illustrated early in the novel by the character Josef Rosner, the son of a minor official from the Wieden suburb. He has been absorbed into a circle of acquaintances whose sympathies are either Christian Socialist or German Nationalist, and who include the son of the city councillor Jalaudek, an influential member of the Christian Socialist Party, and a close acquaintance of the editor of the *Christliche Tagesbote*. Josef's story has been seen to represent the capture of a whole social group by the anti-Semitic movement.[4]

Schnitzler's main concern in this novel, however, is less with the phenomenon of anti-Semitism itself, than with the response to it on the part of a wide variety of Jewish characters. Their attitudes are monitored through the observations of the non-Jewish central character, Baron Georg von Wergenthin. Initially the Jews are viewed from a distance, and even with some amusement, particularly the Ehrenberg family. Salamon Ehrenberg is the wealthy proprietor of a munitions factory, and has acquired an elegant apartment in the fashionable third district overlooking the Schwarzenbergpark, not far from the Belvedere Palace of Archduke Franz Ferdinand.[5] The members of his family are making desperate attempts to assimilate into respectable society. His daughter Else has harboured hopes of marrying Georg von Wergenthin. His son Oskar, an officer of the reserve, seeks the company of young aristocrats, and has assumed an aristocratic manner and tone of voice. Frau Ehrenberg is pretentious and snobbish, and in her ambition to become a society hostess, she has attempted to establish her drawing room as an imitation aristocratic salon. Artists, civil servants, officers, aristocrats and industrial magnates are encouraged to call to engage in conversation on cultural matters, or, more likely, to indulge in social gossip. By contrast Ehrenberg has dissociated himself from his family's social aspirations, and has retained his Jewish identity. He embarrasses his daughter with tactless jokes; he mocks his wife's pretensions as a hostess, and resents his privacy being invaded by all and sundry; he is hostile towards his son's attempts at assimilation into the detested aristocracy. In the face of the threat posed by the anti-Semites Ehrenberg is attracted by Theodor

Herzl's recently formed Zionist movement. He is sceptical of any attempts by the Jews to influence the political scene in Austria, having witnessed the decline of Jewish liberalism and the betrayal of the Jews by the German Nationals. He foresees that the same fate will await the Jewish members of the Social Democrats. Meanwhile, though, he is prepared to finance Therese Golowski's political activities, simply in opposition to his wife's social aspirations!

Ehrenberg is pleased that his Zionist views are shared by Leo Golowski, and it is Leo who describes at length, and with enthusiasm, the longing for Palestine on the part of the Jewish people, in terms of a sacred mission. But Schnitzler's novel also contains sharply critical views of the whole Zionist movement. Edmund Nürnberger perceives that by being seen to unite against the enemy the Jews have brought many of their problems upon themselves, and Leo even admits that his assertion of the division between Jew and Gentile contains within it an implied justification of Viennese anti-Semitism. But the case against Zionism is put most fully and most passionately by the writer Heinrich Bermann, for whom the notion of a Jewish homeland in faraway Palestine is anathema, an artificial concept born solely of political and religious dogma. Bermann feels that his true 'home', his *Heimat*, is in Austria, in the culture in which he has been born and raised, and he cannot identify with other peoples simply on the basis of a shared persecution. Bermann is sceptical of the viability of the 'group solution'. It is up to the individual to find his own private 'Weg ins Freie'. Bermann's views clearly reflect those of Schnitzler himself, who rejected the Zionist solution for the same reasons.[6]

Much of *Der Weg ins Freie* is concerned with the psychological repercussions upon the members of the Jewish community of the growing anti-Semitism in social and political life. Early in the novel Schnitzler draws a sharp distinction between the unconcerned apathy of Edmund Nürnberger and Ehrenberg's obsessive awareness of the potential dangers. Nürnberger feels he has shed his Jewishness altogether, and has never felt threatened personally. Likewise he cannot take seriously the possibility of any threat towards Ehrenberg, the rich industrialist. Were Ehrenberg a common pedlar, he might have greater reason for concern. Ehrenberg, however, suffers from the Jewish 'national illness', a persecution complex that senses anti-Semitism around every corner, and even within his own family. Hence his violent reaction to what he must perceive as his son's treachery, when Oskar attempts to identify himself outwardly as a Catholic. Ehrenberg's extremism is rejected by the writer Heinrich Bermann, the Jewish character whom Georg von Wergenthin comes to know most intimately in *Der Weg ins Freie*. But though Bermann is capable of discussing the Jewish problem rationally and objectively, he too is highly sensitive to the anti-Semitic atmosphere in Vienna, which has been exacerbated for him by criticisms of his recent play in conservative and clerical journals. This has clearly affected his personality. He is touchy, and even tactless in his observation to Georg that the latter, as an aristocrat, would not suffer the same fate in similar circumstances. When Georg accuses him of exhibiting signs of persecution mania in his tendency to view his personal problems constantly in terms of the Jewish question, he responds that this is an inevitable result of current attitudes to Jews. If a Jewish person is criticized, in whatever field or for whatever reason, the critic never fails to mention his Jewish origins, whereas this does not happen with individuals of other races or religions. What Bermann finds most galling is the sense of shame that is inculcated into so many Jews from the moment of their birth. They are educated to avoid the despised Jewish characteristics, and so may come even to hate each other and accept with resignation the discomforts, abuse and injustices to which they are subjected in social and political life.

As Georg von Wergenthin listens to the Jews discussing their problems and their eventual fate, he begins to achieve a vague understanding of what it actually means to be a Jew: to be persecuted and abused in the land in which one has grown up and with whose culture one senses an inner bond; to be torn constantly between the fear of asserting one's identity and personality, lest one be accused of a vanity beyond one's station, and the bitter resentment at having to defer to barbarous ruffians. Through Georg's perception we gain a measure of insight into the Jewish consciousness, though he never achieves full understanding, and in the final analysis Bermann remains a strange and baffling creature, sick in soul and slightly mad. Reading Schnitzler's analysis later in the century, and with the benefit of hindsight, it is impossible not to view it within the context of later developments in Germany and in his native Vienna. Schnitzler never lived to experience the holocaust, but the forecast by Leo Golowski of the return of the pogroms and his vision of a time when Jews would once again be burned at the stake strike a chilling note. That Schnitzler sensed the realities of the danger is suggested when Georg's attempt to reassure his friends that 'such times will never be seen again', is greeted with hollow laughter.

In his autobiography Schnitzler acknowledges that he was interested not so much in the political or social implications of the Jewish question, as in its psychological effects.[7] In this respect his treatment of the theme may be compared with that of Joseph Roth, who was able to look back upon the role played by the Jews in the commercial and cultural life of the empire. In *Radetzkymarsch* Roth's treatment of anti-Semitism is very reminiscent of Schnitzler's approach, as he presents the mindless taunting of the Jewish regimental doctor by Count Tattenbach. But the Jewish problem receives its fullest treatment in *Die Kapuzinergruft* through the figure of the Galician Jew, Manes Reisiger, who arrives in Vienna to secure a place at the Conservatory for his gifted son, the violinist Ephraim. Manes takes it as his son's right to be awarded the place, and the Jew is presented as an enrichment for the city, as he feeds the capital with the inner strength and vitality of the empire at large. The Jews are primeval figures, and the strength of the monarchy is to be found not in Vienna, but in the primal qualities of the provinces.[8] Eventually Ephraim is swallowed up in Vienna and destroyed in the crushing of the workers and the Social Democrats by Chancellor Dollfuss's militia in the 1934 uprising. An anticipation of the fate awaiting the Jews of Vienna in 1938. Apart from isolated comments by Heinrich Bermann Schnitzler's novel stops short of this kind of analysis. Nevertheless *Der Weg ins Freie* presents an intelligent and wide-ranging exploration of the immediate repercussions of the Jewish question upon affected individuals, whether on one side of the battleground or the other.

Der Weg ins Freie also contains frequent references to political activity and to the more general political views of a number of characters. Yet this novel is not a political novel as such. The main issue is a domestic one, the relationship between Georg von Wergenthin and Anna Rosner, and the most gripping passages of the novel are those in which Georg wrestles with his conscience after their child is stillborn. In that Anna is socially his inferior, and Georg's attitude reflects some of the prejudices of the time, Schnitzler's treatment of the relationship does have its *social* implications. But it is totally detached from the background of political activity. Yet the various incidents and conversations which make up this background do not of themselves constitute a fully developed second line of action, or 'sub-plot'. In the opening chapter there is a reference to a question asked in parliament by a young Jewish socialist member, Doctor Berthold Stauber. The question concerned the case of Therese Golowski, one of the leaders of the Social Democratic Party. During a strike of miners in Bohemia Therese had made a speech which had included a defamatory reference to a member of the royal family. She was tried in court, and acquitted. But the public prosecutor appealed, and a second court found her guilty, sentencing her to two months' imprisonment. Meanwhile the original judge was despatched to the Russian border, from whence there is no return. The case clearly smacks of corruption in high places, and Stauber's intervention was howled down by Christian Socialist members, who resorted to hurling anti-Semitic insults at him. But Schnitzler does not pursue the matter further in terms of an analysis of the opposing parties. Stauber resigns his seat in parliament not because of the strength and nature of the hostility shown towards him, but because one of his fiercest opponents had afterwards offered him a drink in the bar. For Stauber this is typical of the half-heartedness of Austrian politics. Parliament is but a frivolous game, a 'Komödienspiel', not a genuine exchange of sincerely held views. In his presentation of Stauber's case Schnitzler shows that he is less concerned with the issues themselves than with an expression of his antagonism towards all political life.

As the novel progresses, Schnitzler's characters time and again express their author's cynical doubts concerning the genuineness of political beliefs and activity. Despite the enthusiasm and persuasiveness of her political speeches, even the highly talented and aggressive Therese Golowski is suspected of lacking genuine conviction. Her brother Leo feels that the long periods during which she frequently detaches herself from her political activities, suggest that her professed sympathy for the poor and wretched is little more than skin-deep. Heinrich Bermann attends a rally of workers in the Brigittenau at which Therese speaks on universal suffrage, as though this were the most important issue in her life. But he wonders if she really believed what she was saying. More maliciously, the cynic Nürnberger has asked her whether at her next trial for 'high treason' she intends to have her hair elegantly styled, or appear in pigtails. But Georg von Wergenthin also senses that her adoption of causes and public speeches amounts to little more than play-acting. Even anti-Semitism is at times seen as something of a pose. Members of a cycling club which is *judenrein* (closed to Jews) forget their politics as they cycle through the mountains, and one of them is actually engaged to a Jewess. Even Lieutenant Sefranek, the scourge of Leo Golowski during his year as a cadet, indulges in anti-Semitic bullying only because it is becoming the fashion. In his private life he frequents Jewish houses, and a Jewish doctor is his intimate friend. That such casual half-heartedness cuts right across the various political parties and factions is perceived by the outsider, the Englishman Skelton. He sees political antagonisms diluted by absurd personal friendships, convictions modified by an all too pervasive tendency to assimilate the exceptions. In parliament he has the impression that the most fiercely divided opponents wink at each other as they exchange insults, a clear indication that they are only playing at politics.

Generally speaking, those characters not actively engaged in politics themselves remain largely indifferent to the political life of the nation. As Georg and Heinrich discuss the composition of parliament, the squabbles between the German Nationalists and the Czechs, and the attacks by the Christian Socialists upon the Minister of Education, they do so with feigned enthusiasm, and neither can remember afterwards which particular side he has taken. Others have a powerful sense of the futility of political activity. For the civil servant Hofrat Wilt, the Austrian political machine is like a complex musical instrument played on by uncomprehending amateurs; in the absence of the master hand it will play on until its strings break and its framework collapses. The political world of *Der Weg ins Freie* consists largely of insincerity, incompetence and indifference. The machinery of government is simply going through the motions of running the empire's affairs, its representatives paying lip-service to ideals and principles in which they do not whole-heartedly believe.

In *Der Weg ins Freie* the political theme is treated largely through discussions between various interested characters, with occasional references to individual events and episodes to provide illustration. By contrast, Schnitzler's other major work treating the contemporary political scene, the drama *Professor Bernhardi*, focuses on one major incident and follows a single line of action through to its conclusion. Again the Jewish question is to the forefront, and though written in 1912, the play is set around the turn of the century, and was prompted by problems experienced by Schnitzler's own father.[9]

Professor Bernhardi is the Jewish director of a private clinic, the Elisabethinum. During the course of the play his position is undermined by his political enemies, whose intrigues eventually force his resignation and even cause him to serve two months in prison. The process is set in motion when Bernhardi treats a young girl who is suffering from the effects of an illegal abortion. Her condition worsens, and a priest is summoned to administer the last rites. But the girl is unaware of the seriousness of her condition, and has entered a state of euphoria. Fearing that the arrival of a priest might shock her into a realization of the truth and turn her dying moments into a nightmare, Bernhardi refuses to allow the priest to go to her bedside. Bernhardi has acted purely on humanitarian grounds, but in the eyes of the Catholic Church he has deprived her of the last sacrament and of the comforts of religion at the moment of her death. Bernhardi is accused in clerical circles, both within and outside the hospital, of offending the Church, the clinic is threatened with withdrawal of patronage and funds, and even a parliamentary question is tabled.

Opposition to Bernhardi is intensified because of his Jewish identity, and the case acts as a catalyst for anti-Semitic intrigue. As his Jewish colleague Doctor Löwenstein points out, if Bernhardi had been a Christian, thousands would have rallied to his support, including German Nationals and Christian Socialists who are now marshalling forces against him. Likewise the sensible and moderate Doctor Cyprian recognizes that simply because of his racial identity Bernhardi should have been more careful, and Doctor Schreimann, an assimilated and baptized Jew, condemns Bernhardi for his 'tactlessness'. Finally Doctor Pflugfelder exposes the campaign against Bernhardi for what it is: nobody really believes that Bernhardi was consciously taking an anti-clerical stance, or making a political point, but some people have welcomed the opportunity of making political capital out of the case. Eventually Bernhardi has to stand trial on a charge of violation of religious feelings. Within the hospital itself the anti-Semite Doctor Filitz wages an open campaign against Bernhardi, whilst Doctor Ebenwald, Bernhardi's deputy, attempts to exploit the situation to ensure the appointment to the hospital staff of a non-Jewish doctor over a better qualified Jewish candidate. Ebenwald's student Hochroitzpointer, a German National from the Tirol, is determined that the affair should cost Bernhardi 'his neck', and gives false evidence at the trial to bring about Bernhardi's conviction. Of all Schnitzler's anti-Semitic characters he is the one who most obviously anticipates the rise of Austro-fascism in the 1920s and 1930s.[10] In the political world at large the anti-Semitic parties use the case to demand that henceforth the appointment of Jews to responsible positions be severely restricted; protests are voiced in parliament about Jewish influence in the University; and complaints are made that Bernhardi's clinic, in which 85 per cent of the patients are Catholics, should employ such a high proportion of Jewish doctors. After the trial Bernhardi is greeted by mindless anti-Semitic chants which lump Jews and freemasons together as groups hostile to the Church. Such scenes were indeed all too frequently a feature of Lueger's Vienna.[11] But in the face of the anti-Semitic opposition the Jewish factions also marshal their forces. In the clinic itself Doctor Löwenstein intends to use the case to rally support for the Jewish 'cause', and after Bernhardi's conviction even the moderate Pflugfelder intends making a direct appeal to the people. Zionists organize demonstrations, the liberal press presents Bernhardi as a political martyr, and the whole affair is an Austrian version of the Dreyfus case.[12] Eventually, after his release from prison, it emerges that Bernhardi was convicted on the basis of false evidence. Yet by now Bernhardi views the possibility of a reopening of the case with positive distaste, and prefers to retire from the public stage into the relative obscurity of private practice.

In 1912, shortly after its appearance in print, *Professor Bernhardi* was banned from performance in Vienna, not because of its specific racial or religious implications, but because of its political applicability.[13] In the play itself the cynical machinations of Bernhardi's enemies at the meeting of the hospital Kollegium in Act Three, are actually described as a parody of parliamentary proceedings. The Bernhardi case takes place against a background of political intrigue, not only within the Elisabethinum itself, but in the wider political circles of the city. As a private clinic the Elisabethinum is heavily dependent on patronage for funds, and it is vital to retain the goodwill of its wealthy and influential supporters. The clinic is governed by the Kuratorium, consisting of two royal princes, a bishop, a bank manager and a high civil servant. The resignation of the Kuratorium in the wake of the Bernhardi incident therefore represents a severe blow to the clinic, depriving it of respectability and funds from a large number of benefactors. The process leading to the resignation begins when Princess Stixenstein, the wife of the president of the Kuratorium, withdraws her patronage from the clinic's annual ball. The bishop likes Bernhardi personally, but acknowledges Bernhardi's serious error in offending the Church. Prince Konstantin holds liberal views, but is aware of the dangers of taking an individual line, and votes in the Herrenhaus with the conservative parties. Hofrat Winkler, a Social Democrat and the most enlightened member of the Kuratorium, will also have to follow the establishment line. And so the clerical and political circles close ranks.

The political repercussions of the Bernhardi affair go far beyond the immediate confines of the Elisabethinum and its governing body, and eventually threaten the reputation of the Minister of Education, Flint. Flint is Schnitzler's version of the typical smooth-talking politician. Ambitious, opportunistic, essentially unprincipled, Flint's sole aim is to turn all situations to his own advantage in the interests of his political career. Flint is a former doctor, and as a young man was a colleague of Bernhardi's. But even then the future politician was clearly in evidence. Bernhardi recalls an occasion when their professor had failed to diagnose the condition of a patient, who had subsequently died. Flint later admitted that he (Flint) had actually made the correct diagnosis, but had kept his information to himself lest he incur the professor's displeasure. He justifies his behaviour on the grounds of expediency: the death of the patient was an unfortunate but necessary sacrifice in the interests of his subsequent medical and political career, which has been to the benefit of so many. When Bernhardi founded the Elisabethinum, Flint, who had by now entered political life and become a minor member of the government, followed the official line and bitterly opposed this new, private initiative. But now that he has risen to high office, Flint intends to make his mark with a series of far-reaching reforms in the medical service, for which he requires the support of all parties.

When Bernhardi and Flint come face to face in the final scene of Act Two, the interview is, then, an important one for both men. Flint reveals that the Bernhardi affair is the subject of an intervention to be made in parliament by the clerical and anti-Semitic parties, to which he, as minister, must respond, and which could be politically embarrassing to him. Were Bernhardi to defuse the situation, with, for example, a personal visit to the priest, or the appointment of the non-Jew Hell to his staff (as Doctor Ebenwald has already suggested), then the opposition assault might be deflected. Bernhardi counters with an eloquent refusal to forsake his principles, but Flint realizes that he could still turn the situation to his own advantage were he to use Bernhardi's principles himself in parliament to 'see off the opposition. Flint regards himself as a master parliamentary tactician. For him it is a matter of choosing the right word at the right time to score points off his political opponents; as Bernhardi perceives, Flint does not really believe in the views he puts forward or in the causes he espouses. They are simply means towards the achievement of his own personal success.

In the event Flint cynically abandons Bernhardi, for when the parliamentary going gets rough he retreats rapidly in the face of mounting opposition, and, apparently even to his own surprise, announces that he will confer with the Minister of Justice as to whether legal proceedings should be instituted against Bernhardi. Later he attempts to justify his sacrifice of Bernhardi, in terms of a sudden realization that his own political downfall at this particular moment would have amounted to a betrayal of his political mission to reform the education system. Flint claims, then, that for him the all-important factor was the greatness of his 'idea'. For the time being, however, his projected reforms seem to be little more than hot air. For a conversation with his senior civil servant reveals that he has recently curried favour with the Christian Socialists by agreeing to increase the hours of religious instruction in schools. Flint claims that he is caught in a precarious balancing act as he attempts to steer a way between the various opposing factions. It does not pay in politics to advertise one's own principles, that is the mistake of the political dilettante, he says. The professional politician has to be pragmatic, and if he behaves in a manner contrary to his own beliefs and ideals, then this is justifiable in the interests of long-term policy. Flint's argument amounts to a highly questionable justification of political expediency. But in his mouth his words ring even more hollow. For he has neither belief nor principle, nor, one suspects, a long-term policy. For Flint is concerned solely with his personal reputation and career.

In many ways Flint represents a caricature of the unprincipled politician whom Schnitzler detested so much. But during the course of the play other, more sympathetically drawn characters argue that in some situations it is necessary, and even honourable, to desert one's principles. Recognizing the paramount importance of placating the clinic's financial backers, Doctor Cyprian urges Bernhardi to express officially his regrets over the incident with the priest. Even the priest shows himself to be something of a political animal. Privately he acknowledges that Bernhardi acted correctly and honourably as a doctor in denying him access to the dying girl, but he did not voice this opinion publicly at Bernhardi's trial lest the enemies of the Church exploit his words for their own political purposes. Bernhardi views this omission as a betrayal of the truth.

In the face of the political machinations of the various opposing factions Bernhardi remains the guardian of uncompromising individualism and fundamental moral values. Politically, in fact, he maintains a neutral and apparently disinterested stance. It is indeed the principal irony of the play that such an apolitical and essentially private man should so unintentionally become the instigator and object of a political *cause célèbre*. Bernhardi's initial act, to spare the girl knowledge of her coming death, is a spontaneous and humane gesture in his capacity as a doctor. Throughout the affair Bernhardi refuses to betray his own conscience. He declines to assuage the opposition by officially apologizing for his behaviour, or by appointing to his staff the inferior Catholic rather than the superior Jew. Yet after his conviction he likewise refuses to appeal, and will not condone the attempts of the press to make of him an example in the fight for progress and freedom. Bernhardi's more pragmatic colleagues may find his determination to preserve his integrity at all costs exasperating, and symptomatic of a foolish stubbornness, that is ultimately self-defeating in a situation requiring compromise. Yet Bernhardi's uprightness and honesty clearly have his author's approval, particularly when set beside the cynical expediency of the professional politician. The impetus for the dramatic complications which arise during the course of the play is provided by the Jewish question. But essentially the play represents the fate of an apolitical man in the unsavoury world of politics.

Schnitzler's cynical view of politics is expressed more satirically in the comedy *Fink und Fliederbusch* (1916). Ostensibly the play is levelled at the press and standards of reporting. The people are fed a diet of petty social gossip, and it is assumed that the average reader is interested in politics only when scandal is afoot. Censorship of political items still prevails, and newspapers are generally wary of criticizing government ministers. For example, a report of a parliamentary debate which has made fun of the Minister of Justice is censored. On the other hand a reference to an intervention by Social Democratic members is condemned for its objectivity! The political editor of *Die Gegenwart*, a liberal paper run by two Jewish immigrants, is continually on the verge of dismissal or resignation because his editorials are considered too pointed. Schnitzler's depiction of the dilemma experienced by *Die Gegenwart* clearly reflects the problems facing the liberal press at the time. Liberal papers such as the *Neue Freie Presse* were largely in the hands of big business, and were used by the government as informal communicators of government policy.[14] The government could put pressure on the press because of the considerable powers of censorship that it still possessed, and through concessions to the financial interests with which the press had close links. Consequently the liberal press was generally regarded as corrupt.

Schnitzler's play also asserts the shallowness of political reporting, and descends to the level of farce when a duel is arranged between two political journalists of opposite persuasions, who are in fact the same person, writing alternately for two rival newspapers. Fliederbusch is the parliamentary reporter of *Die Gegenwart* but as Fink he also writes for the Catholic weekly *Die Elegante Welt*. In his latter capacity he has defended a speech made in parliament by Count Niederhof, on the occasion of a young boy being shot dead by security forces during civil disturbances in Strakonitz. Niederhof has stated that the principle of the authority of the state is more important than the life of an individual subject. He has consequently been attacked by the socialist *Arbeiterzeitung*, but supported by the Catholic and nationalist press, whereas the liberal press has practised self-censorship and moderation, and remained silent. Fliederbusch breaks this silence by writing a reply to Fink's reactionary article, attacking Niederhof politically and personally, and also Fink and the paper he represents, in the most insulting terms. Fink responds by challenging Fliederbusch to a duel, and when, inevitably, the truth of their common identity is revealed, Fliederbusch is accused of having taken politics and the institution of the duel to the point of absurdity. Yet in so doing he has of course revealed an element of truth about them both.

In exposing the shallowness of political reporting, Schnitzler is once again calling into question the depth and sincerity of all political views. The issue is also treated in a conversation which takes place between Fliederbusch and Count Niederhof in Act Three, when Niederhof offers Fliederbusch a journalistic post on a new paper he is founding. As far as the count is concerned one political view is as valid as the next. There are no absolute truths in politics, and views expressed may bear little relationship to actual opinions. In fact a journalist, like a politician, is likely to be more successful without inner convictions, for he may then control his utterances with greater objectivity and efficiency. The only difference between the count and Fliederbusch is that the former has no convictions at all, whereas the latter is apparently capable of holding opposing views simultaneously. Thus Fliederbusch is ideally suited to the count's new paper, which will be reactionary, conservative, anarchic, socialist and liberal all rolled into one, a comic anticipation of the new free press! Again, then, Schnitzler is suggesting through the words of this highly unlikely mouthpiece that the world of politics is merely a façade.

Schnitzler's hostile portrayal of the political scene as a vacuous world, characterized by superficiality, insincerity and expediency, represents a very negative and one-sided viewpoint. To some extent the picture he draws reflects the political impotence of the Austrian parliament at the turn of the century, and the futility of many of the debates that were held there. But it does little justice to the great political movements and causes of his age, which inspired such passions in a Vienna about to experience a major political upheaval. Schnitzler's scepticism is evocative of the resignation of the liberals, and of their acceptance of the decline of their political influence. It is also an extension of his recognition that as a writer he could not influence the course of political events. Like Grillparzer and Bauernfeld before him he felt hampered by censorship, of which he had some personal experience in his early years, and which consequently discouraged him from including overt political comment in his works.[15]

Schnitzler's preoccupations in the two major 'political' works, *Der Weg ins Freie* and *Professor Bernhardi*, suggest that his interest in political issues was limited only to those that directly affected him as an individual: the rise of nationalist and religious factions, which exacerbated anti-Semitic tensions in the late 1890s. Certainly in his younger days he was too preoccupied with the social and private world of Vienna itself to pay too much attention to political developments.[16] Like his character Heinrich Bermann, he was also more interested in his cultural *Heimat* than in the mythical 'fatherland' beyond, and he remained largely indifferent towards the Habsburg Empire as a political unit. He displayed little interest in foreign policy, and from his earliest days as an officer cadet felt no patriotic enthusiasm for Austria's military initiatives.[17] When the empire finally collapsed and the Habsburgs departed in 1918, he experienced no feelings of regret, but no sense of jubilation either at the proclamation of the Republic.[18] Yet none of this indifference means that he himself was totally devoid of principles. His hostility towards the military, for example, was engendered by deeply held pacifist convictions that were present from an early age.[19] It was mainly because of these views that he did not associate himself with the upsurge of patriotism in Vienna at the outbreak of the First World War. As he came to hear of the senseless horrors of the trenches and the battlefields, his penetrating and lengthy comments, which he recorded in his notes at the time, testify to his profound insight into events.[20] He also recognized that the various peace initiatives represented a step in the direction of the victory of democracy over absolutism.[21] It should not be assumed, however, that it was only during the war itself that Schnitzler suddenly became 'politically aware'. The diaries of the years immediately preceding the war are full of references to discussions with acquaintances on political trends and events, on Zionism, on the death of Lueger, on parliamentary debates, on Czech nationalism, on socialism, on Franz Ferdinand, on the Habsburgs, on 'Austrian affairs'. Certainly his main preoccupations were with music, the theatre and literature, but he was also an avid reader of *Die Fackel*, despite its hostile articles about Schnitzler himself. In his middle years, then, he by no means ignored the political issues of his day, and he even did his duty as a citizen when he cast his vote for the Social Democrats, in the elections to the Austrian parliament in 1907,[22] and again in local elections in 1912.[23]

Though clearly aware of the political developments around him, and of their significance for Austria's future, Schnitzler remained very much the passive onlooker, and refused to become positively involved in political life. To a major extent his aversion may be explained in terms of a fundamental antipathy towards the very nature of the professional politician. He expresses this most forcibly in his portrayal of the minister Flint, but he also puts into the mouth of one of his few more sympathetically drawn political figures his most outspoken condemnation of the political animal. In *Der Weg ins Freie* Doctor Berthold Stauber, having resigned his seat in the Reichsrat, is contemplating a political come-back through his candidacy for the Lower Austrian Provincial Assembly, where he intends to concern himself with reforms in public hygiene. His father suggests that for such a role Berthold lacks the necessary humanitarian qualities, but Berthold retorts that in the field in which he is contemplating working, a love of humanity, especially if expressed in the form of pity for individual people, is possibly even a disadvantage. When dealing with anonymous groups of people one must be prepared to be hard and cruel in the interests of the common good. No details are given of what Berthold intends, but his programme appears to condone the sacrifice of the weak and sick to prevent the spread of infection. At the moment he does not advocate the actual 'murder' of such dangerous and 'superfluous' people, but he is convinced that his ideas 'belong to the future'. Stauber is a Jew, and a professed socialist, but his words, taken out of context, provide a chilling anticipation of the selective removal of those designated as the 'subhumans' in Nazi Germany. And more pointedly, they reflect the disregard for the individual on the part of the mass political movements of the time, that were to play such a dominant role in the twentieth century to come.

9

REALIST AND CRITIC

Our examination of Schnitzler's works began with his psychological studies, an acknowledegement in itself that one of his most prominent features is his ability to plumb the depths of human psychological experience. That Schnitzler's interest is focused most immediately upon the individual human being is beyond dispute. Nevertheless to deny any interest on his part in social problems or trends beyond the individual consciousness, or to state categorically that he concentrates on 'Man – not Society',[1] would seem to ignore a significant dimension to his works. Many commentators have indeed asserted a correlation between the mental states of his characters and the values, attitudes and behavioural habits of a specific social order.[2]

Clearly there is a danger in assuming that, simply because Schnitzler sets so many of his works in his own contemporary world, his characters are 'socially conditioned'. Such an assumption can draw one all too easily into a circular critical stance, namely of contending on the one hand that a full understanding of Schnitzler's characters is dependent on actual knowledge of the social context, on the other of claiming that the psychological analysis in itself affords insight into social values and structures. Nevertheless so many of his characters strike one as social 'types', or representative figures of specific groups such as the Jewish bourgeoisie, the military, or the *Kleinbürgertum*, that it would seem perfunctory not to take the social context into account in any overall assessment of his works. For example, *Leutnant Gustl* rightly owes its reputation as one of Schnitzler's most important works to its author's original and brilliant use of the internal monologue technique, but the monologue itself is anchored in the attitudes and values of the Imperial Army, and Gustl comes across as a socially determined type.[3] Other characters, such as Fedor Denner (*Das Märchen*) and Adolf Losatti (*Das Vermächtnis*), represent all too clearly the prejudices and hypocrisies of their social class. Even the heroine of *Therese*, which is essentially the study of individual experience, is identified as a representative figure through the novel's subtitle *Chronik eines Frauenlebens*, suggesting that her fate is to be taken as a typical example of sexual discrimination and oppression.[4] Moreover the very fact that this novel, like other works written in the post-war period such as *Spiel im Morgengrauen*, *Traumnovelle* and *Der Sekundant*, is set in Schnitzler's favourite turn-of-the-century context, suggests his conscious preoccupation with a particular time-anchored milieu. Indeed, in the eyes of the post-war generation, Schnitzler came to be regarded more and more as *the* recreator of a social world long since past.

That the social import of several of Schnitzler's works was certainly apparent to his contemporaries is suggested by the reception afforded a number of his plays. In bourgeois circles it was felt that *Das Märchen* advocated immorality and female emancipation;[5] the misgivings of Max Burckhard, the director of the Burgtheater, over the effect that *Liebelei* might have on the more genteel members of his audience, were amply justified by the scandal that the play provoked;[6] *Das Vermächtnis*, a success in the Burgtheater, was regarded as 'modern';[7] *Das weite Land* was accepted as a progressive criticism of society, and was greeted, for example, with considerable enthusiasm by one of the young archdukes, who then hastily distanced himself from the applause.[8] Meanwhile Schnitzler had acquired a degree of notoriety, particularly through the publication of *Leutnant Gustl* and *Reigen*, which aroused public hostility precisely because they were accepted as social pieces, and Schnitzler came to be detested by those who sensed that he was openly criticizing them. Schnitzler's social criticism was not of course relevant only to conditions in his own native city. The fact that *Reigen* created such a scandal in Berlin, where it was first performed in 1921, is indicative of the fact that he was tackling issues concerning the epoch as a whole, and not just a local, Viennese phenomenon. But the attacks on the play were at their fiercest in Vienna itself. The Viennese première (also in 1921) led to violent scenes in the theatre, fire extinguishers were turned on to the stage, and stink bombs were exploded; outside there were demonstrations in the streets and at the Rathaus, and even angry exchanges in parliament.[9] Much of the hostility, both in Berlin and in Vienna, was anti-Semitic in origin, but it is clear that Schnitzler's exposure of sexual hypocrisy had touched a raw nerve, even after the collapse of the political and social order that had presided over it.

The *Reigen* scandal demonstrated in particular both the specific and the general connotations of Schnitzler's works, his ability to capture aspects of his own milieu that were also those of the epoch at large. The social divisions in Vienna, the prejudices and hypocrisies of its citizens, were clearly paralleled elsewhere, so that Schnitzler cannot be dismissed simply as a regional writer. The success of his plays in Berlin in particular, where many had their first performances under Otto Brahm, testifies to their wider appeal. Furthermore, Schnitzler's understanding of human nature and his skill as an interpreter of the individual consciousness lend his works the quality of universality, which has ensured their enduring success and popularity. In short, they have textual meaning, without reference to the social context. Nevertheless Vienna is so often his chosen scenario, and his characters fit so perfectly, according to their social rank or origin, into the sociological fabric of the city, that he cannot escape entirely his reputation as Vienna's foremost and most prolific chronicler. He has indeed been justly praised for his capacity to recreate the figures of his own environment.[10] He has elevated the figure of the 'süße Mädel' into a recognizable Viennese phenomenon, Leutnant Gustl now stands as the typically empty-headed officer of the Imperial Army, the indolent way of life pursued by Theodor and Fritz is now regarded as being typically Viennese. It would be wrong to assert that such figures existed only in Vienna. But their manner of speech and behaviour identify them as Viennese, and as such they have come to represent a particular location. It was perhaps Schnitzler's misfortune that the image presented of Vienna had already become a cliché in his own lifetime, as he himself acknowledges in *Der Weg ins Freie*. When Georg von Wergenthin takes up his post in Detmold, he is regarded with a mixture of sympathy and mockery when it is learned he comes from Vienna, with its assumed associated phenomena of Strauß waltzes, coffeehouses, 'süße Mädel', roast chicken, hackney-carriages and parliamentary scandals. In a sense Schnitzler both confirms and contributes to the myth. But his critical analysis of the social mores of the imperial city offers something more than just a catalogue of clichés.

Schnitzler's predilection for a specific milieu places him within a tradition of social realists who dominated European prose writing from the 1830s on, and whose influence has been felt well into the twentieth century. It is tempting indeed to suggest that Schnitzler has done for Vienna what Balzac did for Paris, Dickens for London and Fontane for Berlin. Nevertheless it is important to appreciate the limitations of Schnitzler's 'social realism' before indulging in such comparisons. In the first place, Schnitzler's account of his milieu is by no means a comprehensive one in terms of the various social strata of the city. Apart from a number of excursions into the circles of the lower aristocracy, and various references to the plight of the lower classes, Schnitzler's world is predominantly that of the bourgeoisie. Although he by no means ignores or neglects the larger world beyond the confines of his own immediate sphere,[11] essentially his realism is very selective. Secondly, whereas Schnitzler makes frequent reference to specific localities, he does not indulge in lengthy descriptions of the city itself. For example, when Berta Garlan arrives in the city for her meeting with Emil Lindbach, he traces the route of her walk through the streets and along the Ring, and names the buildings that she passes, but he does not describe their appearance for their own sake. When Fritz looks out of Christine's window towards the Kahlenberg, he does not describe what he sees. Clearly Schnitzler did not need to add such details for his Viennese readers. Thus his realism is also a very limited form of referential realism, and though it is arguable that his works may appeal more to those who know the city well than to those who do not, they can certainly be appreciated and understood without undue consideration of their specific background. The reader must not be misled into taking pleasure at local references as an end in themselves, for Schnitzler is interested not so much in the streets, parks and buildings that constitute the city sights, as in the individuals who inhabit them.

That Schnitzler's prime concern is with the personae of his milieu, rather than with their actual physical surroundings, is well illustrated by a comparison of the first chapter of his novel *Der Weg ins Freie* with the opening paragraphs of Theodor Fontane's novel *Irrungen Wirrungen* (1888). Fontane opens with a descriptive account of the house and garden where the early stages of the novel will be set. He gives the precise location at the intersection of Berlin's Kurfürstendamm with the Kurfürstenstraße, and launches into a detailed description of the house's peculiar architectural style, which renders it a curiosity in itself. The whole scene is presented from the perspective of an interested, but objective observer. In the opening paragraphs of *Der Weg ins Freie* Schnitzler's realism is essentially subjective and impressionistic. Georg von Wergenthin is alone in the apartment that he shares with his brother, and is preoccupied with thoughts of his father, who has recently died. As he paces about the room, he glances out of the window over the scene in the park below. But as yet the park is not identified, and only later are we told that this is the Stadtpark, and that beyond it is the Ring, and a view of the Stefansdom. From this information the Viennese reader will deduce that the Wergenthins inhabit one of the imposing mansions of the Heumarkt,[12] but Schnitzler makes no specific reference to this. Nor does he provide a detailed pictorial account of the park, but conveys only Georg's fleeting impressions, as he reflects on the events of his youth, and on his current social isolation. The park is viewed through Georg's consciousness, and his desultory contemplations of the scene reflect his aimless, lazy mood. Georg then leaves the house, and walks across the park, out on to the Ring and along to the Café Imperial. Briefly, then, Schnitzler captures a moment from the indolent life-style of the privileged upper classes. The reader familiar with the milieu will be able to visualize his walk, and may even react to his behaviour as being typically Viennese. But as Georg walks, Schnitzler's real preoccupation is with his state of mind, and little attention is paid to the world immediately beyond his consciousness. Schnitzler's Vienna is a forum for an exploration of its individual inhabitants, who together make up part of the social fabric of the city.

Examples of Schnitzler's referential realism abound in all his works, as he evokes, rather than describes the atmosphere of his native city. None more so than when his characters visit the institution that has become synonymous with the image of Viennese gaiety, the Prater entertainment park. Georg von Wergenthin strolls through the Prater with his friend Heinrich Bermann, and is immediately caught up in the mood of lighthearted frivolity generated by the music emanating from the beer-gardens and amusements. They encounter an acquaintance, Oskar Ehrenberg, accompanied by his 'süße Mädel' Amy, and the four go together on the giant wheel, which carries them majestically aloft, and then on to the switchback, on which they rush up and down in the darkness of the night. Eventually, in excellent humour, they dine in a chambre séparée in one of the restaurants of the inner city, where Oskar buys the champagne, Georg improvises on the piano, and Amy sprawls on the chaise-longue in contentment. A typically Viennese evening of pleasure and frivolity, but for Georg it ends in melancholy ruminations, as he becomes painfully aware of the futility and emptiness of their existence:

> Plötzlich hielt Georg im Spielen inne. Ein Gefühl von der Traumhaftigkeit und Zwecklosigkeit des Daseins kam über ihn, wie manchmal, wenn er Wein getrunken hatte.
> (ES I, 677)
>
> (Suddenly Georg stopped playing. He was overcome by a sense of the unreality and pointlessness of their existence, as often happened when he had drunk wine.)

The evening at the Prater thus takes on a symbolic significance, as Schnitzler evokes its familiar atmosphere to make a social point about those who enjoy its facilities. But not all who go to the Prater form part of the lively, pleasure-seeking throng. Therese Fabiani goes there alone, and walks past the gardens and the restaurants filled with music and gay crowds. The Prater provides an appropriate setting to emphasize her loneliness, and also her vulnerability, for it is there that she has her fateful first meeting with Kasimir Tobias, who is to become the father of her child.

Although Schnitzler's references to named localities in Vienna are always accurate in terms both of the physical and social geography of the city, there are obviously times when he does not feel the need to provide such precise detail. For example, the account of Therese's arrival in Vienna, and walk into the inner city, is sketchy and vague as to locality, as Schnitzler concentrates on her state of mind and problems. Moreover in this novel the speed of the narrative often allows no interruption for accounts of milieu, other than very general references to the living conditions of the various houses in which she is employed. Often Schnitzler's references to city life are not intended to evoke a specifically Viennese atmosphere. When Berta Garlan returns to the Vienna of her youth, the account of the noise and bustle of the station, the confusion of carriages and people on the crowded streets, the references to elegant gentlemen and ladies in pretty dresses, could refer to any city. Similarly when Georg von Wergenthin returns to Vienna in the early morning and takes a carriage to his apartment, he sees people going to work and shutters being hoisted, affording us a brief glimpse of a waking city. On the other hand the nocturnal wanderings of Fridolin in the story *Traumnovelle*, with its references to students on the Rathausplatz who clearly belong to a German Nationalist fraternity, to a prostitute in Buchfeldgasse, a café on the corner of Wickenburgstrasse, then the secret house in Ottakring, all make it clear to the reader that Schnitzler is referring specifically to the sordid night life of Vienna's sexual underworld.

Schnitzler's attention to the geographical and social actualities of contemporary Vienna helps to distinguish him from the majority of his Viennese contemporaries. This is not to maintain that he is the only Viennese writer at the turn of the century to set his works in a clearly definable social or historical context.[13] Hermann Bahr, in his social dramas, and Peter Altenberg, in some of his sketches of Viennese life, do offer something of a challenge to this view. Nevertheless Schnitzler's assured account of his immediate environment does indeed suggest that he shared little of the uncertainty of *fin-de-siècle* writers such as Hofmannsthal over the writer's ability to describe reality with precision, or to express personal feelings and opinions. The predilection for Schnitzler's plays of Otto Brahm, the director of the Deutsches Theater in Berlin and producer of Hauptmann and Ibsen, also sets Schnitzler apart from his fellow Viennese. At the same time it must be stressed that his highly selective brand of referential realism scarcely aligns him with the exponents of German Naturalism of the final two decades of the nineteenth century.[14] Just as his novels lack detailed description of settings, so too do his stage directions contrast with the lengthy accounts to be found at the beginnings of so many Naturalist dramas. Generally speaking his stage directions are concerned with characters' gestures and behaviour, and settings are indicated with brief references to the locality, often simply to denote the social level of the characters. Similarly, there is little use of dialect in his works, and the language of his characters generally maintains a reasonable level of sophistication and good taste. In this respect, then, his presentation of reality amounts to a form of refined realism. References in *Thérèse* to Franz's 'bad language' serve only to prove the point, for Schnitzler avoids giving details of the words which shock his mother. Schnitzler's plays are generally presented in standard German, with just a tinge of Viennese accent and local colour. To be sure, he is able to conjure up through realistic dialogue and speech mannerisms, a convincing party atmosphere as Fritz and Theodor entertain Christine and Mizzi in the opening act of *Liebelei*, and he also captures the tone of polite conversation in such plays as *Das weite Land* and *Der einsame Weg*. But his language is handled so delicately that the implications of characters' emotions are often expressed in subtle modifications of speech, or even through non-verbal communication. As Anatol and Gabriele meet on the dark streets of the inner city, and he tells her of his latest 'süße Mädel', they communicate through innuendo 'between the lines', rather than through an open confession of emotion:

> ANATOL Sehen Sie . . . in der kleinen Welt werd' ich nur geliebt; in der großen – nur verstanden – Sie wissen ja . . .
> GABRIELE Ich weiß gar nichts . . . und will weiter nichts wissen!
>
> (DW I, 44)
>
> ANATOL You see . . . in the little world I am simply loved; in the big world I am only understood – as you well know . . .
> GABRIELE I know nothing at all . . . and do not wish to know any more!

Despite her denial, Gabriele clearly understands the nature of Anatol's accusation, and her peremptory insistence that this conversation must cease, betrays all too clearly her own interest in Anatol, which, because of her cowardice in the face of the pressures of convention, she must suppress.

Schnitzler's frequent use of dashes and dotted lines is a feature of his dramatic style, and provides a visual indication of the importance which he attaches to the significant pauses in conversation, with their half-spoken messages and suggestions of undisclosed emotions. They are also illustrative of the tact and discretion with which he normally treats sexual feelings and behaviour. Often he stops short of explicit reference to sexual activity, as in the case of the relationship between Fritz and Christine in *Liebelei*. Even when it is obvious that a couple are sexually intimate, for example Georg von Wergenthin and Anna Rosner in *Der Weg ins Freie*, he avoids treating the physical aspect of the relationship. Despite his preoccupation with sexual themes, there is little attempt to shock the reader or audience with the kind of explicit details provided, for example, in the rape and masturbation scenes of Wedekind's *Frühlings Erwachen* (1891), though references in *Traumnovelle* to naked nuns, or to a prostitute who brazenly opens her bathrobe to disclose the voluptuous shape of her body, might possibly have this effect. In his *Frauengeschichten*, *Frau Berta Garlan*, *Frau Beate und ihr Sohn*, and *Therese* he does provide a more explicit insight into the sexual development and activity of the central characters. The reawakening in Frau Berta of sexual urges is described, for example, in candidly physical terms, as she experiences the sensation of her blood circulating throughout her body, reminding her of a particular phase of her youth. Later in the story he even gives a graphic description of the onset of her periodic pains to inform the reader that her encounter with Emil has not resulted in pregnancy:

> Plötzlich flimmerte es ihr vor den Augen, eine wohlbekannte plötzliche Schwäche kam über sie, ein Schwindel, der sich gleich wieder verlor. Zuerst bebte sie leise, dann aber atmete sie tief wie erlöst auf . . .
> (ES I, 312)

(Suddenly she felt in a daze, a sudden familiar feeling of weakness came over her, a dizziness which rapidly cleared. At first she gave a slight shudder, but then came a sigh of profound relief, as though she had been redeemed . . .)

But even this revelation of an intimate physical process is treated with great discretion, and is incorporated into the artistic texture of the story as a symbol of her escape from, and ultimate rejection of, her sexual adventure. For Berta's thoughts proceed as follows:

> denn mit dem Hereinbrechen dieser Ermattung fühlte sie ja auch, daß in diesem Augenblick nicht nur ihre Befürchtungen von früher, sondern der ganze Wahn dieser wirren Tage, die letzten Schauer einer verlangenden Weiblichkeit, alles, was sie für Liebe gehalten, in nichts zu verströmen begannen.
> (ES I, 312)

(for with the onset of this weariness, she also felt that at this moment not only her earlier fears, but all her muddled illusions of the past few days, those final yearnings of womanhood, everything that she had assumed represented feelings of love, began to ebb away into nothingness.)

In the later novel *Therese* he provides a lengthy catalogue of his heroine's sexual career, including references to sexual diseases and lesbianism, and her son Franz tells of summer nights where youths and girls sleep together in the Prater meadows. Schnitzler also gives a graphic account of Therese's search for a back-street abortion, describes the onset of labour pains when she gives birth to Franz, and later mentions that she does have an abortion when she becomes pregnant a second time, though he passes over this incident relatively quickly and discreetly. *Therese* is written in a more matter-of-fact style than the earlier works, and he clearly felt freer in the 1920s to give a more frank account of events.

Schnitzler's most notorious account of sexual activity is *Reigen*, which first had to be published privately, and was read secretly in Vienna as a piece of pornography.[15] Subsequently, the first performance in Berlin led to the famous court case of November 1921, in which the acting company was charged with displaying the basest and most objectionable of human impulses. Clearly the play refers repeatedly and explicitly to the sexual act. But the defence argued that just as the instances of sexual activity are indicated only by dotted lines in the text, so too did the lowering of the curtain in the theatre at the crucial moment add a note of discretion to the proceedings. The prosecution countered that this in itself stimulated the imagination, moreover that the music played while the curtain was down reproduced the rhythm of the sexual act. Impressionable members of the audience might thereby be incited to indulge in promiscuous behaviour. Eventually, however, Schnitzler was rehabilitated on the (rather vague) grounds of having artistic intentions, though the defence might have argued rather more effectively that the play presents the banalities of the sexual act and the illusory, and ultimately unsatisfactory, nature of the pleasure it affords.[16]

Occasionally Schnitzler strays from his own brand of refined realism to touch on uglier aspects of reality. At the close of the short story *Das neue Lied*, the blind heroine Marie plunges to her death, and the gushing of blood from her head and the twitching of her lips and nostrils in her dying moments are reported in naturalistic detail. Even more grotesque is the detailed description in *Traumnovelle* of the body of the aristocratic lady laid out in the mortuary, apparently already in an early state of decomposition:

Er sah einen gelblichen, faltigen Hals, er sah zwei kleine und doch etwas schlaff gewordene Mädchenbrüste, zwischen denen, als wäre das Werk der Verwesung schon vorgebildet, das Brustbein mit grausamer Deutlichkeit sich unter der bleichen Haut abzeichnete, er sah die Rundung des mattbraunen Unterleibs, er sah, wie von einem dunklen, nun geheimnis- und sinnlos gewordenen Schatten aus wohlgeformte Schenkel sich gleichgültig öffneten, sah die leise auswärts gedrehten Kniewölbungen, die scharfen Kanten der Schienbeine und die schlanken Füße mit den einwärts gekrümmten Zehen.

(ES II, 500)

(He saw a yellowish, wrinkled neck, he saw two breasts, small, like those of a young girl, but no longer firm, between which the breastbone could be seen outlined with dreadful clarity under the pale skin, as though the process of decomposition were already advanced. He saw the curve of the dullish brown lower part of the body, he saw the shapely thighs, open with apparent indifference from a dark shadow, now meaningless and no longer mysterious; he saw the curve of the knees, turned slightly outwards, the sharp edges of the shin-bones and the slim feet with toes bent inwards.)

In these instances Schnitzler is clearly intent on conveying to the reader the horrified reactions of the two onlookers, guilt in the case of Karl, disgust and disillusionment in the case of Fridolin.[17] It has frequently been noted that the prevalence of death, illness and decay is an important factor in Schnitzler's works, his morbid fascination representing perhaps his heightened sense of death in a decadent and dying society.[18] But the physical details he discloses in these graphic descriptions go somewhat beyond his normal practice.

Despite these excursions into a more blatantly realistic mode, it is in his psychological case studies that Schnitzler may be seen as embodying most faithfully the spirit of Naturalism. Just as the principles of Naturalism were based on scientific observations of human behaviour, so too did Schnitzler draw on his professional knowledge and experience as a doctor for his explorations of individual psychology. Schnitzler's use of a particular milieu as a setting for his characters' mental states also aligns him closely with the Naturalists, but here the similarity ends. For although many of his characters may be seen as typical representatives of their environment, Schnitzler does not place undue emphasis on either hereditary or environmental influences upon the individual consciousness. Only in Franz Fabiani (*Therese*) does he deliberately explore the case of an individual, whose behaviour and character are moulded and determined by his environment and upbringing. In his depiction of characters who are unmistakably the product of their milieu, Schnitzler focuses on social values and social norms. Thus he comes across as the social commentator and social critic rather than the realist *per se*.[19]

It has long been a debatable point as to whether Schnitzler is consciously offering in his works a direct criticism of aspects of his own society. His lack of positive interest in the major social and political movements of his day scarcely cast him in the role of a social revolutionary, and students of his works have been warned not to mistake his 'diagnostic observations' for 'conventional social criticism'.[20] But although Schnitzler is never didactic in the sense of advocating positive solutions to social ills, he has nevertheless been widely acknowledged as a social analyst, who perceived the shortcomings of his fellows as expressions of the values, attitudes and habits of a clearly defined social world.

It is true that particularly in his prose works, Schnitzler tends to depict the scene without overt thematic discussion, and social issues are generally embedded within the texture of individual relationships. The tendency to present events through the individual consciousness of a central character, rather than from the perspective of a moralizing narrator figure, also implies an absence of explicit social comment. In a story such as *Frau Beate und ihr Sohn*, for example, the readers are left to draw their own conclusions with regard to social implications from the evidence that is available in the text. Schnitzler's sympathetic presentation of characters who are the victims of social norms and values also carries with it the implication of social criticism on his part. Occasionally characters in his prose works perceive such implications themselves, and comment in effect from 'within' their own stories. At the end of *Frau Berta Garlan* the heroine gives explicit expression to her awareness of a social injustice that has become apparent to the reader throughout her relationship with Lindbach. In *Leutnant Gustl* Schnitzler's technique is far more subtle, as Gustl is himself scarcely conscious of the implications of some of the thoughts on the code of honour, that occur to him during the course of his mental ramblings. In *Der Weg ins Freie* Schnitzler employs a number of characters who comment on events from 'outside', ranging from the various short, cutting remarks of Therese Golowski, to the objective analysis of Austrian half-heartedness by the Englishman Skelton. The prevalence of such comments, and the frequent discussions that take place in this novel, produce the effect of an ongoing commentary on events.

It is in his plays, however, that Schnitzler makes most striking use of the *raisonneur* type of character. In *Das Vermächtnis* Emma Winter castigates Losatti for his hypocrisy and snobbery, and in *Das weite Land* Doctor Mauer criticizes the frivolity and superficiality inherent in the social and sexual relationships that he sees around him. The function of these enlightened characters is to cast others in an unfavourable light. Some, such as Fedor Denner in *Das Märchen*, are themselves caught up in events, and become the unwitting objects of their own criticism. Occasionally there is a genuine and active vehicle of social protest, such as Paul Rönning of *Freiwild*, who eventually pays the ultimate price for his opposition to the institution of the duel. Even more effective are those brief, but dramatic expressions of outrage, that occur at the conclusion of several of his plays. In the final moments of *Das Märchen* Fanny Theren rounds on Denner for his vanity and social cowardice, and departs for St Petersburg in a dramatic rejection of the society whose values he has now come to embody. Similarly, in *Liebelei*, Christine's bitter attack on Theodor for his assumptions of the insignificance of her role in Fritz's life and of the shallowness of her feelings for him, represents a fierce castigation of prevailing social structures and prejudices:

THEODOR Ich hab' das nicht geahnt . . .
CHRISTINE Was nicht geahnt? – Daß ich ihn *geliebt* habe? – Führen Sie mich zu seinem Grab!
THEODOR Christine . . . später . . . morgen . . . bis Sie ruhiger geworden sind –
CHRISTINE Morgen? – Wenn ich ruhiger sein werde?! – Und in einem Monat ganz getröstet, wie? – Und in einem halben Jahr kann ich wieder lachen, was –? *Auflachend* Und wann kommt denn der nächste Liebhaber?

(DW I, 263)

(THEODOR I didn't realize . . .
CHRISTINE Didn't realize what? – That I *loved* him? – Lead me to his grave!

THEODOR Christine . . . later . . . tomorrow . . . by then you'll be less upset –
CHRISTINE Tomorrow? – When I'm less upset?! – And in a month I'll have got over it altogether, won't I? – And in six months time I shall laugh again, right –? *Laughing* And when will the next lover come along?)

Less dramatic, but no less destructive, is Genia Hofreiter's response to her husband when he reveals to her that he has just shot Otto Aigner in an 'honourable' duel. She accuses him of inhuman vanity, of villainy even, and though her words, like those of Christine, are aimed at a specific individual, they carry with them the implication of an attack upon a social code and ethic.

In assessing Schnitzler's achievement as a social writer, it is important to bear in mind that his is essentially a personal view of those segments of Viennese society that he knew best. Indeed, from numerous references in his autobiography and diaries, it is apparent that a large number of his characters are based on friends and acquaintances, several of whom objected to the transparency of the links between fiction and reality! The details of Schnitzler's life that have emerged through the publication of autobiographical material, also suggest that he drew much of his material for his literary works from his own experiences. In his student days he led a life similar to that described by Fritz to Christine in *Liebelei*, a seemingly empty existence, consisting largely of social visits, afternoons spent idly reading and playing cards in coffee-houses, piano-playing at home, 'occasional' attendance of lectures. His autobiography and the first volume of his diaries, covering the years 1879–92, give a full account of a bohemian life-style that he had to conceal from the disapproving eyes of his strait-laced father. There are references to late-night dances, coffee-houses such as the Café Central, the Café Ruthmayr, the Café Tuchlauben, the Arkadencafé and countless more. There are evenings spent in wine cellars and wine bars, taverns and beer-gardens; he describes boisterous excursions to the races at the Freudenau, to the Prater, to the Casino Zögernitz in Döbling; he dances to gypsy music in Heiligenstadt, dines in the restaurant on the Kahlenberg, strolls through the Vienna woods to Klosterneuburg. But just as Fritz acknowledges the triviality and futility of his life, so too was Schnitzler frequently aware of the shortcomings of this aimless and profligate 'Wiener Leben'. Clearly he lived the 'Viennese life' to the full, but was frequently depressed at his lack of real achievement through the perpetual pursuit of superficial pleasures.[21]

But Schnitzler's activities were not confined to these mindless and philistine pursuits. His cultural interests meant a continual round of visits to theatres, concerts, operas and art galleries. As he became absorbed into the Jung Wien circle in the 1890s, references to discussions and readings in the Café Griensteidl began to predominate over his accounts of the earlier, more superficial activities. When, by the turn of the century, he had established his reputation in his own right, he began to form his own group of acquaintances in the cultural and intellectual circles of the city. Of the Griensteidl poets, Hofmannsthal, Salten and Beer-Hofmann remained as his closest friends. To these he added the young novelist Jakob Wassermann, the author and publisher Felix Speidel, the writer Raoul Auernheimer, the philosopher Arthur Kaufmann, and the leading light of the new generation, Stefan Zweig. In theatrical circles he was closely acquainted with the producer Otto Brahm, the actor Josef Kainz, the secretary of the Burgtheater Richard Rosenbaum. Very musical himself, he was on friendly terms with a number of conductors and composers, including Bruno Walter and Clemens von Franckenstein, he met Brahms, Bruckner, Richard Strauß and Mahler, and was in later life acquainted with Mahler's widow Alma.

As he grew older and more financially secure Schnitzler became ever more absorbed into the professional and cultured bourgeoisie of the inner city, though his relationship with his own class remained an ambivalent one. In his youth he had rebelled at his parents' strictness, at the social conventions that stifled his relationship with Franziska Reich, at his father's snobbishness over his sister's marriage to a young upstart Jewish doctor. Schnitzler's father had viewed his son's literary aspirations with increasing scepticism and hostility, and even after he had achieved fame and success, members of his immediate family maintained a sceptical view of his activities. His brother Julius, who had married into a good bourgeois family and kept up the Schnitzler family tradition as a highly successful surgeon, regarded him as a wastrel, and Marcus Hajek, the doctor who had married his sister Gisela, thought his works indiscreet.[22] Despite his hostility to his bourgeois upbringing, however, Schnitzler was the first to acknowledge that many of his attitudes were 'bourgeois'. As a student he was vain and snobbish, he habitually lunched in the Riedhof, a high-class restaurant near the University, he enjoyed cutting a dash as a military cadet, and in his dealings with girls of the *Kleinbürgertum* remained firmly anchored in the prejudices of his class.[23] With his marriage in 1903 to Olga Gussmann, an aspiring actress and singer, Schnitzler gave his life-style some semblance of orderliness. Though not yet wealthy, and ever concerned about his finances, he lived comfortably, if not luxuriously. He had servants, and from 1909 a secretary, though he could not initially afford expensive holidays abroad, and he was never able to purchase a motor car. When in 1910 he bought his new house in the Sternwartestrasse, he did so with the help of a loan from his brother. But he was now moving in relatively exalted circles, both financially and socially. The names of senior civil servants, merchants and bankers, eminent academics and medical consultants, even barons and baronesses, all feature in abundance in the diaries of 1909–19, the years of his prosperity and fame. Bohemian coffee-houses, taverns and wine bars are all behind him, as he and Olga now dine out at the Hotel Savoy, or the restaurant in the Türkenschanzpark, they take tea in the Hotel Imperial and move on for the evening to the Hotel Sacher. A car is hired to take them to Grinzing.[24]

Schnitzler's very active social life and wide circle of acquaintances within his particular sphere, his profound interest in human nature and powers of observation of his fellows, have all contributed to provide in his literary works a uniquely extensive, if by no means exhaustive critique of the social life of his city. Primarily he exposes the artificial rigidity of the class divisions. He attacks a harsh code of sexual behaviour, which makes such unnatural demands on individuals, resulting in frustration, hypocrisy and deception. In particular he perceives women as the victimized members of his culture, and exposes the prejudices that create artificial barriers of respectability between different social groups. Within the circles of the bourgeoisie he probes the veneer of bourgeois respectability, and the harmony of family life is seen to be no more than a sham. His use of gesture and interior monologue to expose the façade of social intercourse also forms an integral part of his social criticism. At times he gives an impression of frivolity, as his characters indulge in superficial and short-lived emotional attachments; at others he exposes the inhuman and unnatural brutality of the still persistent code of honour. Some of his works reflect the growing anti-Semitism, others reveal the half-heartedness and lack of genuine principle pervading Austrian political life. Schnitzler's analysis of the social structures and mores of his day, reveals a society whose codes of conduct contribute to a social façade that is inimical to the natural and healthy development of the individual, and incompatible with openness, sincerity and genuineness in public life.

NOTES

1 THE SETTING

1. Stefan Zweig, *Die Welt von Gestern. Erinnerungen eines Europäers* (Fischer, Berlin, 1962), p. 24.
2. Arthur J. May, *The Habsburg Monarchy 1867–1914* (Harvard U.P., Cambridge, Mass., 1965), pp. 305–6.
3. See Edward Crankshaw, *The Fall of the House of Habsburg* (Longman, London, 1963), pp. 318–19; May, pp. 308–9.
4. Frank Field, *The Last Days of Mankind. Karl Kraus and his Vienna* (Macmillan, London, 1967), pp. 32–41; Edward Timms, *Karl Kraus, Apocalyptic Satirist* (Yale U.P., New Haven, 1986), pp. 10–18.
5. A. J. P. Taylor, *The Habsburg Monarchy 1809–1918. A History of the Austrian Empire and Austro–Hungary* (Hamish Hamilton, London, 1948), p. 199.
6. For an account of his personality and life-style, see May, pp. 144–50.
7. A. Janik and S. Toulmin, *Wittgenstein's Vienna* (Weidenfeld and Nicolson, London, 1973), p. 40.
8. Crankshaw, p. 347. Crankshaw gives a more sympathetic account of Franz Josef's personality and problems, and of his relationship with wife and son.
9. May, p. 158.
10. For an account of the life of the nobility, see May, pp. 156–64; see also Ilsa Barea, *Vienna. Legend and Reality* (Secker and Warburg, London, 1966), p. 323.
11. See William M. Johnston, *The Austrian Mind. An Intellectual and Social History 1848–1938* (University of California Press, Berkeley, 1972), pp. 53–4.
12. Zweig, pp. 93–4.
13. May, pp. 174–5.
14. Zweig, pp. 13–15.
15. Zweig, pp. 31–2.
16. For a full account of the Ring and of its development, see Carl E. Schorske, *Fin de Siècle Vienna. Politics and Culture* (Weidenfeld and Nicolson, London, 1980), pp. 24–115.
17. Schorske, pp. 50-1.

NOTES

18. Barea, p. 244.
19. Edward Crankshaw, *Vienna. The Image of a Culture in Decline* (Macmillan, London, 1938), p. 226.
20. Timms, pp. 21–2.
21. Hilde Spiel, *Vienna's Golden Autumn* (Weidenfeld and Nicolson, London, 1987), p. 36.
22. May, p. 177; Janik and Toulmin, p. 59.
23. Zweig, pp. 21–2.
24. Janik and Toulmin, p. 53.
25. Zweig, pp. 13–14.
26. Crankshaw, *The Fall of the House of Habsburg*, pp. 302–3; the decline of Austrian liberalism and its psychological repercussions are analysed by Schorske, pp. 5–10.
27. Zweig, pp. 65–6.
28. Janik and Toulmin, p. 53.
29. Timms, pp. 16–17.
30. May, p. 312.
31. Janik and Toulmin, p. 58.
32. For an account of the disadvantages suffered by the Jews, see May, pp. 178–81.
33. Field, p. 62.
34. This is based on Zweig's account, pp. 33–6.
35. Frederic Morton, *A Nervous Splendour. Vienna 1888–1889* (Weidenfeld and Nicolson, London, 1980), p. 57.
36. May, p. 307.
37. Timms, p. 15.
38. Crankshaw, *The Fall of the House of Habsburg*, p. 312.
39. See Barea, pp. 286–9.
40. See Spiel, p. 63.
41. Spiel, p. 162.
42. Timms, p. 6.
43. Spiel, p. 191.
44. Crankshaw, *The Fall of the House of Habsburg*, p. 317.
45. Zweig, p. 69.

2 THE LITERARY IMAGE

1. Claudio Magris, *Der habsburgische Mythos in der österreichischen Literatur* (Müller, Salzburg, 1966), p. 9.
2. See Jens Malter Fischer, *Fin de Siècle. Kommentar zu einer Epoche* (Winkler, Munich, 1978), pp. 15–20.
3. Hermann Bahr, *Zur Ueberwindung des Naturalismus. Theoretische Schriften 1887–1904* (Kohlhammer, Stuttgart, 1968), pp. 35-102.
4. Bahr, pp. 190–1.
5. Magris, p. 173.

NOTES

6. Magris, p. 191.
7. Reinhard Urbach, 'Hermann Bahrs Wien', *Literatur und Kritik* 199/200 (1985), pp. 404–8.
8. Donald G. Daviau, *Hermann Bahr* (Twayne Publishers, Boston, 1985), p. 14.
9. Bahr, pp. 37–8.
10. Daviau, pp. 114–15.
11. Timms, *Karl Kraus*, p. 36.
12. Timms, p. 58.
13. Kraus's appreciation of Altenberg is expressed in an essay 'Peter Altenberg' (1909), in Karl Kraus, *Die Chinesische Mauer* (Langen and Müller, Munich, 1964), pp. 188–9 (Vol. 12 of Karl Kraus, *Werke*, ed. Heinrich Fischer).
14. Quoted in Fischer, p. 159.
15. Andrew Barker, 'Die weiseste Oekonomie bei tiefster Fülle – Peter Altenberg's *Wie ich es sehe*' in B.O. Murdoch and M.G. Ward (eds), *Studies in Nineteenth Century Austrian Literature* (Scottish Papers in Germanic Studies, Glasgow, 1983), p. 83.
16. Magris, pp. 218–19.
17. Mary Gilbert (ed.), Hugo von Hofmannsthal, *Der Tor und der Tod* (Blackwell, Oxford, 1942), pp. xxviii–xxx.
18. C.E. Williams, *The Broken Eagle. The Politics of Austrian Literature from Empire to Anschluß* (Elek, London, 1974), p. 22.
19. Hugo von Hofmannsthal, *Selected Essays* (Blackwell, Oxford, 1955) pp. 92–3.
20. W.E. Yates (ed.), Hugo von Hofmannsthal, *Der Schwierige* (Cambridge, Cambridge University Press, 1966), pp. 26–7.
21. Janik and Toulmin, *Wittgenstein's Vienna*, p. 36.
22. Magris, p. 285.
23. Williams, p. 176.
24. See A.F. Bance (ed.), Joseph Roth, *Die Kapuzinergruft* (Harrap, London, 1972), pp. 145, 149–50.
25. Williams, p. 130.

3 THE FREUDIAN CONNECTION

1. As early as December 22, 1882 he writes in his diary that his work in the military hospital is abhorrent to him, Arthur Schnitzler, *Tagebuch 1879–1892* (Oesterreichische Akademie der Wissenschaften, Vienna, 1987), p. 144. There are many such negative comments during the ensuing years. His growing disaffection from his medical studies is recorded in his autobiography, Arthur Schnitzler, *Jugend in Wien. Eine Autobiographie* (Molden, Vienna, 1968), pp. 227ff.
2. Theodor Reik, *Arthur Schnitzler als Psycholog* (Bruns, Minden, 1913).
3. R.O. Weiss, 'The Psychoses in the works of Arthur Schnitzler', *Germanic Review* 41 (1969), pp. 394–5.
4. For a full analysis of the 'cure', see P. Russell, 'Schnitzler's *Blumen*. The Treatment of a Neurosis', *Forum for Modern Language Studies* 13 (1977), pp. 289–302.
5. Weiss, pp. 394–5.

NOTES

6. Letter to Hofmannsthal, December 10, 1903. Hugo von Hofmannsthal, Arthur Schnitzler, *Briefwechsel* (Fischer, Frankfurt, 1964), p. 179.
7. Freud's letters to Schnitzler were first quoted by V.A. Oswald and V. Pinter-Mindess, 'Schnitzler's *Fräulein Else* and the Psychoanalytic Theory of Neurosis', *Germanic Review* 26 (1951), pp. 279–80. See also W. Nehring, 'Schnitzler, Freud's alter Ego?', *Modern Austrian Literature* 10 (1977), p. 180.
8. Quoted by F.J. Beharriell, 'Freud's Double: Arthur Schnitzler', *Journal of the American Psychoanalytic Association* 10 (1962), p. 723.
9. Theodor Reik also recognizes that there is a type of mourning following the death of a spouse or beloved which, because of its extreme form, gives the impression of a psychological disorder, Reik, p. 43.
10. First discussed by Reik, pp. 51–2, and followed by various commentators, e.g. Nehring, p. 183; Beharriell, pp. 724–5.
11. F.J. Beharriell, 'Schnitzler's Anticipation of Freud's Dream Theory', *Monatshefte* 45 (1953), pp. 81–9; Reik, pp. 226ff., analyses Berta Garlan's 'wish-dream' (see Chapter 4 of the present study, p. 74).
12. Johnston writes that Meynert typified the 'therapeutic nihilism' of the time, *The Austrian Mind*, pp. 231–2.
13. Nehring, pp. 187–8; Johnston, pp. 242–3.
14. Russell, p. 291.
15. Weiss, pp. 381–2.
16. William H. Rey, *Arthur Schnitzler. Die späte Prosa als Gipfel seines Schaffens* (Schmidt, Berlin, 1968), p. 175.
17. Rey, p. 164. Rey's study is particularly enlightening in highlighting the social implications of Robert's madness.
18. Oswald and Pinter-Mindess, pp. 281–2.
19. R. Bareikis, '*Fräulein Else*. A Freudian Novelle?', *Literature and Psychology* 19 (1969), p. 27.
20. Rey, p. 79. Rey's study of *Fräulein Else* draws attention in particular to the social implications of the story.
21. Michaela L. Perlmann, *Arthur Schnitzler* (Metzler, Stuttgart, 1987), pp. 144–6.
22. Reik, pp. 155–8.
23. S. Bolkosky, 'Arthur Schnitzler and the Fate of the Mothers in Vienna', *Psychoanalytic Review* 73 (1986), p. 8.
24. Hilde Spiel, 'Im Abgrund der Triebwelt oder kein Zugang zum Fest. Zu Schnitzlers *Traumnovelle*' in G. Farese (ed.), *Arthur Schnitzler und seine Zeit* (Lang, Berne, 1985), pp. 164–9.
25. M.H. Sherman, 'Reik, Schnitzler, Freud and *The Murderer*. The Limits of Insight in Psychoanalysis', *Modern Austrian Literature* 10 (1977), p. 199.
26. Nehring, p. 186–7; see also M.W. Swales, *Arthur Schnitzler. A Critical Study* (Clarendon, Oxford, 1971), p. 125.
27. Letter to Hofmannsthal, November 26, 1895, Hofmannsthal, Schnitzler, *Briefwechsel*, pp. 63–4; see also Dorit Cohn, 'Als Traum erzählt. The Case for a Freudian Reading of Hofmannsthal's *Märchen der 672. Nacht*', *Deutsche Vierteljahrschrift* 54 (1980), pp. 284–305.
28. Oswald and Pinter-Mindess, pp. 287–8, end their article with the following observation: '*Fräulein Else* is also a story about a family, about a society, and

even about a civilization. It is, by implication, a scathing denunciation of the values by which so many men have lived, and not only in Vienna!'
29. Perlmann, pp. 136–7.
30. Views summarized by Freud in his essay 'Civilized Sexual Morality and Modern Nervous Illness' (1908) in S. Freud, *Collected Works*, Vol. 9 (Hogarth Press, London, 1959ff.), pp. 181–204.
31. See Janik and Toulmin, *Wittgenstein's Vienna*, pp. 46–7; Morton, *A Nervous Splendour*, p. 69, discusses the high incidence of suicide in Vienna; Johnston, pp. 238–40, discusses the affinities between instances of neurotic illness and the Viennese milieu.

4 THE SEXUAL CONTEXT

1. Scenes from the *Anatol* cycle were broadcast on BBC Radio during the Christmas period 1987; *Liebelei* had a successful run as 'Dalliance' in London's West End during the previous summer; productions of *Reigen* took place in Manchester and London after its release for public performance in 1982, when it was also screened on BBC Television.
2. Heinz Politzer, 'Arthur Schnitzler. The Poetry of Psychology', *Modern Language Notes* 78 (1963), p. 358.
3. Diary entry of July 31, 1880, *Tagebuch 1879–1892*, p. 77; in his account of his friendship with Olga Waissnix in his autobiography, he refers to her husband's desperate fears of social gossip, *Jugend in Wien*, pp. 252–3.
4. Zweig, *Die Welt von Gestern*, p. 74.
5. In his diary the young Schnitzler complains bitterly at the convention that did not permit him even to kiss Franziska Reich in her parents' presence, November 19, 1880, *Tagebuch 1879–1892*, p. 89.
6. Taken from Stefan Zweig's account of prostitution in Vienna, *Die Welt von Gestern*, pp. 84–8.
7. Renate Wagner, *Arthur Schnitzler. Eine Biographie* (Molden, Vienna, 1981), p. 79.
8. Rolf-Peter Janz, Klaus Laermann, *Arthur Schnitzler. Zur Diagnose des Wiener Bürgertums im Fin de Siècle* (Metzler, Stuttgart, 1977), p. 37.
9. A fashionable restaurant near the city hospital, where Schnitzler often took lunch or dinner in his younger days.
10. See Johanna Bossinade, 'Wenn es aber . . . bei mir anders wäre. Die Frage der Geschlechterbeziehung in Arthur Schnitzlers *Reigen*', in G. Kluge (ed.), *Aufsätze zur Literatur und Kunst der Jahrhundertwende* (Rodolphi, Amsterdam, 1984), pp. 273–328.
11. E.g. Lou Andreas Salomé, letter to Schnitzler, May 15, 1894, quoted by Barbara Gutt, *Emanzipation bei Arthur Schnitzler* (Spiess, Berlin, 1978), p. 113; in his letter to Schnitzler of August 21, 1896 Hugo von Hofmannsthal comments on Schnitzler's 'oft besprochene Ueberschätzung der weiblichen Individualitäten', Hofmannsthal, Schnitzler, *Briefwechsel*, p. 73.
12. A. Doppler, 'Der Wandel der Darstellungsperspektive in den Dichtungen Arthur Schnitzlers. Mann und Frau als sozialpsychologisches Problem', in Farese (ed.), *Arthur Schnitzler und seine Zeit*, p. 46.

NOTES

13. See Gutt, pp. 166, 178–81; Renate Möhrmann, 'Schnitzlers Frauen und Mädchen. Zwischen Sachlichkeit und Sentiment', in Farese (ed.), *Arthur Schnitzler und seine Zeit*, p. 97.
14. A. Fuchs, *Geistige Strömungen in Oesterreich 1867–1918* (Löcker, Vienna, 1978), pp. 143–5.
15. Olive Banks, *Faces of Feminism* (Robertson, Oxford, 1981), p. 68.
16. See R.J. Evans, *The Feminist Movement in Germany 1894–1933* (Sage Publications, London, 1976), pp. 116ff; Peter Labanyi, 'Die Gefahr des Körpers. A Reading of Otto Weininger's *Geschlecht und Charakter*', in G.J. Carr and E. Sagarra (eds), *Fin de Siècle Vienna* (Trinity College Dublin, 1985), p. 161.
17. R. Pascal, *From Naturalism to Expressionism. German Literature and Society 1880–1918* (Weidenfeld and Nicolson, London, 1973), p. 157.
18. See Timms's account of Kraus's critique of sexual hypocrisy in Vienna, Timms, *Karl Kraus*, pp. 63–93.
19. Letter to Georg Brandes, April 25, 1901, Georg Brandes, Arthur Schnitzler, *Briefwechsel* (Francke, Berne, 1956), pp. 83–4.
20. Wagner, p. 77.
21. Diary entry, May 26, 1909, *Tagebuch 1909–1912* (Oesterreichische Akademie der Wissenschaften, Vienna, 1981), p. 69.
22. Arthur Schnitzler, *Gesammelte Werke. Aphorismen und Betrachtungen* (Fischer, Frankfurt, 1967), p. 318.
23. Gutt, pp. 166–7.
24. Gutt, p. 106; but see Rey's reservations, William H. Rey, 'Schnitzlers Erzählung *Casanovas Heimfahrt*. Eine Strukturanalyse', in E. Schwarz et al. (eds), *Festschrift für Bernhard Blume* (Vandenhoeck and Ruprecht, Göttingen, 1967), p. 200.
25. Gutt, p. 95; Anton Pelinka, 'Die Struktur und die Probleme der Gesellschaft zur Zeit Arthur Schnitzlers', *Literatur und Kritik* 163/4 (1982), p. 62.
26. Janz, Laermann, p. 68.
27. Janz, Laermann, p. 60.
28. Ilse H. Reis, 'Eine emanzipierte Frau im Fin de Siècle. Zu Schnitzlers Fragment *Ritterlichkeit*', *Literatur und Kritik* 119/20 (1977), p. 542.
29. Gutt, p. 85.
30. Rey, *Arthur Schnitzler*, pp. 143–8.
31. *Aphorismem und Betrachtungen*, p. 333.
32. Gutt, p. 79; Doppler, p. 51; but Beverley Driver points out that it is Berta herself who draws her own moral lesson at the close of the story, and not Schnitzler's narrator, B.R. Driver, 'Arthur Schnitzler's *Frau Berta Garlan*. A Study in Form', *Germanic Review* 46 (1971), p. 290.
33. See Bossinade's analysis of the husband-wife scene, Bossinade, pp. 302–4.
34. Renate Möhrmann, 'Impressionistische Einsamkeit bei Schnitzler. Dargestellt an seinem Roman *Der Weg ins Freie*', *Wirkendes Wort* 23 (1973), p. 396; C.E.J. Brinson, 'Searching for Happiness. Towards an Interpretation of Arthur Schnitzler's *Doktor Gräsler, Badearzt*', *Modern Austrian Literature* 16 (1983), p. 58; Waltraud Gölter, 'Weg ins Freie oder Flucht in die Finsternis – Ambivalenz bei Arthur Schnitzler', in Hartmut Scheible (ed.), *Arthur Schnitzler in neuer Sicht* (Fink, Munich, 1982), pp. 257, 265.

NOTES

35. Dieter Sevin, 'Arthur Schnitzlers Gestalt des erotischen Abenteurers', *University of Dayton Review* 10 (1973), pp. 61–2.
36. Martin Swales, 'Nürnberger's Novel. A Study of Arthur Schnitzler's *Der Weg ins Freie*', *Modern Language Review* 70 (1975), pp. 571–3.
37. Renate Wagner, *Frauen um Schnitzler* (Jugend und Volk, Vienna, 1980), p. 115.
38. Andrew Török suggests that the connections between Georg and Schnitzler are only superficial, A. Török, 'Arthur Schnitzlers *Der Weg ins Freie*. Versuch einer Neuinterpretation', *Monatshefte* 64 (1972), p. 373; Schnitzler himself indicated that the original was in fact the conductor Clemens Franckenstein, Wagner, *Arthur Schnitzler*, p. 186.
39. Manes Sperber, 'Arthur Schnitzler. Epilogische Bemerkungen zu seinem 50ten Todestage', *Literatur und Kritik* 163/4 (1982), p. 19.
40. *Jugend in Wien*, pp. 175–6.
41. *Jugend in Wien*, p. 309.
42. *Jugend in Wien*, pp. 261, 304.
43. For example, *Jugend in Wien*, p. 263.
44. The account is given in Wagner, *Frauen um Schnitzler*, pp. 19–20.
45. Gerlinde Weiß (Review), Adele Sandrock, Arthur Schnitzler, *Geschichte einer Liebe in Briefen, Bildern und Dokumenten* (Fischer Taschenbücher, Frankfurt, 1983), in *Germanistik* 27 (1986), pp. 696–7.
46. See the diary entry for May 19, 1903, quoted by Gutt, p. 159.
47. Hedy Kempny, Arthur Schnitzler, *Das Mädchen mit den dreizehn Seelen. Briefe und Tagebücher* (Rowohlt, Hamburg, 1984). See particularly pp. 107, 123, 137, 167.
48. Michaela Perlmann writes: 'Gesellschaftskritik ist bei Schnitzler Kritik an der eigenen Schicht und damit auch Selbstkritik', Perlmann, p. 61.
49. K.H. Kramberg (ed.), *Josefine Mutzenbacher. Die Lebensgeschichte einer wienerischen Dirne, von ihr selbst erzählt* (Rowohlt, Hamburg, 1978), pp. 5–6. In a diary entry of April 10, 1911, Schnitzler reports that he too was at one stage presumed to be the author, *Tagebuch 1909–1912*, p. 233.
50. Frequent diary references from 1887 to 1892 record in brackets after the daily account the number of his successful sexual performances for the day with Jeanette Heger or Marie Glümer. At one point, on August 10, 1890, he is clearly alarmed at his own 'impertinente Sinnlichkeit', *Tagebuch 1879–1892*, p. 301.
51. Timms, p. 90.
52. See Labanyi, op. cit.
53. Merryn Williams, *Women in the English Novel 1800–1900* (Macmillan, London, 1984), p. 41.
54. A.B. Willeke, 'Wedekind and the *Frauenfrage*', *Monatshefte* 72 (1980), p. 28.
55. Fischer, *Fin de Siècle*, pp. 53-65.
56. Theodor W. Adorno, *Minima Moralia. Reflexionen aus dem beschädigten Leben* (Berlin, 1951), p. 42, writes: 'Die süßen Mädel hat es in angelsächsischen und anderen Ländern technischer Zivilisation eh nicht gegeben', quoted by Gutt, p. 151.
57. *Jugend in Wien*, pp. 292, 303–4.
58. *Jugend in Wien*, pp. 287–8; Schnitzler also notes that the year 1883 began

with a strict moral lecture from his father, January 2, 1883, *Tagebuch 1879–1892*, p. 146.
59. Morton, *A Nervous Splendour*, p. 150.

5 THE BOURGEOISIE

1. Schnitzler experienced the same feelings in his relationship with the actress Marie Glümer, Wagner, *Arthur Schnitzler*, pp. 55–6. He expressed his own misgivings at the prospect of meeting her former lover socially in his letter to her of November 18, 1890, Arthur Schnitzler, *Briefe 1875–1912* (Fischer, Frankfurt, 1981).
2. B. Coghlan, 'The Turn of the Century' in J.M. Ritchie (ed.), *Periods in German Literature*, Vol. 1 (Wolff, London, 1966), p. 68.
3. For example, Hartmut Scheible writes: 'Da Fichtner, der gealterte impressionistische Künstler, kläglich versagt, wird die Aufwertung der bürgerlichen Lebensform Wegrats . . . unausweichbar', Hartmut Scheible, *Arthur Schnitzler in Selbstzeugnissen und Bilddokumenten* (Rowohlt, Hamburg, 1976), p. 86.
4. Details are given in Chapter 4 of the present study, p. 79.
5. A full treatment of Johanna's relationship with Sala and the motivation for her suicide are not relevant to the present study, but I have discussed both of these aspects of the play elsewhere, B. Thompson, 'The End of the Lonely Road. A Study of Schnitzler's *Der einsame Weg*', in B.O. Murdoch and M.G. Ward (eds), *Studies in Nineteenth Century Austrian Literature*, Scottish Papers in Germanic Studies, Vol. 3 (Glasgow, 1983), pp. 102–18.
6. It has, for example, even been compared in passing to the award of the child Michel to the surrogate mother Grusche in Brecht's *Der kaukasische Kreidekreis*, Ernst L. Offermanns, *Arthur Schnitzler. Das Komödienwerk als Kritik des Impressionismus* (Fink, Munich, 1973), p. 208 (note 6); Reinhard Urbach, *Arthur Schnitzler* (Friedrich, Hanover, 1968), p. 82.
7. See Note 3 above.
8. See, for example, *Jugend in Wien*, p. 44.
9. See Chapter 1 of the present study, p. 5; the treatment of the duel in Schnitzler's works is discussed in Chapter 7, pp. 133–44.
10. A point made by Martin Swales in his sensitive discussion of the play, Martin Swales, 'Schnitzler's Tragi-Comedy. A Reading of *Das weite Land*', *Modern Austrian Literature* 10 (1977), pp. 233–45.
11. Perlmann, *Arthur Schnitzler*, p. 109.

6 THE SOCIAL FAÇADE

1. Alfred Doppler, 'Die Problematik der Sprache und des Sprechens in den Bühnenstücken Arthur Schnitzlers' in Alfred Doppler, *Wirklichkeit im Spiegel der Sprache. Aufsätze zur Literatur des 20. Jahrhunderts in Oesterreich* (Europa, Vienna, 1975), pp. 31–52; Helmut Prang, 'Arthur Schnitzlers Regieanweisungen', *Jahrbuch der Grillparzergesellschaft* 12 (1976), pp. 257–75.
2. See pp. 95–6 of the present study.
3. See pp. 70–1 of the present study.

4. In his autobiography Schnitzler describes his relationship with a married lady whilst on holiday in Ostend, in which each acts out the 'Komödie der Verliebtheit', without really convincing the other, *Jugend in Wien*, pp. 306–7.
5. Perlmann, *Arthur Schnitzler*, p. 121.

7 SOCIAL GROUPS

1. *Jugend in Wien*, pp. 143, 149.
2. *Jugend in Wien*, pp. 172–4. One diary entry in question is that of December 1, 1882, *Tagebuch 1879–1892*, p. 144.
3. In answer to a questionnaire on the duel by the Ethische Gesellschaft in 1905, Schnitzler did not object to the principle of duels between consenting parties, but only to the obligation to duel placed upon unwilling civilians, *Aphorismen und Betrachtungen*, pp. 321–3. In his literary works Schnitzler appears to imply an essentially more hostile attitude on his part.
4. Rönning's decision to confront Karinski has been seen as a capitulation on his part to the demands of the code, Janz, Laermann, *Arthur Schnitzler*, p. 142. But Rönning himself views his action more positively than this.
5. As Françoise Derré points out, in sheer dramatic terms the ending as it stands is far more hard-hitting than if Rönning had escaped, Françoise Derré, *L'oeuvre de Arthur Schnitzler. Imagerie viennoise et les problèmes humains* (Didier, Paris, 1966), p. 109.
6. *Allgemeine Sportzeitung*, February 13, 1898, quoted in the programme to the production of *Freiwild*, Theater in der Josefstadt, Vienna, 1987/8, pp. 60–1.
7. In 1889 Schnitzler himself avoided such a 'violent consequence' when he refused to challenge a colleague in the Poliklinik. Schnitzler had interfered in the order of dances at the hospital ball, and the colleague had demanded, in highly insulting terms, that he apologize to the organizing committee. Schnitzler thought it absurd to put his life at stake over such a petty affair, but recognized that if matters had been taken further he would have lost his rank as a reserve officer rather earlier than he eventually did, *Jugend in Wien*, pp. 313–15.
8. Schnitzler's account of the atmosphere leading up to the *Waidhofener Beschluß* is given in *Jugend in Wien*, pp. 155–8.
9. This is Gustl's own view of the situation. According to Janz and Laermann, who give a detailed account of Gustl's predicament, Gustl needed only to have threatened the baker on the spot with his sword, in order to force his 'withdrawal', Janz, Laermann, p. 131.
10. In fact Schnitzler refused to appear before the tribunal, and was eventually stripped of his rank as an officer on April 21, 1901, partly because his story had insulted the honour of the Imperial Army, and partly because he himself had refused to respond 'correctly' (i.e. with a demand for satisfaction) to the insults levelled at him by a journalist in the army newspaper *Die Reichswehr*. Wagner, *Arthur Schnitzler*, pp. 121–3, 127–8.
11. See pp. 70–1 and 118–19 of the present study.
12. Janz, Laermann, pp. 152–3.

NOTES

13. The episode is examined in detail by Janz and Laermann, pp. 148–50.
14. Joseph Roth, *Radetzkymarsch* (Kiepenheuer and Witsch, Amsterdam, 1950), p. 135.
15. I owe this and subsequent points in this section to a paper given by Susan Wimmer (University of Vienna) entitled 'The Influence of Military Life on Austrian German Writers at the Turn of the Century', given at a symposium on 'The Habsburg Monarchy in Transition, 1890–1914', held at the University of London, 1985.
16. E. Schwarz, 'Arthur Schnitzler und die Aristokratie' in Scheible (ed.), *Arthur Schnitzler in neuer Sicht*, p. 66.
17. See p. 38 of the present study, and note 10 to Chapter 3.
18. See particularly Elsbeth Dangel, *Wiederholung als Schicksal. Arthur Schnitzlers Roman 'Therese. Chronik eines Frauenlebens'* (Fink, Munich, 1985).
19. See Norbert Leser, 'Literatur und das soziale Problem in Wien', *Literatur und Kritik* 193/4 (1985), pp. 131–40.
20. Timms, *Karl Kraus*, p. 24.
21. See Note 45 to Chapter 4 of the present study.
22. Jeffrey B. Berlin, 'Political Criticism in Arthur Schnitzler's *Aphorismen und Betrachtungen*', *Neophilologus* 57 (1973), p. 173.
23. *Aphorismen und Betrachtungen*, pp. 231–40.

8 POLITICS AND THE JEWISH QUESTION

1. See H.R. Klieneberger, 'Arthur Schnitzler and the Jewish Question', *Forum for Modern Language Studies* 19 (1983), pp. 261–73.
2. See Note 22 to Chapter 1.
3. *Jugend in Wien*, pp. 155–8.
4. Klieneberger, p. 264.
5. See Janz and Laermann's treatment of the Ehrenbergs' aspirations, *Arthur Schnitzler*, pp. 157–9.
6. Klienerberger, p. 265.
7. *Jugend in Wien*, pp. 96–7.
8. Roth, ed. Bance, *Die Kapuzinergruft*, p. 150.
9. Wagner,*Arthur Schnitzler*, p. 63.
10. W.H. Rey, *Arthur Schnitzler. Professor Bernhardi* (Fink, Munich, 1971), p. 16; Perlmann, *Arthur Schnitzler*, p. 98. In fact Schnitzler based the character partly on a fellow student from the Tirol called Mäusetschläger, *Jugend in Wien*, p. 158.
11. Perlmann, p. 98.
12. Schnitzler was well aware of the similarities between the two cases whilst at work on the play, as indicated by his diary entry of August 10, 1910, *Tagebuch 1909–1912*, p. 168.
13. Reinhard Urbach, *Schnitzler. Kommentar zu den erzählenden Schriften und dramatischen Werken* (Winkler, Munich, 1974), p. 186.
14. Field, *The Last Days of Mankind*, pp. 42–7.
15. Berlin, 'Political Criticism in Arthur Schnitzler's *Aphorismen und Betrachtungen*', p. 173.

16. In his diary entry of March 11, 1880, he confesses to regarding the political world with only 'sidelong glances', *Tagebuch 1879–1892*, p. 31.
17. *Jugend in Wien*, pp. 276–7; see also the diary entry of April 28, 1880, *Tagebuch 1879–1892*, pp. 45–6.
18. Wagner, pp. 307–8; diary entry of November 12, 1918, *Tagebuch 1917–1919* (Oesterreichische Akademie der Wissenschaften, Vienna, 1985), p. 201. His cynicism continued into the post-war years, as indicated by the diary entry of June 3, 1919, *Tagebuch 1917–1919*, p. 257.
19. *Jugend in Wien*, p. 100.
20. Numerous diary entries from the war years, *Tagebuch 1913–1916* (Oesterreichische Akademie der Wissenschaften, Vienna, 1983), and *Tagebuch 1917–1919*; and a long section in *Aphorismen und Betrachtungen*.
21. *Aphorismen und Betrachtungen*, p. 223.
22. Diary entry of May 14, 1907, quoted by Gutt, *Emanzipation bei Arthur Schnitzler*, p. 163.
23. Diary entry of April 23, 1912, *Tagebuch 1909–1912*, p. 321.

9 REALIST AND CRITIC

1. R.O. Weiss, 'The Human Element in the Works of Arthur Schnitzler', *Modern Austrian Literature* 5 (1972), p. 31.
2. For example, Martin Swales, 'Schnitzler als Realist', *Literatur und Kritik* 161/2 (1982), p. 56.
3. Swales, 'Schnitzler als Realist', pp. 57–8.
4. Leser, 'Literatur und das soziale Problem in Wien', p. 133.
5. Wagner, *Arthur Schnitzler*, p. 70.
6. Wagner, p. 79.
7. Wagner, p. 102.
8. Wagner, pp. 240–1.
9. A full account of the *Reigen* scandal is given by Ludwig Marcuse, *Obscene. The History of an Indignation*, trans. Karen Gerschan (McGibbon and Kee, London, 1965).
10. Egon Schwarz, 'Milieu oder Mythos? Wien in den Werken Arthur Schnitzlers', *Literatur und Kritik* 163/4 (1982), pp. 22–35.
11. As suggested by C.E. Williams, *The Broken Eagle*, pp. 148–9.
12. Janz and Laermann's *Arthur Schnitzler* includes a nineteenth-century map of Vienna in which the dwellings and movements of the characters of *Der Weg ins Freie* are clearly marked for the information of the reader.
13. Swales, 'Schnitzler als Realist', p. 56.
14. Schnitzler himself preferred to be compared with Chekhov, rather than with Hauptmann. He also made a 'pilgrimage' to his much-admired Ibsen in 1896.
15. In a letter of February 15, 1903, headed 'lieber Pornograph', Hofmannsthal praised *Reigen* as Schnitzler's best work hitherto, and urged him to publish it, Hofmannsthal, Schnitzler, *Briefwechsel*, pp. 167–8.
16. Marcuse, p. 212.
17. In his autobiography Schnitzler describes his first experience in the mortuary,

but as a medical student he quickly became accustomed to the sight of corpses, *Jugend in Wien*, pp. 126–7.
18. Perlmann, *Arthur Schnitzler*, pp. 136–42.
19. Lutz-W. Wolff, 'Bürger der Endzeit. Schnitzler in sozialistischer Sicht' in Scheible (ed.), *Arthur Schnitzler in neuer Sicht*, p. 352.
20. Weiss, p. 31.
21. See especially *Jugend in Wien*, pp. 205–12, and the diary entries for July 24, 1885 and February 1, 1886, *Tagebuch 1879–1892*, pp. 181–2, 188.
22. Wagner, pp. 189, 255.
23. Wagner, p. 169.
24. See, for example, the diary entries of June 9, 1909 and January 1, 1910, *Tagebuch 1909–1912*, pp. 72, 116.

SELECTED BIBLIOGRAPHY

PRIMARY SOURCES

Schnitzler

Schnitzler, Arthur, *Gesammelte Werke. Die Erzählenden Schriften*, 2 vols, Fischer, Frankfurt, 1961. (References to this edition are indicated in the text by the initials ES, followed by the volume number.)
—— *Gesammelte Werke. Die Dramatischen Werke*, 2 vols, Fischer, Frankfurt, 1962. (References to this edition are indicated in the text by the initials DW, followed by the volume number.)
—— *Gesammelte Werke. Aphorismen und Betrachtungen*, Fischer, Frankfurt, 1967.
—— *Jugend in Wien. Eine Autobiographie*, Molden, Vienna, 1968.
—— *Tagebuch 1909–1912*, Oesterreichische Akademie der Wissenschaften, Vienna, 1981.
—— *Tagebuch 1913–1916*, Oesterreichische Akademie der Wissenschaften, Vienna, 1983.
—— *Tagebuch 1917–1919*, Oesterreichische Akademie der Wissenschaften, Vienna, 1985.
—— *Tagebuch 1879–1892*, Oesterreichische Akademie der Wissenschaften, Vienna, 1987.
—— *Briefe 1875–1912*, Fischer, Frankfurt, 1981.
——, Georg Brandes, *Briefwechsel*, Francke, Berne, 1956.
Hofmannsthal, Hugo von, Schnitzler, Arthur, *Briefwechsel*, Fischer, Frankfurt, 1964.
Sandrock, Adele, Schnitzler, Arthur, *Geschichte einer Liebe in Briefen, Bildern und Dokumenten*, Fischer Taschenbücher, Frankfurt, 1983.
Kempny, Hedy, Schnitzler, Arthur, *Das Mädchen mit den dreizehn Seelen. Briefe und Tagebücher*, Rowohlt, Hamburg, 1984.

Other authors

Altenberg, Peter, *Auswahl aus seinen Büchern von Karl Kraus*, Atlantis, Zurich, 1963.

SELECTED BIBLIOGRAPHY

Andrian, Leopold von, *Der Garten der Erkenntnis*, Fischer, Frankfurt, 1970.
Bahr, Hermann, *Zur Ueberwindung des Naturalismus. Theoretische Schriften 1887–1904*, Kohlhammer, Stuttgart, 1968.
—— *Das Konzert*, Reclam, Stuttgart, 1961.
Beer-Hofmann, Richard, *Der Tod Georgs*, Reclam, Stuttgart, 1980.
Ebner-Eschenbach, Marie von, *Der Herr Hofrat. Eine Wiener Geschichte* in Ebner-Eschenbach, *Erzählungen. Autobiographische Schriften*, Winkler, Munich, 1958, pp. 422–63.
Freud, Sigmund, '"Civilized" Sexual Morality and Modern Nervous Illness' (1908) in Freud, *Collected Works*, Hogarth Press, London, 1959ff., Vol. 9.
Hofmannsthal, Hugo von, *Der Tor und der Tod*, ed. M.E. Gilbert, Blackwell, Oxford, 1942.
—— *Der Schwierige*, ed. W.E. Yates, Cambridge University Press, 1966.
Kraus, Karl, *Die letzten Tage der Menschheit* in Kraus, *Werke*, Kösel, Munich, 1957, Vol. 5.
Musil, Robert, *Der Mann ohne Eigenschaften*, Rowohlt, Hamburg, 1952.
Roth, Joseph, *Radetzkymarsch*, Kiepenheuer and Witsch, Amsterdam, 1950.
—— *Die Kapuzinergruft*, ed. A.F. Bance, Harrap, London, 1972.
Saar, Ferdinand von, *Novellen aus Oesterreich* in von Saar, *Sämtliche Werke*, Hesse, Leipzig, 1908, Vols 7–12.
—— *Geschichte eines Wiener Kindes* in *Sämtliche Werke*, Vol. 9, pp. 213–72.
—— *Schloß Kostenitz* in *Sämtliche Werke*, Vol. 9, pp. 277–345.
—— *Die Familie Worel* in *Sämtliche Werke*, Vol. 12, pp. 11–31.
Zweig, Stefan, *Phantastische Nacht*, Fischer Taschenbuch, Frankfurt, 1954.

SECONDARY LITERATURE

On Schnitzler

Amery, J., 'Inmitten des alten Oesterreich. Arthur Schnitzler', *Literatur und Kritik* 151, 1981, pp. 37–45.
Dangel, E., *Wiederholung als Schicksal. Arthur Schnitzlers Roman 'Therese. Chronik eines Frauenlebens'*, Fink, Munich, 1985.
Derré, F., *L'oeuvre de Arthur Schnitzler. Imagerie viennoise et les problèmes humains*, Didier, Paris, 1966.
Doppler, A., 'Der Wandel der Darstellungsperpsektive in den Dichtungen Arthur Schnitzlers. Mann und Frau als sozialpsychologisches Problem', in Farese, G.(ed.), *Arthur Schnitzler und seine Zeit*, Lang, Berne, 1985, pp. 41–59.
Farese, G. (ed.), see Doppler, A.
Gutt, B., *Emanzipation bei Arthur Schnitzler*, Spiess, Berlin, 1978.
Janz, R-P., Laermann K., *Arthur Schnitzler. Zur Diagnose des Wiener Bürgertums im Fin de Siècle*, Metzler, Stuttgart, 1977.
Kann, R.A., 'Die historische Situation und die entscheidenden politischen Ereignisse zur Zeit und im Leben Arthur Schnitzlers', *Literatur und Kritik* 161/2, 1982, pp. 19–25.
Klieneberger, H.R., 'Arthur Schnitzler and the Jewish Question', *Forum for Modern Language Studies* 19, 1983, pp. 261–73.

Nehring, W., 'Schnitzler, Freud's *alter Ego?*', *Modern Austrian Literature* 10, 1977, pp. 179–94.
Pelinka, A., 'Die Struktur und die Probleme der Gesellschaft zur Zeit Arthur Schnitzlers', *Literatur und Kritik* 163/64, 1982, pp. 59–66.
Perlmann, M.L., *Arthur Schnitzler*, Metzler, Stuttgart, 1987.
Rey, W.H., *Arthur Schnitzler. Die späte Prosa als Gipfel seines Schaffens*, Schmidt, Berlin, 1968.
—— *Arthur Schnitzler. Professor Bernhardi*, Fink, Munich, 1971.
Scheible, H., *Arthur Schnitzler in Selbstzeugnissen und Bilddokumenten*, Rowohlt, Hamburg, 1976.
—— *Schnitzler und die Aufklärung*, Fink, Munich, 1977.
—— (ed.), see Schwarz, E.
Schwarz, E., 'Arthur Schnitzler und die Aristokratie' in Scheible, H.(ed.), *Arthur Schnitzler in neuer Sicht*, Fink, Munich, 1982, pp. 54–70.
—— 'Milieu oder Mythos? Wien in den Werken Arthur Schnitzlers', *Literatur und Kritik* 163/4, 1982, pp. 22–35.
Skrine, P., *Hauptmann, Wedekind and Schnitzler*, Macmillan, Basingstoke and London, 1989.
Swales, M.W., *Arthur Schnitzler. A Critical Study*, Clarendon, Oxford, 1971.
—— 'Nürnberger's Novel. A Study of Arthur Schnitzler's *Der Weg ins Freie*', *Modern Language Review* 70, 1975, pp. 567–75.
—— 'Schnitzler's Tragi-Comedy. A Reading of *Das weite Land*', *Modern Austrian Literature* 10, 1977, pp. 233–45.
—— 'Schnitzler als Realist', *Literatur und Kritik* 161/2, 1982, pp. 52–61.
Urbach, R., *Arthur Schnitzler*, Friedrich, Hanover, 1968.
—— *Schnitzler. Kommentar zu den erzählenden Schriften und dramatischen Werken*, Winkler, Munich, 1974.
Wagner, R., *Frauen um Schnitzler*, Jugend und Volk, Vienna, 1980.
—— *Arthur Schnitzler. Eine Biographie*, Molden, Vienna, 1981.
Weiss, R.O., 'The Human Element in the Works of Arthur Schnitzler', *Modern Austrian Literature* 5, 1972, pp. 30–44.
Wolff, L-W., 'Bürger der Endzeit. Schnitzler in sozialistischer Sicht' in Scheible, H. (ed.), *Arthur Schnitzler in neuer Sicht*, pp. 330–59.

General background

Barea, I., *Vienna. Legend and Reality*, Secker and Warburg, London, 1966.
Coghlan, B., 'The Turn of the Century' in Ritchie, J.M. (ed.), *Periods in German Literature*, Vol. 1, Wolff, London, 1966.
Crankshaw, E., *Vienna. The Image of a Culture in Decline*, Macmillan, London, 1938.
—— *The Fall of the House of Habsburg*, Longmans, London, 1963.
Daviau, D.G., *Hermann Bahr*, Twayne Publishers, Boston, 1985.
Evans, R.J., *The Feminist Movement in Germany 1894–1933*, Sage Publications, London, 1976.
Field, F., *The Last Days of Mankind. Karl Kraus and his Vienna*, Macmillan, London, 1967.

SELECTED BIBLIOGRAPHY

Fischer, J.M., *Fin de Siècle. Kommentar zu einer Epoche*, Winkler, Munich, 1978.
Fuchs, A., *Geistige Strömungen in Oesterreich 1867–1918*, Löcker, Vienna, 1978.
Gainham, S., *The Habsburg Twilight*, Weidenfeld and Nicolson, London, 1979.
Janik, A., Toulmin, S., *Wittgenstein's Vienna*, Weidenfeld and Nicolson, London, 1973.
Johnston, W. M., *The Austrian Mind. An Intellectual and Social History 1848–1938*, University of California Press, Berkeley, 1972.
Leser, N., 'Literatur und das soziale Problem in Wien', *Literatur und Kritik* 193/4, 1985, pp. 131–40.
Magris, C., *Der habsburgische Mythos in der österreichischen Literatur*, Müller, Salzburg, 1966.
May, A.J., *The Habsburg Monarchy 1867–1914*, Harvard University Press, Cambridge, Mass., 1965.
Morton, F., *A Nervous Splendour. Vienna 1888–1889*, Weidenfeld and Nicolson, London, 1980.
Nürnberger, H., 'Wien im Werk Joseph Roths', *Literatur in Wissenschaft und Unterricht* 18, 1985, pp. 193–211.
Pascal, R., *From Naturalism to Expressionism. German Literature and Society 1880–1918*, Weidenfeld and Nicolson, London, 1973.
Polheim, K.K., 'Das Bild Wiens im Werk Robert Musils', *Literatur und Kritik* 191/2, 1985, pp. 37–48.
Schorske, C.E., *Fin de Siècle Vienna. Politics and Culture*, Weidenfeld and Nicolson, London, 1980.
Spiel, H., *Vienna's Golden Autumn*, Weidenfeld and Nicolson, London, 1987.
Taylor, A.J.P., *The Habsburg Monarchy 1809–1918. A History of the Austrian Empire and Austro-Hungary*, Hamish Hamilton, London, 1948.
Timms, E., *Karl Kraus. Apocalyptic Satirist*, Yale University Press, New Haven, 1986.
Urbach, R., 'Hermann Bahrs Wien', *Literatur und Kritik* 199/200, 1985, pp. 404–8.
Williams, C.E., *The Broken Eagle. The Politics of Austrian Literature from Empire to Anschluß*, Elek, London, 1974.
Zweig, Stefan, *Die Welt von Gestern. Erinnerungen eines Europäers*, Fischer, Berlin, 1962.

INDEX

Adler, Victor 9
Allen, Grant: *The Woman Who Did* 87
Altenberg, Peter 13, 21–3, 183; *At Home* 22; *Blumenkorso* 22; *Siebzehn bis dreißig* 88–9; *Wie ich es sehe* 22
Andreas-Salomé, Lou 69
Andrian, Leopold von 13; *Der Garten der Erkenntnis* 17
anti-Semitism 9–11, 21, 26, 28, 136–7, 160–5, 167–9; *see also* Jews
aristocracy 4–5, 6, 11, 23, 24–6, 67, 146–9
Auernheimer, Raoul 191

Bahr, Hermann 13, 16, 19–21, 104, 183; *Das Konzert* 20, 86–7, 106; *Das Theater* 20; *Das Tschaperl* 20; *Der Apostel* 20; 'Die Ueberwindung des Naturalismus' 16; 'Wien' 20
Balzac, Honoré de 180
Barrès, Maurice 16
Baudelaire, Charles 21
Bauernfeld, Eduard von 174
Beer-Hofmann, Richard 13, 104, 191; *Der Tod Georgs* 17
Berg, Alban 12
Bernheim, Hippolyte 32
bourgeoisie: lower middle classes (*Kleinbürgertum*) 8, 9, 11, 60–1, 63, 66, 91–4, 112, 138–9, 148–50, 153–4; upper middle classes (*Großbürgertum*) 5–6, 11, 19–20, 54, 58–61, 65–6, 68, 88, 91–113, 129–30, 149
Bourget, Paul, 16

Brahm, Otto 179, 183, 191
Brahms, Johannes 191
Braun, Lily 70
Breuer, Josef 32, 39
Bruckner, Anton 12, 191
Burckhard, Max 178

Charcot, Jean Martin 32
Crankshaw, Edward 7, 13
cultural life 11–13, 17–18, 19, 23, 25, 99, 105; artists 99–100, 156–9; theatre 60, 67, 68, 70, 92, 100, 153–6

Der neue Tag (journal) 28
Dehmel, Richard 87
Dickens, Charles 180
Doderer, Heimito von 30
Dollfuss, Englebert 165
'Dreyfus case' 161, 169
duels 5, 26, 108, 110–11, 133–46

Ebner-Eschenbach, Marie von 18, 19, 31, 83; *Der Herr Hofrat* 19
Elisabeth, Empress of Austria 3, 4
Engländer, Richard *see* Altenberg, Peter

Fontane, Theodor 88, 180; *Effi Briest* 88; *Irrungen Wirrungen* 88, 180–1
Franckenstein, Clemens von 83 (note 38), 191
Franz Ferdinand, Archduke of Austria 4, 162, 175

210

INDEX

Franz Josef I, Emperor of Austria 3–4, 5, 6, 18, 27, 29, 30
Freud, Sigmund, 12, 32, 33, 38–9, 49, 52–4, 58, 85; '"Civilized" Sexual Morality' 54; 'The Ego and the Id' 49; *The Interpretation of Dreams* 38–9; 'Freudian' 44, 46, 48

Gissing, George: *The Odd Women* 87
Glümer, Marie 84, 93 (note 1)
Grillparzer, Franz 174
Großbürgertum see bourgeoisie
Gussmann, Olga *see* Schnitzler, Olga

Hardy, Thomas: *Jude the Obscure* 87
Hauptmann, Gerhard 15, 87, 183
Hajek, Marcus 191
Heger, Jeanette 83, 84
Herzl, Theodor 10, 162–3
Hitler, Adolf 10, 11
Hofmannsthal, Hugo von 13, 16–17, 21, 23–5, 26, 28, 30, 31, 104, 149, 183, 191; *Das Märchen der 672 Nacht* 53; *Der Schwierige* 24–5, 26, 149; *Der Tor und der Tod* 23; *Der Unbestechliche* 24; 'Preuße und Oesterreicher' 25
Holz, Arno 15

Ibsen, Henrik 183
Imperial Army 5, 26, 27, 28, 29–30, 101, 131–42, 144–6, 167, 177, 179

Jerusalem, Else 70
Jews 7–8, 160, 162–3; *see also* anti-Semitism
Jung Wien writers 13, 15–16, 17, 20, 21, 23, 31, 53, 153, 156, 191

Kainz, Josef 191
Kaufmann, Arthur, 191
Kempny, Hedy 85
Key, Ellen 69
Kleinbürgertum see bourgeoisie
Klimt, Gustav 12
Kokoschka, Oskar 12
Krafft-Ebing, Richard von 85
Kraus, Karl 13, 20–1, 69, 86; *Die Fackel* 20, 175; *Die letzten Tage der Menschheit* 21, 145–6; 'Sittlichkeit und Kriminalität' 69

Lehar, Franz 17
Loeb, Clara 69; *Mimi* 69
Loos, Alfred 12
lower classes 8–9, 11, 18, 22, 66, 149–53
Lueger, Karl 4, 9, 10, 169, 175

Mach, Ernst 12, 16; *Analyse der Empfindungen* 16
Magris, Claudio 15
Mahler, Alma 191
Mahler, Gustav 12, 158, 191
Makart, Hans 12
Mallarmé, Stéphane 21
Mann, Heinrich 87
Mann, Thomas: *Tonio Kröger* 159
Maria Theresa, Empress of Austria 4, 147
Mayreder, Rosa 69
Mendelssohn Bartholdy, Felix 158
Meynert, Theodor 13, 32, 38, 39
middle classes *see* bourgeoisie
Morton, Frederic 89–90
Musil, Robert 25, 30, 31; *Der Mann ohne Eigenschaften* 25–7

Neue Freie Presse (journal) 139, 173

Petzold, Alfons: *Das rauhe Leben* 153
politics 2–3, 8–10, 26–7, 28, 166–7, 169–76

Radetzky, Joseph (Field Marshal) 27
Reich, Franziska 84
Reik, Theodor 33, 46, 52
Reinhard, Marie 82–3
Reuter, Gabriele 70
Rosenbaum, Richard 191
Roth, Joseph 27–8, 31, 144, 165; *Die Kapuzinergruft* 27, 28, 29, 165; *Radetzkymarsch* 27–30, 144–5, 165
Rudolf, Crown Prince of Austria 3, 4

Saar, Ferdinand von 18–19, 31, 89; *Die Familie Worel* 18; *Geschichte eines*

INDEX

Wiener Kindes 18–19, 89; *Novellen aus Oesterreich* 18
Sacher, Anna 4
Sacher-Masoch, Leopold von: *Die Messalinen Wiens* 85
Salten, Felix 191; *Josefine Mutzenbacher* 85
Sandrock, Adele 84, 154
Schiele, Egon 12
Schnitzler, Arthur: as army cadet 10, 13, 131–2, 133; and cultural scene 6, 13, 154, 156, 191; and feminists 69–70, 77, 88; as Jew 8, 10, 160, 163, 165; life-style 5–6, 13–14, 46, 91, 190–2; and medical world 13–14, 32, 38–40, 52–3; and parents 6, 32, 89, 104, 190, 191; politics 159, 166, 171, 174–6; realism as writer 1, 14, 15, 22–3, 31, 177–90; sex life 55, 82–6, 89, 91, 93 (note 1); as student 10, 13, 131–2, 160, 190

WORKS

Anatol 55–8, 61, 77, 78, 91, 93; *Abschiedssouper* 56, 60; *Episode* 56; *Weihnachtseinkäufe* 57–8, 60, 62, 184
Blumen 36, 39, 43, 54
Casanovas Heimfahrt 70
Das Märchen 70, 91–4, 153–4, 159, 178, 189
Das neue Lied 155, 156, 186
Das Schicksal des Freiherrn von Leisenbohg 146, 154
Das Vermächtnis 91, 94–8, 115–16, 178, 189
Das weite Land 98, 105–11, 113, 116–18, 143–4, 178, 184, 189, 190
Der Andere 33
Der einsame Weg 79–80, 98–105, 106, 113, 154, 156–7, 184
Der Ehrentag 155, 156
Der Sekundant 119–21, 133, 142, 178
Der Sohn 38, 152
Der Weg ins Freie 70, 80–3, 136–7, 144, 146, 150, 154, 157–9, 160–7, 174, 176, 179, 180–3, 184, 188–9
Der Witwer 35–6
Die Fremde 33–5
Die Nächste 36–7, 42, 43, 54
Die Toten schweigen 71, 111, 123–7
Doktor Gräsler, Badearzt 78–9
Fink und Fliederbusch 150, 172–4
Flucht in die Finsternis 40–3, 54
Frau Beate und ihr Sohn 46–8, 53, 54, 74, 111, 121–3, 185, 188
Frau Berta Garlan 71–5, 77, 84, 111, 180, 182, 185, 188
Fräulein Else 43–6, 48, 53, 54
Freiwild 132, 133–5, 138, 144, 150, 154–5, 189
Internationale Klinische Rundschau (ed.) 32
Jugend in Wien 55, 83, 84, 104, 132, 165, 190
Komödie der Worte 111
Komtesse Mizzi 147–9
Leutnant Gustl 77–8, 127–9, 137–41, 144, 151, 160–1, 177–8, 179, 188
Liebelei 55, 60–3, 77, 86, 87, 91, 94, 96, 132, 142–3, 149, 178, 179, 180, 184, 189–90
Professor Bernhardi 160, 167–72, 174
Reichtum 150
Reigen 55, 56–7, 60, 63–8, 70, 71, 77, 85, 86, 109, 114–15, 147, 149–50, 151, 154, 156, 178–9, 186
Ritterlichkeit 70
Spiel im Morgengrauen 70–1, 118–19, 132–3, 141–2, 146, 150–1, 178
Stunde des Erkennens 111
Therese. Chronik eines Frauenlebens 72, 75–7, 111–13, 133, 146–7, 151–3, 155–6, 161, 178, 182, 183, 185, 186, 188
Traumnovelle 48–52, 54, 146, 150, 151, 178, 183, 185, 186–7

Schnitzler, Gisela (sister) 191
Schnitzler, Johann (father) 2, 6, 8, 10, 14, 32, 89, 190, 191

Schnitzler, Julius (brother) 191
Schnitzler, Olga (wife) 84–5, 192
Schönberg, Arnold 12, 158
Schönerer, Georg von 9–10, 161
Schratt, Katharina 4
sexual mores 19, 20, 52, 54, 55–68, 85–6, 89–90, 97–8, 109–10
Speidel, Felix 191
Strauß, Johann (the elder) 27
Strauß, Johann (the younger) 11, 12–13, 17, 179
Strauß, Richard 17, 191; *Der Rosenkavalier* 17–18
Sudermann, Heinrich 87

theatre *see* cultural life
Torresani, Baron: *Aus der schönen wilden Leutnantszeit* 145; *Schwarzgelbe Reitergeschichten* 145

Vetsera, Baroness Marie von 4
Vienna: Allgemeines Krankenhaus 13, 32; Alsergrund 7; Augartenbrücke 64; Belvedere Palace 4, 26, 61, 162; Brigittenau 166; Buchfeldgasse 183; Burgtheater 6, 7, 12, 26, 28, 62, 154, 156, 178; Café Central 13, 190; Café Griensteidl 13, 23, 191; Café Imperial 181; Carltheater 135; Deutsches Volkstheater 135; Döbling 7, 19, 190; Donaukanal 150; Dornbach 43, 157; Favoriten 8; Freudenau 190; Grillparzerstraße 22; Grinzing 192; Gürtel 8; Hernals 8, 58, 60; Hernalser Hauptstraße 147; Herrengasse 13; Herrenhaus 5, 26, 148; Heumarkt 181; Hietzing 7; Hofburg 1, 4, 26, 28; Hotel Sacher 4, 60, 192; Hotel Imperial 105, 192; Hotel Savoy 192; Hotel Victoria 84; Josefstadt 7, 64, 149; Josefstadttheater 61; Kahlenberg 149, 180; Künstlerhaus 12; Leopoldstadt 7, 10, 28; Margarethen 7; Mariahilf 7, 149; Mayerhofgasse 147; Michaelerkirche 136; Neustift 12; Ottakring 8, 9, 51, 183; Poliklinik 2; Porzellangasse 64, 114; Prater 11, 31, 64, 69, 94, 158, 181–2, 186, 190; Rathaus 7, 22, 49, 150, 178, 183; Reichsrat 3, 5, 7, 10, 11, 26, 28, 94, 166, 169, 171, 175, 176, 178; Riedhof 64, 192; Ringstraße 2, 4, 6–7, 8, 12, 20, 28, 61, 64, 94, 145, 180, 181; Schiffamtsgasse 150; Schiffgasse 64; Schwarzenbergpark 162; Schwarzenbergplatz 6; Schwindgasse 64, 114; Secession 12, 84; Singerstraße 64; Spiegelgasse 64; Stadtpark 146, 181; Stefansdom 2, 181; Sternwartestraße 192; Strozzigasse 66; Theresianum 4; Türkenschanzpark 192; University 7, 22, 28, 94, 160, 169; Westbahnhof 43; Wickenburgstraße 183; Wieden 7, 151, 162; Wollzeile 43

Wagner, Otto 12
Waidhofener Beschluß 136
Walter, Bruno 191
Wassermann, Jakob 191
Webern, Anton 12
Wedekind, Frank 87–8; *Frühlings Erwachen* 184–5
Weininger, Otto 86
Werfel, Franz 30
Wildgans, Anton: *Armut* 153
Womens' Movement 20, 69–70

Zweig, Stefan 5, 7, 8, 30–1, 58, 191; *Die Welt von Gestern* 1, 30; *Phantastische Nacht* 30–1